SURVEYOR OF THE SEA

The Life and Voyages of Captain George Vancouver

SURVEYOR

OF THE SEA

The Life and Voyages of Captain
George Vancouver

By Bern Anderson

University of Washington Press · Seattle

G
246
V 3
A7
1960

Preface

M Y INTEREST IN Captain George Vancouver and his work was first aroused while I was in command of a small naval vessel engaged in tending and servicing outlying radio stations in Oregon, Washington, and Alaska during the middle 1930's. As I cruised in Puget Sound and the inland waters of British Columbia and southeastern Alaska, I became curious about the origin of the predominantly English names borne by islands, channels, headlands, and other geographical features in those restricted waters. Only a little searching revealed that most of these names were given in the course of a single British naval exploring voyage in 1791-95, under the command of Captain Vancouver. I soon became convinced that this was one of the most remarkable voyages in the history of navigation, and my admiration for Vancouver and his accomplishments during the voyage has been enhanced by my own experience in hydrographic surveying with modern equipment.

Several abridged accounts of Vancouver's voyage were available when I began further study, but of Vancouver himself I could find little information. Aside from the late Professor Edmond S. Meany's *Vancouver's Discovery of Puget Sound,* which is an annotated reproduction of a part of Vancouver's own account of his voyage, there have been only two brief and sketchy biographical studies published. Most of the standard reference works, such as William Laird Clowes's *The Royal Navy—A History* and the *Dictionary of National Biography,* depict Vancouver as a man of considerable ability but lacking in other command qualifications. Specifically, he is described as a harsh and even cruel disciplinarian who mistreated some of his midshipmen. The belief that this characterization does not harmonize with Vancouver's actual accomplishments has led to my own study of the man and his work, and, in view of the cloud that has covered Vancouver's reputation, I have made a special point of including every instance of criticism and questionable conduct, reserving judgment until all of the incidents have been considered.

A shortcoming of most books about explorers and exploration is the tendency to confine the narrative to an account of the expedition itself, with too little consideration of contemporary political and economic events. Often the real reason for a voyage of exploration such as Vancouver's is based on deeper political, scientific, or personal motives than are revealed in the formal orders for the voyage. In my own study, therefore, I have kept in mind the broad economic and political aspects of the period and have endeavored to introduce briefly other major historical events of the time.

The original version of this study was submitted as a doctoral thesis in history and is now in the archives of Harvard University. In making revisions I became indebted to Professor Robert G. Albion and Professor Samuel E. Morison, of Harvard, both of whom read the original and gave me numerous valuable comments and suggestions. Mr. Tuckerman Day also gave me useful editorial advice. The opinions and conclusions expressed, however, are my own.

Most of my material came from eighteenth-century records and the surviving manuscript logs and journals of members of the Vancouver expedition. Many of the manuscripts are now in the British Museum and the Public Record Office in London; microfilms of many of them were made available to me through the assistance of the late Mr. Charles W. Smith, founder of the Pacific Northwest Collection in the University of Washington Library, and later through Mr. J. Ronald Todd, reference librarian in the same library. The originals of those not studied in microfilm were examined by me in London in the spring of 1953.

I am indebted to Mr. C. R. H. Taylor, librarian of the Alexander Turnbull Library, Wellington, New Zealand, for a microfilm of the Edward Bell journal, the original of which is in that library. Miss K. Lindsay MacDougall, curator of manuscripts at the National Maritime Museum at Greenwich, England, supplied me with microfilms of three of Vancouver's own journals kept while he was a lieutenant in the Caribbean. The Yale University Library also provided me with microfilms and gave permission to reproduce the Vancouver letter and the Manby personal journal, both of which are in that library's collection of Western Americana. I owe special thanks to Mrs. Emily C. Heffernan, librarian of the U.S. Naval War College Library in Newport, Rhode Island, for the liberal use of an excellent set of the first edition of Vancouver's *Voyage of Discovery,* which enabled me to make a thorough study of that scarce but key source. The Reverend R. S. Mill, Vicar of Petersham, kindly provided me with much background information on Petersham and its history. For the maps, adapted from Vancouver's original charts, my thanks are due to Mr. Raymond Gaudet and Mr. Michael E. Berg.

BERN ANDERSON

Rear Admiral, U.S. Navy (Ret).

Newport, R. I.
May, 1959

Contents

CONTENTS

Illustrations

ILLUSTRATIONS

SURVEYOR OF THE SEA

The Life and Voyages of Captain
George Vancouver

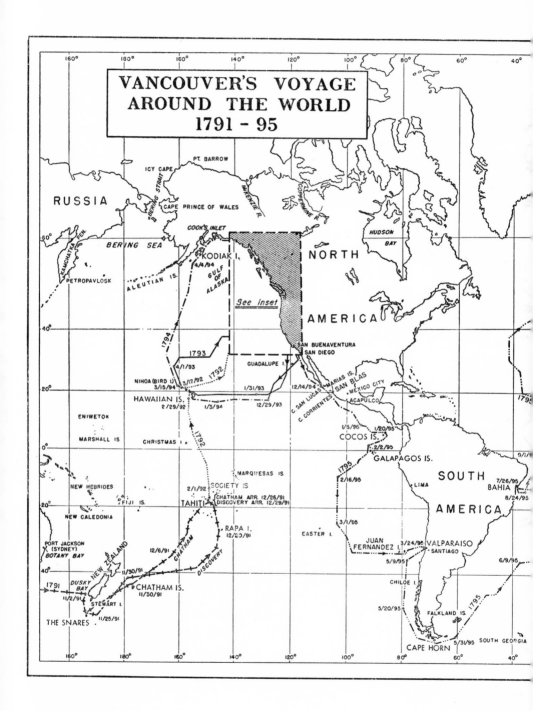

VANCOUVER'S VOYAGE AROUND THE WORLD 1791 - 95

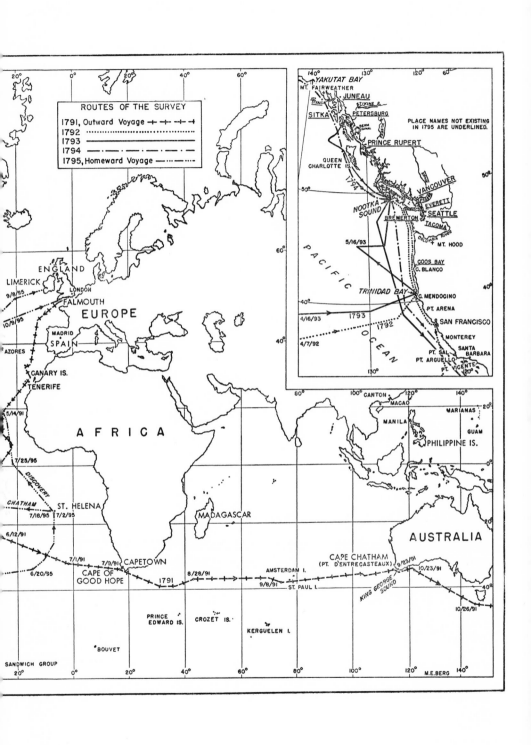

ROUTES OF THE SURVEY

1791, Outward Voyage ＋ ＋ ＋ ＋
1792 ·····························
1793 ─────────
1794 ── ── ── ──
1795, Homeward Voyage ──·──·──

PLACE NAMES NOT EXISTING
IN 1795 ARE UNDERLINED.

Inset map labels: YAKUTAT BAY, MT. FAIRWEATHER, JUNEAU, SITKA, STIKINE R., PETERSBURG, PRINCE RUPERT, QUEEN CHARLOTTE IS., NOOTKA SOUND, VANCOUVER, EVERETT, SEATTLE, BREMERTON, TACOMA, COLUMBIA RIVER, MT. HOOD, COOS BAY, C. BLANCO, TRINIDAD BAY, C. MENDOCINO, PT. ARENA, SAN FRANCISCO, MONTEREY, SANTA BARBARA, PT. SAL, PT. ARGUELLO, PT. VICENTE

5/16/93, 4/16/93, 1793, 4/7/92, 1792

PACIFIC OCEAN

World map labels: ENGLAND, LIMERICK, LONDON, FALMOUTH, EUROPE, MADRID, SPAIN, AZORES, CANARY IS., TENERIFE, AFRICA, DISCOVERY, CHATHAM, ST. HELENA, MADAGASCAR, AUSTRALIA, CAPETOWN, CAPE OF GOOD HOPE, AMSTERDAM I., ST. PAUL I., CAPE CHATHAM (PT. D'ENTRECASTEAUX), KING GEORGE SOUND, PRINCE EDWARD IS., CROZET IS., KERGUELEN I., BOUVET, SANDWICH GROUP, CANTON, MACAO, MANILA, MARIANAS, GUAM, PHILIPPINE IS.

9/8/95, 10/9/95, 5/14/91, 7/25/95, 7/18/95, 7/2/95, 6/12/91, 6/20/95, 7/1/91, 7/9/91, 8/26/91, 9/8/91, 9/23/91, 10/23/91, 10/26/91, 1791

M.E.BERG

1

Youth at Sea
(1757-80)

THE SETTING

THE SPAN OF George Vancouver's life, from 1757 to 1798, included some of the greatest events in the development of the British Empire. In 1757 the Seven Years' War was in its second year, with England and France the chief antagonists. That war cost France Canada and established British domination in India. By 1798 England had been at war with France again for five years, and after the defeat of Napoleon in 1815 Britain emerged as undisputed mistress of the seas. The revolution of the American colonies was the only major setback during that period of expanding British imperial power.

It was a martial era, in which naval warfare was a decisive factor, but victorious wars alone do not account for the advance which England made during those years. Her commercial empire had been and was continuing to be built largely by the risk and private enterprise of her subjects, operating through the great monopolistic overseas trading companies. Supporting the individuals was a government usually willing and able to protect and encourage such enterprise and to convert commercial penetrations into political gains.

The era saw the beginning of the Industrial Revolution, agricultural reforms, and social movements that would slowly transform England from the privileged class society of George III to the monarchial democracy that she has since become. Added to that was a lively interest, centered in the Royal Society, in every aspect of science. The government itself showed a practical interest in science, revealed by a standing offer of rewards of up to £20,000 for the discovery of a method of finding the longitude at sea.

In this study we are concerned with certain aspects of military, political, economic, and scientific developments during the second half of the eighteenth century and with the story of one of those loyal and energetic servants whose efforts were a material contribution to the building of the British Empire.

George Vancouver was born at King's Lynn, Norfolk, a North Sea port about one hundred miles north of London, on June 22, 1757. He was the sixth and youngest child and third son of Bridget and John Jasper Vancouver. His father was of Dutch descent and his mother a member of an old manorial family whose seat was at nearby Wiggenhall St. Mary. His older brothers, Charles and John, presumably twins since they were baptized on the same day, had brief but important parts in George's later life.

John J. Vancouver was the deputy collector of customs and collector of town dues at King's Lynn. The deputy collector was an appointee of the customer and collector, whose own office was a sinecure. The deputy was the active administrator of the customs in the port and as such was an important citizen who enjoyed a lucrative income in an inefficient and wasteful system that was characteristic of the period. King's Lynn at the time was one of the major ports of England, especially important in the coasting trade, and it ranked fifth in customs duties in all of the ports of the country. In his position in such an important port George Vancouver's father was a man of prestige and considerable political influence.

Almost nothing is known of George's boyhood. A member of a prominent well-to-do family, he probably attended the local grammar school. In the bustling port that was his home no healthy and active youngster could fail to know something of the activity, language, lore, and spirit of the sea. From his fifteenth year to his death his life was devoted to the sea and to the Royal Navy rather than to King's Lynn. The beginning of his career at sea came at about the time of his fourteenth birthday, soon after the return of Captain James Cook from his first voyage of exploration.

In 1768, Captain Cook was selected to command an important scientific expedition, which had been organized at the request of the Royal Society for the purpose of making observations in the South Seas of a transit of the planet Venus across the face of the sun. In addition to his scientific orders, Cook was given secret instructions to explore the South Pacific in search of new lands and to examine the land then shown vaguely on the maps as New Zealand.

Behind those secret orders was a British-French rivalry in a race to discover new territory in the southern seas. Since the end of the Seven Years' War, French and British explorers had been active in the Pacific, and both governments equipped one expedition after another in their attempts to discover and claim new lands. Cook, leaving England in August, 1768, on his first expedition, made the astronomical observations as he had been directed, established the insularity of New Zealand, mapped the east coast of Australia, and discovered some minor islands in the South Pacific.

On this voyage at his own request was a wealthy young botanist, Joseph Banks. He was the naturalist of the expedition, and he had three years before been elected a member of the Royal Society at the age of twenty-three. His personal party on this voyage consisted of ten, including himself. Banks made extensive studies of plant life in the Pacific, and he brought back to England many botanical specimens. He also brought back a lifelong interest in Pacific botany and geography, and from that time his name was prominent among those promoting and preparing for official scientific expeditions to that ocean. Among the many projects to which he devoted much time and effort was the colonization of Australia.

Banks was elected president of the Royal Society in 1778, and in that office he ruled over its affairs and destiny as an autocrat for more than forty years. He was an intimate of George III and was given a baronetcy in 1781. He was very popular socially, and toward the end of the eighteenth century he was a powerful and influential figure in British life. He introduced Cook to many of the leading social figures of the day, including the Earl of Sandwich, then First Lord of the Admiralty. Banks was a valuable friend, and, by the same token, his enmity was to be feared, as Vancouver would learn to his sorrow.

Little public notice was taken of Cook's first voyage, but, shortly after his return, plans were made for another expedition to the South Seas. Cook's discovery that New Zealand was an island group revived an age-old question of Southern Hemisphere geography. Did a great unknown and habitable continent exist in that part of the world? *Terra Australis Incognita,* the unknown southern land of the ancients, had by then excited the attention of theoretical geographers and practical navigators for nearly two centuries. As yet no Englishman had searched for the southern continent, but English geographers were asserting its existence, and French activity in the area after 1769 stimulated British interest. Cook was now instructed to search for this southern continent by circumnavigating the globe as close to the South Pole as possible.

A paragraph in Cook's instructions reveals England's watchfulness over her maritime rivals and the spirit of imperial expansion that was behind these voyages of exploration:

You are with the consent of the natives to take possession of convenient situations in the country in the name of the King of Great Britain, and to distribute among the inhabitants some of the medals with which you have been furnished to remain as traces of your having been there. But if you find the country uninhabited you are to take possession of it for His Majesty by setting up proper marks and inscriptions as first Discoverers and Possessors.[1]

On Cook's recommendation the *Resolution,* of 426 tons,[2] and the *Adventure,* of 336 tons, were obtained for the expedition. They were almost new north-country ships from the coal trade, strong and sturdy, and able to withstand severe storms and possible groundings in remote and unknown waters. Small ships, they carried relatively small crews, but they could stow a large stock of provisions and supplies, most important on a long voyage to waters where supply bases were nonexistent. Cook commanded the *Resolution* and Lieutenant Tobias Furneaux, the *Adventure*.

On board the *Resolution* under Cook, George Vancouver began his apprenticeship for a commission in the navy. He must have been personally selected by his new commander, since that was the manner of the times. Just how and by whom the youth was brought to Cook's attention is not now known. Somehow, through his father's connections, the necessary arrangements were made.

An officer's career was an attractive one in the eighteenth century for younger sons of the nobility and sons of the well-to-do upper class. In a day when public morality was generally low, nepotism, favoritism, and influence were used freely to launch boys on that career. The regulations implied that a boy should be fourteen years old at the time of entering; but there were many abuses, and it was not uncommon for a very young boy, still in elementary school, to be entered on the roll of a ship in order to have extra "service" count toward the required service for a commission. A boy was required to serve six years at sea, with at least two years in the grade of midshipman, before he was eligible to take examinations for and be commissioned a lieutenant.

Once accepted for service a youth had to serve for two years before he could be designated a midshipman. Consequently he was first entered by some convenient title, usually "volunteer" on the larger ships. A very young boy might be on the rolls as a "captain's servant." On smaller ships, as was the case with Vancouver, he might be entered simply as "able seaman." These designations were for pay purposes and were only nominal, not descriptive. The boys were "young gentlemen," and as such they enjoyed a special place and treatment on board ship. Destined for officers' commissions, they were members of the officer class, and except for the training routine they were treated as such. Until they reached the midshipman's grade they lived in or near the gunroom under the watchful eye of the gunner.

Midshipmen had their own messing and berthing compartment in the after part of the ship under the officer's spaces, near or even below the water line. It was a bleak and crowded space; the midshipmen's sea chests and a table were the only furniture. The midshipmen slept in hammocks as did the crew, but each had his "hammock man," one of the older seaman who, for a weekly payment of grog, lashed and stowed the boy's hammock and performed other personal services for him. The midshipman's pay was low, and most of his expenses had to be met from personal funds. He had little leisure, and his pleasures were self-made within the limits of the ship and his berth.

He was in training for an officer's responsibilities, and that was never forgotten. At sea he stood regular watches on deck as assistant to the lieutenant of the watch, running messages for him and keeping the hourly record of the weather and navigational data on the slate provided for the purpose. He had a station aloft helping and supervising the yardmen in their tasks of making, furling, or changing sail. Most important for the younger boys was the daily forenoon session with the schoolmaster, studying trigonometry, navigation, and the sea arts and sciences. Every midshipman had to prove his proficiency in those subjects in his examination for lieutenant.

George Vancouver and his fellows in the *Resolution* were especially fortunate in their schoolmaster, William Wales, the astronomer of the expedition and one of the leading astronomers of the era. He had helped to develop the astronomical method for finding longitude at sea which Cook was one of the first to use, and he was eminently qualified to teach that subject to the youths in the ship. That he succeeded in at least one case we are assured by Vancouver who, during his own later voyage, gave to a headland in southeastern Alaska the name Point Wales, "after my much-esteemed friend Mr. Wales of Christ's Hospital; to whose kind instruction, in the early part of my life, I am indebted for the information which has enabled me to traverse these lonely regions." [3]

Cook was one of the more progressive officers of his time, and he had a genuine interest in the welfare of his men. The cause and cure of scurvy were well known, but he made the prevention of the disease in his ships a special challenge. Long voyages at sea, with a ration consisting of salt beef or pork, dried peas, oatmeal, and hardtack, were ideal for the development of scurvy, and it was all too common. Cook carried a supply of special antiscorbutic rations which he used regularly. One of these was malt extract for making beer. A gallon of beer each day, while it lasted, was a standard item in the normal ration. That was a boon, for the fresh water carried was apt to be ordinary river water which soon became putrid when stored on board ship in wooden casks. Other regular measures which Cook used were, as he expressed them, "airing and drying the ship with fires made betwixt decks, smoking &c, and by obliging the people to air their bedding, wash and dry their cloaths, whenever there was an opportunity." [4] These measures were not lost on Vancouver in this, his first voyage, and he used them with equal vigor in his later life and voyages.

The *Resolution* and the *Adventure* sailed from England in July, 1772. After a few weeks at the Cape of Good Hope the expedition sailed toward the Antarctic in November, at the beginning of the summer season in the Southern Hemisphere. Before long the ships began to meet icebergs, and soon after they crossed the Antarctic Circle their southern progress was stopped by pack ice. For the next two months the ships worked eastward along the edge of the ice pack and covered about one third of the circumnavigation, generally near the Antarctic Circle. As winter approached, Cook went to Dusky Bay, on the western side of South Island, New Zealand, where he knew he could obtain fresh fish and greens from shore to supplement the ration. He had but one case of scurvy, and he gave credit for its low incidence to the regular use of sauerkraut, which he preferred to lemon juice.

Another item produced at Dusky Bay was "spruce beer." The very name suggests an unattractive and bitter beverage, yet contemporary writers mention spruce beer frequently in accounts of voyages such as this, generally praising its flavor and potable qualities. It was made by boiling a batch of small branches of spruce or other evergreens in a large caldron for several hours, then adding molasses, water, and a fermenting agent such as yeast or wort, and putting the strained mixture into casks to ferment. In a few days it was considered fit to drink and ready for issue.

The two ships sailed for an exploring cruise through the South

Pacific in June, 1773, and in mid-August reached Tahiti, where two weeks were spent trading for provisions, cleaning the ships, and checking the rate of error of the chronometers.

Cook was one of the first explorers to have chronometers and the means for finding the longitude at sea. Heretofore navigators could only guess at the longitude by keeping a careful record of the compass courses steered and of the speed of the ship through the water. When the ship's track was plotted on the chart by "reckoning," its position in latitude and longitude could be taken from the chart by "dead reckoning." The latitude could be determined daily by a simple astronomical observation, and errors could be corrected at once. Until about 1763 there was no comparable way in which the longitude could be found. Without that knowledge there was no way of knowing of, or allowing for, ocean currents. Large errors in the longitude determined by reckoning were the rule, and the positions of new discoveries reported by explorers before Cook's time were subject to such errors.

Beginning in the seventeenth century the maritime nations of Europe offered large rewards for a solution to the problem of longitude. Shortly after the middle of the eighteenth century two methods were introduced. One, called the lunar method, was astronomical, and it was based on the fact that the moon changes its position very rapidly with respect to the sun and other heavenly bodies. When the angle between the moon and one of those bodies was measured and suitably corrected, the Greenwich time when that angle occurred could be obtained from tables computed in advance. By a comparison of the local time at the ship, which could also be found by simple observations, with the Greenwich time, the longitude east or west of Greenwich could be found in time and converted to degrees (one hour of time equals fifteen degrees of arc). Cook used this method on his first voyage.

A second and much simpler method was developed about the same time by an English cabinetmaker named John Harrison. He produced the chronometer, a timekeeper capable of keeping extremely accurate time. With the chronometer set to keep Greenwich time the longitude could be found merely by comparing the local time with that of Greenwich. The weakness of the chronometer was that if it stopped for any reason or suffered an accident it was useless. On his second and third voyages, Cook had chronometers, with which he kept a daily record of his positions. He had established the true longitude of Tahiti by the transit of Venus on his first voyage, and thus had a known point with which he could check the error of his chronometers on Greenwich time.

Solving the problem of finding the longitude at sea was a great milestone in the development of navigation. Because of it Cook and those who followed him had an advantage over their predecessors that cannot be overstated.

Leaving Tahiti, the ships returned to New Zealand, and the *Resolution* returned alone to search for the Antarctic continent. Twice it penetrated below the Antarctic Circle, and late in January, 1774, it made the deepest penetration of the voyage, to latitude 71°10' south. There Cook was forced to turn north again.

One of the young gentlemen on board, sensing the significance of the occasion, went to the head of the bowsprit before the turn was made, waved his hat in the air, and cried out, *"ne plus ultra."* Thus George Vancouver could claim in later life that he had been nearer the South Pole than any other man.[5]

The rigors of those months in high latitudes was vividly described by George Forster, the assistant naturalist, who pointed out that most voyages were made in generally mild weather:

Ours was just the reverse of this; our southern cruises were uniform & tedious in the highest degree, the ice, the fogs, the storms and ruffled surface of the sea formed a disagreeable scene, which was seldom cheered by the reviving rays of the sun; the climate was rigourous & our food detestable. In short, we rather vegetated than lived; we withered and sacrificed our health, our feelings, our enjoyments, to the honour of pursuing a track unattempted before.[6]

During the second Antarctic winter the *Resolution* made another sweeping cruise through the South Seas, during which was made the most important physical discovery of the voyage, New Caledonia. The polar circumnavigation was completed during the third summer season. Cook was convinced that this voyage left little to be explored in the Southern Hemisphere and that it should end the search for a southern continent. Besides demonstrating to his own satisfaction that Antarctica, if it did exist, was inaccessible to sailing ships, this, Cook's most difficult voyage, was the first circumnavigation of the globe from west to east.

COOK'S THIRD VOYAGE

The *Resolution* returned to England in July, 1775, and within six months plans were well advanced for a third voyage under Cook's command. The objective of the third voyage was a search for the Northwest Passage, to be made in the Pacific. For many years there had been a standing Parliamentary reward of £5,000 for any ship that reached within one degree of latitude of the North Pole. In 1776, when Cook obviously might be a beneficiary, Parliament offered a new reward of £20,000 for the discovery of a Northwest Passage north of latitude 52° north. Cook hoped to win both. The latitude limitation was influenced by Samuel Hearne's overland journey in 1771 from Hudson Bay to the Arctic Ocean at the mouth of the Coppermine River, well north of the Arctic Circle.

Cook resumed command of his old ship *Resolution,* and the *Discovery,* of about three hundred tons, was purchased as her consort. The *Discovery* was commanded by Commander Charles Clerke, who had been second lieutenant of the *Resolution* on the second voyage. George Vancouver went in the *Discovery* as a midshipman. The ships sailed independently from Plymouth for the Cape of Good Hope in July, 1776.

That such an expedition should be undertaken at the outset of the American Revolution is eloquent evidence of how little appreciated in England was the depth of the movement already irrevocably launched on the far side of the Atlantic. On the day after the Declaration of Independence was adopted, when a convoy of transports bearing Hessian troops was forced into Plymouth by storms, Cook expressed his feelings:

It could not but occur to us as a singular and affecting circumstance, that at the very instant of our departure upon a voyage, the object of which was to benefit Europe by making fresh discoveries in North America, there should be the unhappy necessity of employing others of His Majesty's ships, and of conveying numerous bodies of land forces, to secure the obedience of those parts of that continent which have been discovered and settled by our countrymen in the last century.[7]

After leaving the Cape of Good Hope the expedition cruised leisurely through the South Seas, leaving Bora Bora, in the Society group, in December, 1777. A month later land was sighted which proved to be Kauai, one of the western islands of the Hawaiian group—the Sandwich Islands, Cook named them, for his patron, the Earl of Sandwich. This is now generally accepted as the first European discovery of the Hawaiian Islands, but there has been much speculation in the past that they might have been seen earlier by one of the Spanish galleons in the trade between Manila and Acapulco, Mexico. The question was to occupy Vancouver and his officers fifteen years later.

Pausing only briefly in the western islands for fresh water and provisions the ships continued to the mainland coast of what is now Oregon, which they followed northward. One of Cook's early and most significant finds in that region was Nootka Sound, on the southwest coast of Vancouver Island about one hundred miles northwest of the Strait of Juan de Fuca. With an abundance of fresh water and wood, including mast and spar timber, it was the most accessible and convenient harbor for the sailing ships that were drawn to the northwest coast in search of furs after the American Revolution. Cook remained there nearly a month before he sailed up the outer coast, naming such prominent Alaskan landmarks as Mount Edgecumbe, near Sitka, and Mount Fairweather, a fourteen-thousand-foot peak a few miles north of the upper end of the Inside Passage. He explored Cook Inlet, which he decided was a river, and continued along the south coast of the Alaskan Peninsula. While passing the southern end of Kodiak Island a sharp-eyed midshipman in the *Discovery* noted a small island which was "not noticed in Captain Cook's chart of his journal . . . it was however seen in that voyage from on board the Discovery and then placed by me 5' to the south of its situation deduced from the result of our present observations." [8] In the same waters sixteen years later George Vancouver made a more thorough survey than Cook's.

Late in June the ships entered the Bering Sea and made their way along the Alaskan coast, through Bering Strait, and along the Arctic coast of Alaska until they were stopped by pack ice near Icy Cape (latitude 70°29′ north), only about 130 miles from Point Barrow, the northernmost point in Alaska. Cook was almost as close to the North Pole as he had been to the South Pole in his second voyage. He next searched along the Siberian coast for a Northwest Passage but was again stopped by pack ice at Cape North, about 250 miles northwest of East Cape, Siberia. He then headed for the Hawaiian Islands, where he expected to spend the winter. After crusing among them in search of a good harbor the ships anchored in Kealakekua Bay, on the west coast of the island of Hawaii, in January, 1779.

The expedition was received enthusiastically by the islanders, and Cook was treated like a chief of the highest rank and even like a god. The work of preparing for a return to the Arctic went on so well that the ships sailed early in February, but they returned a week later to repair a sprung foremast in the *Resolution*. Their reception was now very different; the natives were sullen, and it was understood that the king of the island had placed the bay under a *kapu*, or taboo. Trouble soon started and came to a climax when Cook was killed in a melee on the beach while trying to induce the king on board the *Resolution* as a hostage for the return of a boat that had been stolen the night before.

The story of the death of Captain Cook has been told many times and at great length.[9] Here we are more concerned with the part played by George Vancouver in that incident. The afternoon before the boat was stolen a native snatched some tools in the *Discovery* and escaped in a canoe. Thomas Edgar, master of the ship, and Vancouver were sent in chase in the cutter, but the native made the shore. Joined by a pinnace from the *Resolution*, Edgar saw Cook on shore and took both boats into a nearby cove where he seized the canoe in which the thief escaped. One native, trying to prevent the seizure, was hit on the head with an oar, and this brought a shower of stones onto the boat's crews from a growing crowd of natives, forcing the boats to pull off. While getting clear the pinnace grounded on a submerged rock and her crew swam to some nearby rocks where Edgar's boat tried to embark them. The natives closed in on the Englishmen and one swung a broken oar at Edgar. As Edgar later recorded it:

[The native] most certainly would have knocked me off the rock, and into the water, if Mr. Vancover, the Midshipman had not this Inst Step'd out of the pinnace between the Indian and me, & received the Blowe, which took him on the side & knocked him down. . . .[10]

Edgar next made his way to Cook on shore, leaving Vancouver to guard the grounded pinnace. When he returned he found that the young midshipman had courageously protected the boat but had been beaten and knocked down by the natives, who had taken his cap and tried to steal some fittings from the boat. Later in the day the cap was returned and a truce was restored, only to be broken the next morning when the *Discovery*'s cutter was stolen.

Captain Clerke succeeded to command of the expedition on the death of Cook, and on the following morning he sent Lieutenant King and Vancouver, with five heavily armed boats, to try to recover Cook's body. The two men were chosen because they had already acquired a fair understanding of the native language. Only parts of Cook's dismembered body were recovered during the next few days, and these were interred at sea.

After leaving Kealakekua Bay, Clerke cruised among the islands until the middle of March, when he sailed for Petropavlovsk, on the Kamchatka Peninsula of Siberia. There the ships received an unexpectedly warm welcome from the commander of the district, Major Behm, a German in Russian employ. Vancouver was so impressed with his manner that in 1793 he named a channel in southeastern Alaska Behm's Canal, "to commemorate the weighty obligations conferred by Major Behm on the officers and crews of the Resolution and Discovery at Kampschatka in the year 1779." [11]

Early in July the ships were again in the Arctic, but they were soon stopped by pack ice in almost the same spot that they had reached the year before. For several days the ships battled the ice attempting to break through, and both received damage to their hulls. Clerke gave up the search for the Northwest Passage to return to Petropavlovsk for repairs. He died two days before they reached the port, and Lieutenant Gore, next in rank, assumed command of the *Resolution;* Lieutenant King took over the *Discovery.*

Sailing southward after repairs, the ships skirted the coast of Japan and reached Macao early in December, moving later to Whampoa, the anchorage for Canton. There a brisk trade developed between Chinese merchants and members of the crews who had traded bits of iron to natives of the northwest coast for sea otter skins. Prices were bid up daily, and Captain King estimated that about £2,000 was realized for the limited number of skins that were in the ships. "The rage with which our seamen were possessed to return to Cook's River, and, by another cargo of skins, to make their fortunes, at one time, was not far short of mutiny," he reported.[12] More than anything else, the commercial experience of the crews of the two ships at Whampoa attracted general interest to this voyage when the account of it was published. It became the foundation on which was built the history of the northwest coast of North America for the next twenty years.

The long voyage home past the Cape of Good Hope was uneventful, and the ships reached England in October, 1780, after an absence of more than four years. By then England was deep in a war that had spread from a colonial revolt to a world-wide conflict. It was a dark year in the colonies themselves, but Spain had joined France against England and the decisive events of the war were soon to come. Forgotten for the time being were voyages of exploration, and Cook's ships and men went to war.

George Vancouver had then spent nearly seven and a half venturesome years at sea and was ready for his examination and first commission. His passing certificate for the rank of lieutenant was dated October 19, 1780, just two weeks after the ships reached Deptford dockyard, on the Thames just below London. He was then twenty-three years of age.

2

Caribbean Service
(1781-89)

THE YEAR 1781 was a dark one in British history. In the struggle with the colonies across the Atlantic, British forces suffered a long series of reverses. Cornwallis' surrender at Yorktown in October virtually ended the American Revolution, although a formal peace treaty was delayed for another year. In Europe, Britain faced a hostile coalition led by France, and in the Baltic region Russia, Sweden, and Denmark, later supported by Prussia, Austria, and Holland, formed the Armed Neutrality to protect their shipping from interference by British warships. Outnumbered, the British were on the defensive everywhere.

In that far from cheerful atmosphere George Vancouver, less than two months after receiving his passing certificate for lieutenant, joined the *Martin,* sloop of war, Captain William Wardlaw, at Sheerness in December, 1780. The *Martin* was then engaged in escorting convoys between the east-coast ports of England and Ostend, Belgium, and until early in 1782 the ship conducted convoys and patrolled in the North Sea, frequently chasing and occasionally capturing small French vessels.

In 1782 the *Martin* was sent to the Caribbean. She reached the Windward Islands in March, and a few days later sailed from the island of St. Lucia in company with the *Invincible,* a seventy-four-gun ship of the line, escorting ten merchant ships to Jamaica.

Soon after reaching Jamaica the *Martin* was sent with a supply ship for the garrison of Swan Island, a small and isolated island about 350 miles west of Jamaica and 100 miles north of Honduras. It proved to be a fruitless trip, for about a month earlier the island had been seized by a Spanish squadron, and all the people, except a few slaves who escaped into the bush, had been taken off.

While returning to Jamaica from Swan Island the *Martin* fell in with a strange sail and gave chase. Late in the afternoon the ship was hailed, and according to Vancouver's journal:

> [The captain] answered he came from Carthagena bound to the Havanna. Capt. Merrick then desired him to shorten sail immediately. He answered he would, but he fired a broadside at us which we immediately answered & both ships kept continually firing for near two hours.[1]

With two men dead and several wounded, and with his rigging and sails damaged, Captain Merrick, who had taken command of the ship just before she left England, broke off the engagement until daylight. At daybreak the action was renewed, and half an hour later the Spaniard struck his colors and surrendered. The Spanish ship was badly battered, but a prize crew was put on board and she was sent into Port Royal, on the southern coast of Jamaica.

Port Royal, at that time the principal British naval base in the western Caribbean, lay at the tip of a long spit, called Palisadoes, which forms the outer side of an extensive and protected harbor. On the inner shores of the harbor is the city of Kingston. Port Royal was the principal center on the island during the early British occupation of Jamaica, but an earthquake in 1692 wrecked most of the town. After a hurricane further damaged it in 1722 Kingston became the center of commerce, but Port Royal continued to be used as the naval base.

In May, Vancouver was appointed fourth lieutenant of the *Fame,* Captain George Wilson, a seventy-four-gun ship of the line.

As fourth lieutenant, Vancouver commanded a part of the *Fame*'s battery of guns and took his regular turn standing watches on deck handling the ship. A ship of Rear Admiral Sir Samuel Hood's division, the *Fame* sailed habitually in close order formation with the other ships of the division. The watch officer's chief task was to watch the position of his ship in the column and to trim the sails to keep her in exact station on her next ahead. Precision in that respect was then, as it still is, a matter of great pride to the admirals and captains of the fleet, and the lieutenants standing watch learned to be highly skilled seamen. It was much more than a paradelike maneuver, for ships properly closed up and in station were in mutually supporting positions in battle.

Vancouver's journal for this period is only a bare outline record probably kept simply to comply with an order; it lacks the descriptive power, imagination, and conviction that mark his account of the later voyage under his own command. Nevertheless, the journal for the tour of duty in the *Fame* contains records of the death of a man every day or two from fevers and scurvy, the greatest hazards to crews in the Caribbean at that time. Yellow fever, in particular, was rampant and seems to have reached epidemic proportions in the *Fame*. During his service in the *Martin*, Vancouver had found time to experiment successfully with treatment of scurvy according to methods devised in the Hawaiian Islands on Cook's third voyage, but many of the captains in the Caribbean fleet were not as careful as Cook had been. There were nearly fifteen hundred cases of scurvy in the ships by the time the fleet reached New York in September.[2]

In July Admiral Hugh Pigot arrived at Jamaica to assume command of the fleet in the Caribbean. According to an unexpressed mutual agreement, both the British and the French fleets moved north during the hurricane season in the Caribbean, and shortly after his arrival Pigot sailed his entire fleet of thirty-seven ships to New York. On the way north, the fleet acted as convoy to homeward-bound merchant ships, and the *Fame* played an active part in beating off and chasing Spanish ships in waters off Havana. After a month and a half in New York harbor, the British fleet returned to the Caribbean late in October.

For five months the fleet was kept active cruising off the French islands of the eastern Caribbean, the monotony of the patrolling broken from time to time by the sighting and chasing of strange sails. Early in April, 1783, the king's proclamation of peace, resulting from preliminary treaties at Paris in January, was received on the station. Within two weeks the *Fame* sailed for

Plymouth, and in July, 1783, she was put out of commission.

For the next sixteen months Vancouver was on inactive service and on half pay, a condition, common to thousands of officers, resulting from the general demobilization that followed the end of the war. Nothing is known of what he did during that time, except that he was seeking another assignment at sea. In the introduction to his *Voyage of Discovery* he merely stated that his life after the age of thirteen, except for fifteen months, was devoted to naval service. In November, 1784, he managed to secure an active assignment in a ship at a time when the navy was fully reduced to its peacetime strength. Competition for the available billets was keen under the circumstances, but Vancouver's record and connections, though now unknown, were apparently good enough to commend him for one.

Many former midshipmen, with their passing certificates for lieutenant in hand, volunteered for duty in the Caribbean as midshipmen with the morbid hope that deaths among the lieutenants on the station would create vacancies for them. *Falconer's Marine Dictionary* states that in 1813, three decades later than the time we are considering but still a war year of full mobilization, there were two thousand midshipmen who had passed their examinations for lieutenant but for whom there were no vacancies. It is not surprising, therefore, that the former midshipmen of the mid-1780's were willing to risk the high mortality rate that could be expected in the Caribbean for a chance at promotion. Many lieutenants, with little chance for active duty in their own service, turned to the merchant marine or volunteered for service in a foreign navy.

SECOND CARIBBEAN CRUISE

When Vancouver joined the *Europa,* a fourth-rate ship of fifty guns, Captain Richard Fisher, she was preparing to proceed to the Caribbean flying the flag of Rear Admiral Alexander Innes, newly appointed commander in chief of the Jamaica station. She sailed from England at the end of 1784 and reached Port Royal the following February.

With only a few ships on the station, these mainly to show the flag and represent royal authority, and with little real active service to perform, station duty in years of peace tended to be a monotonous routine. For the flagship, in particular, it meant long periods at anchor in Port Royal while the other ships cruised along the coast of Jamaica on the lookout for smugglers. In the middle of 1786 Commodore Sir Alan Gardner arrived on the station in the *Expedition* to become commander in chief in place of Rear Admiral Innes, who had died the preceding January. At about the same time Captain Edward Marsh replaced Captain Fisher in the *Europa*.

Gardner's arrival on the station was a fortunate event for Vancouver, for it brought him to the notice of a man who was to become his good friend, and who, as one of the Lords of the Admiralty, would later sponsor him for his own command. Under Commodore Gardner, also, there was a noticeable change in naval activity on the Jamaica station.

Gardner was one of the more progressive officers of his time, taking an interest in the health and welfare of his men. Shortly after he arrived in Jamaica he found that there was no sauerkraut or portable soup (a concentrate, forerunner of bouillon cubes) in the squadron. One of his first requests to the Admiralty was for a supply of those antiscorbutics. In July, in keeping with the annual practice on the station, he shifted his ships to the inner harbor for the hurricane season. In September he shifted his pennant to the *Europa,* and by October he was busy with plans for evacuating English settlers from Latin America along the Mosquito Coast, an adjustment required by a treaty with Spain of July, 1786, fixing boundaries in that region.

The *Expedition* and the *Europa* were the only ships of the line in Gardner's command. The commodore remained at Port Royal or Kingston with his pennant flying in one of them while the other cruised about the island. In October Gardner ordered Captain Sawyer, of the *Expedition,* to cruise off the northern coast of Jamaica to prevent illicit trade with the United States. When the *Expedition* returned to Port Royal in January, 1787, Gardner shifted to her and sent the *Europa* on a similar cruise. For the next several months the two ships alternated between resting at anchor in Port Royal and cruising off the island enforcing the Navigation Acts. In March the Honorable John W. Chetwynd relieved Captain Sawyer in command of the *Expedition*.

Late in 1786 Gardner received instructions from the Admiralty directing all ships to make accurate surveys of harbors visited. This was one of the early steps by the Admiralty in taking official action to improve hydrographic knowledge, although a hydrographer's office was not formed until 1795. Shortly after the orders were received in Jamaica, entries in the captain's journal of the *Expedition* noted that boats were employed in surveying Bluefield Bay and Port Antonio. Vancouver's name is not mentioned in connection with those surveys, but it is possible that he may have been loaned for them because of his experience with Cook. If so, his work at the smaller harbors may well have drawn the attention of Gardner to his skill in that type of work. Gardner's journal notes that in May, 1787, he received a letter from Captain Chetwynd from Bluefield Bay, "with a small plan of Pedro Keys and Portland Rock." [3]

In July the ships of the squadron were again moved into Kingston Harbor for the hurricane season, and cruising ended. Early in September, by Gardner's order, Vancouver and Joseph Whidbey, master of the *Europa,* were engaged in surveying Kingston Harbor. The usable part of that extensive harbor is about seven miles long and from one to two miles wide, and the surveying of it was therefore no small task.

From the time he was assigned to survey Kingston Harbor, Vancouver's name appears more frequently in Gardner's journal, and his advancement was rapid. A patron in high position was essential for a lieutenant who hoped to reach high rank in the navy, and Vancouver found his in Sir Alan Gardner. Gardner appointed him second lieutenant of the *Europa* late in November, 1787, and only two months later Vancouver was made first lieutenant of the ship. As such he was second in command and the captain's executive assistant.

The association with Whidbey which began in the *Europa* was to continue throughout Vancouver's active naval service. Little information about Whidbey has been found, but since he was master of a ship of the line at that time, in the lean years of the middle 1780's, he must have been an experienced navigator and was probably considerably older than his fellow officers on the later voyage under Vancouver's command. It is probable that he remained a master throughout his naval service, for he was master attendant at Sheerness in 1802. He joined the *Europa* in September, 1786, shortly after Captain James Vashon assumed command in place of Captain Marsh, who had died.

The title "master" may be confusing, for that term is sometimes used to designate the commander of a ship. Here its meaning is that of the very old "sailing master" or navigating officer of the ship. The master was the specialist and expert in the art of navigation, somewhat similar to the "pilot" of Spanish ships. He ranked after the lieutenants and ahead of the warrant officers on board ship, a special position that has no close counterpart in modern naval rank. The master's duties were to check the stores and supervise the stowing of the holds, to "have care of Navigating the ship under the direction of his superior officer, and to see that the Log and Logbook be duly kept." He was also to provide himself "with proper instruments charts and books and keep an exact journal, noting therein the coming and going out of all Stores and Provisions," according to the King's Regulations.[4] The master could and sometimes did take his examinations and go on through the rank of lieutenant to the higher ranks of the navy, but many elected to remain in their special rank.

The master often had a number of assistants known as "master's mates." They normally came from the ranks of the brighter seamen and formed a grade intermediate between midshipman and lieutenant. They were usually a little older than midshipmen and, being qualified to navigate, were better paid. For that reason many midshipmen took certificates as master's mates as soon as they had the necessary qualifications. Another inducement was that the mate could navigate a prize into port and thus qualify for a greater share of prize money. By the end of the eighteenth century the two grades, master's mate and midshipman, were so intermixed that they messed and berthed together on board ship, and they can be considered as one group in the ship's company. The mate could take an examination for lieutenant and thus enter the commissioned ranks in the same manner as the midshipman.

After a brief interruption in the survey, while Gardner's ships prepared for sea duty in response to reports of French build-ups in the area, Vancouver and Whidbey, in January, 1788, continued their surveying in Port Royal and among the keys outside the harbor. That was another job of major proportions, for outside the entrance and south of it is an extensive group of keys and reefs forming a labyrinth included in a rectangle about four by five miles in extent. The well-executed chart resulting from the work of Vancouver and Whidbey is now in the Admiralty's library in London.

In June Commodore Gardner, with his pennant in the *Europa,* took his whole squadron to sea for exercises together and cruised off the north coast of Jamaica, visiting several of the outlying ports. The squadron returned to Port Royal late in July and to the regular inner moorings for the hurricane season. There, with only normal shipboard routine to be carried out, the ships lay until November and the end of the hurricane threat.

In January, 1789, the *Europa* made a cruise to Navassa Island, between Jamaica and Haiti, and then to Cartagena, on the South American coast of Colombia; this was the first time she had been away from the island of Jamaica during her whole tour on the station. While the *Europa* was cruising to the south Captain Peter Rainier, for whom the mountain in Washington was named, in the *Astrea,* looked into Havana and brought back encouraging reports of the light Spanish strength there. Returning to Port Royal in February the *Europa* remained there until June, when Rear Admiral Affleck arrived to take command of the station. The day after his arrival, Commodore Gardner, in the *Europa,* with the *Expedition,* the *Astrea,* and the *Cygnet* in company, sailed for England by way of the west coast of Cuba and the Straits of Florida. They arrived in England late in August, and Commodore Gardner moved on to become one of the Lords of the Admiralty. On September 15 Vancouver was paid off from the *Europa* after a cruise lasting almost five years. He went on half pay for a few months but was soon selected for a much more important task than any he had yet had.

An incident which gives us an interesting sidelight into Vancouver's character may have occurred at about this time. In 1818 there appeared in London a handbill caricature of the eccentric Lord Cochrane called "Belasarious the Counterfeit and Belasarious of the Ancients Contrasted." [5] Cochrane had refused to pay a fine in 1816 and it was paid by a popular penny subscription. In 1818 there were many former sailors in distress in London and Cochrane spoke out for their relief. The caricature shows him holding out a begging can and a sailor is about to drop a penny in it. His companion calls on him to wait and among other things says: "How did he sarve poor Vancouver, when he wanted the money he'd lent him in Charity, to rig him for a Midshipman? why just as he sarved his poor old Father, for tho' his lockers were well stored, he only jeered and denied him." [6] Nowhere does Vancouver mention Lord Cochrane, but the latter did enter the navy in about 1789 and had a long and contentious career.

Vancouver's Caribbean cruises were on the whole dull and routine in nature. A watchful suspicion of potential enemies provided the only excitement. The greatest hazard of the cruises was the ever present threat of fever with its high mortality rate. Anyone reading the various journals of the officers at that time is impressed by the appalling rates of deaths from diseases—yellow fever and other tropical fevers, aggravated by the crowded living conditions on board ship. The hospitals were little better than the ships in treating the diseases, as nothing was then known of their causes or of the preventive measures that could bring them under control. Admiral Innes, Gardner's predecessor, and several of the captains died during Vancouver's tour on the station. His own advancements were due to the deaths of lieutenants senior to him on the list or to similar promotions for them in turn. There is no indication that he was sick at any time during his whole tour, and indeed his health must have been good because he was chosen for an arduous task that required the best of health to see it through.

27

The greatest benefit that Vancouver gained from his tours in the Caribbean, aside from experience gained and skill in seamanship acquired, was his association with Sir Alan Gardner. Since he performed his duties with ability and thoroughness, Gardner made him a favorite, gave him increased responsibilities, and became his friend and benefactor. This had an immediate effect for at the Admiralty plans were in preparation that would require officers with the precise skills Vancouver had already demonstrated. Sir Alan Gardner was in an ideal position to work him into those plans.

3

The Spanish Armament
(1786-90)

BRITISH TRADERS IN THE NORTH PACIFIC (1786-89)

AFTER THE GENERAL demobilization in 1783 of the principal navies and the resulting unemployment of many officers, merchant marine service in the Pacific attracted a number of half-pay or retired lieutenants. The publication in 1784 of the account of Cook's third voyage directed the attention of many venturesome sailors to the possibilities of the sea otter fur trade from the northwest coast of America to China.[1] Aside from activities of the Russians, who began to expand their trading operations to mainland Alaska in 1784, the first trading voyage after the Revolution was made by Captain John Hanna in 1785, from China to Nootka Sound, the port on Vancouver Island first described by Cook. That profitable voyage was the beginning of an expanding trade that in only four years was to make Nootka Sound a focal point of world attention over which a major war was narrowly averted. In 1786 five or more British ships were on the northwest coast in the fur trade, but only one of them is of special interest here. This is the *Nootka*, which sailed from Bengal for the Gulf of Alaska in March, 1786, under the command of Captain John Meares, an adventurer who had formerly been a lieutenant in the navy. After a summer season's trading, the ship spent the following winter in a cove on Hinchinbrook Island, at the entrance to Prince William Sound in the upper Gulf of Alaska.

29

There, in May, 1787, she was found by Captain George Dixon, of the *Queen Charlotte,* with the survivors of her crew suffering severely from scurvy; twenty-three of them had already died from the malady.

The *Queen Charlotte* was one of two ships sent out from England in 1785 by a group of London merchants, Etches and Company, to engage in the fur trade. The leader of the expedition was Captain Portlock, in the *King George.* Like Meares, both Portlock and Dixon were former naval officers, and both had been with Cook on his third voyage. After wintering in Hawaii the two ships had just returned to Prince William Sound for a second season of trading when Meares was found. Portlock and Dixon gave Meares what provisions they could spare and helped him to get his ship in condition for sailing. Before Meares sailed in June, Captain Portlock exacted from him a bond in which Meares agreed to stop all trading and to leave the northwest coast. Meares's account of his voyage, published in 1790, was highly critical of his treatment by Portlock and Dixon and resulted in a public pamphleteering battle between Dixon and Meares.

The important part of that argument is simply stated, and it is the key to most of Meares's future troubles. In order for an English ship to trade legally on the northwest coast and in China, it was necessary for her to carry two special licenses from the great English overseas trading monopolies. The charter of the South Sea Company, of 1711, gave that company exclusive British trading privileges on the western coast of America for a distance of three hundred leagues offshore. Although the Great South Sea Bubble burst in 1720, and the company never recovered from that financial collapse, its charter was still active in the late eighteenth century. English ships were required to have its license to trade on the northwest coast. The powerful East India Company had similar exclusive rights over the markets of China. Its licenses were especially galling and restrictive for the company required the ship to be placed completely under its domination and all business in China had to be conducted through the company's agents.[2] The ships were subjected to the arbitrary rulings of company officials and agents, and the company took none of the risks, although it stood to profit richly from every successful fur-trading voyage. These license restrictions caused severe financial hardships to English traders and are at least part of the reason that American traders took over the bulk of the northwest coast fur trade in the late 1790's.

When Captain Portlock required Meares to give bond to stop trading in 1787, it was because Meares held no licenses while Portlock's two ships were duly licensed by both companies. As Judge Frederick W. Howay, who devoted most of his life to an intensive study of the early history of the Pacific, has pointed out Meares was a poacher in English eyes and his ship could have been seized as a lawful prize.[3] After that experience Meares continued to evade the licensing restrictions by ostensibly operating out of Macao under the Portuguese flag.

Early in 1788 Meares, then commanding the *Felice,* and Captain Douglas, in the *Iphigenia,* sailed from China for Nootka Sound. Meares and his backers had taken on a Portuguese partner, one Cavalho, of Macao. Through him the ships were outfitted with Portuguese papers and captains, although the Portuguese captains were supercargoes in the real organization. Meares later explained the device as one to evade excessive port charges which the Chinese imposed on all but the Portuguese, but it is obvious from the course of events that the real reason was to evade the licenses required by the English companies. The *Iphigenia* went directly to Alaska on a trading cruise, while the *Felice* reached Nootka in May. On board were a number of Chinese artisans and material for a small trading vessel or tender to be built at Nootka. A house and workshop were built in one of the coves of Nootka Sound for the use of Meares's men. While his tender was being built, Meares himself went off on a trading cruise from which he returned in July.[4] The new vessel, named the *North West America,* and the first to be built in that part of the world, was launched near the end of September. The *Iphigenia* and the *North West America* sailed soon afterward for the Hawaiian Islands to spend the winter while Meares, in the *Felice,* returned to China with the season's take of furs. No trouble had been experienced with other traders, for whenever there was any doubt the Portuguese colors were used, especially when launching the *North West America*. Meares later denied this, and a plate in his *Voyages* shows the vessel on the stocks wearing outsize English colors, but there is too much evidence to the contrary to accept his denial at face value.

In China Meares engineered a merger of his group with the legitimate Etches company, which had two ships in China at the time. That gave the new group four vessels for trading, two of them wintering in the Hawaiian Islands with dual nationality. But Meares then had a share in the Etches company's licenses, at least for two ships. In early 1789 Captain James Colnett, in the *Argonaut*, and the *Princess Royal*, Captain Hudson, were to go to Nootka and there build a permanent factory, using Chinese craftsmen whom Colnett would take with him. Detailed instructions for the project were contained in sailing orders given to Colnett by Meares, who chose to remain in China for the season. Those orders brought Colnett, and Meares's project, into direct conflict with the Spaniards, who by that time were getting more and more concerned over foreign encroachments in regions they considered their own.

THE NOOTKA INCIDENT

Since 1774 the Spaniards had sent exploring expeditions from Mexico northward and had taken formal possession of several places along the coast for Spain. Members of expeditions in 1774, 1775, 1788, and 1789 spent the summer months exploring and surveying the coast, and they were gradually mapping the whole coast as far north as the Gulf of Alaska. When La Pérouse, the French explorer, visited Monterey, California, in September, 1786, after being on the Alaskan coast, he produced a Russian map showing four Russian posts in Alaska, with one indicated to be established at Nootka Sound. In 1788 the Spanish government decided to investigate the Russian activities in Alaska and sent Captain Estaban José Martinez from Mexico to the northwest coast for that purpose. He reached as far north as Prince William Sound. On his return Martinez, alarmed by the extent of trading activity he had seen, recommended to Viceroy Flores that Nootka be occupied to forestall any Russian expansion toward California.

The viceroy commissioned Martinez to occupy the port, and his action was later approved by the Spanish government. Flores not only wanted to check Russian expansion southward from Alaska but also was fearful that the new American republic or England might get a foothold on the northwest coast. Blocking the growing threat to the security of the California missions, rather than trade, was the real purpose of the move.

Martinez arrived in Nootka Sound early in May, 1789, prepared to establish a permanent Spanish colony complete with a garrison and fortifications. The buildings Meares had erected the year before were no longer there. Two weeks before Martinez reached Nootka, Captain Douglas, in the *Iphigenia,* returned there with the *North West America* from Hawaii. The *North West America* was sent off on a trading cruise, but the *Iphigenia,* wearing her Portuguese colors, was still in port when Martinez arrived. Also present was the American trading ship *Columbia,* Captain Ingraham. The statement of Ingraham, as the only neutral present, so to speak, was important in later negotiations concerning what took place at that time.

Martinez soon became suspicious of the apparent double nationality of the *Iphigenia* and asked to see her papers. He became even more suspicious over a section of Douglas' Portuguese instructions which told him that if any Russian, Spanish, or English ship should attempt to divert him from the purpose of his voyage he was to resist by force. In case he had superior strength he was to seize the ship and bring her into port for proceedings before a prize court. On the strength of that paragraph Martinez seized the *Iphigenia,* but he decided to release her two weeks later because of his lack of men to send her to Mexico. After her release the *Iphigenia* left the harbor on a trading cruise. Douglas claimed that Martinez had tried unsuccessfully to get a letter from him to Captain Funter, of the *North West America,* ordering him to sell the small vessel to the Spaniards. In June the *North West America* returned to Nootka and was seized by Martinez, ostensibly as security for bills owed him by Meares's company for supplies furnished the *Iphigenia.* A few days later Meares's newly acquired ship, the *Princess Royal,* arrived in Nootka from China. Captain Hudson was well received and observed the formalities of taking possession of Nootka Sound by Martinez at the end of June. A few days later he sailed on a trading cruise. In the evening of the same day that the *Princess Royal* left Nootka, Captain Colnett arrived from China in the *Argonaut*. Colnett was prepared to build the Meares-Etches company's new factory but was completely unprepared to find the Spaniards in formal and full possession of the place.

Trouble started at once, but the exact details are uncertain since the various accounts of the affair conflict. Colnett's own journal is vindictive and full of complaints, while Martinez's account, straightforward and factual, is presented in the most favorable light to himself.[5]

On his arrival at Nootka, according to Colnett, he received a letter from Captain Hudson telling him of the seizure of the *North West America* by Martinez. He claimed that he then asked only for permission to build a boat which he had on board in frame, but that was refused. He further asserted that Martinez accused him of being a pirate and arrested him.[6] According to Martinez, Colnett claimed to be a British naval officer and was threatening in his attitude, implying that his proposed factory was a government-sponsored project. Colnett was evasive when Martinez asked to see his papers but finally produced the license from the East India Company. Colnett demanded that he be allowed to sail from the port, threatening to sail under the fire of Martinez' guns if necessary. The conversation became heated, and Martinez recorded that he heard the words "God damned Spaniard." [7] Thereupon Martinez arrested Colnett on the spot and seized his ship, with her officers and crew.

The *Argonaut* was sent to San Blas, Mexico, in the middle of July, with Colnett and the other Englishmen of the ship's company on board as prisoners. With her Martinez sent a full report to the viceroy, telling what had taken place in the form of affidavits. What he really feared was that Colnett, having been beaten into Nootka by the Spaniards, would try to set up his factory at some other place on the northwest coast. And that is very likely what Colnett would have done if he could have slipped out of Nootka. The Chinese on the ship when she was seized were later sent to China. Shortly after the *Argonaut* was sent to Mexico the *Princess Royal* returned to Nootka, was seized by Martinez, and was also sent to San Blas.

When he received Martinez' report on the seizure of the *Argonaut* late in August, the viceroy rushed a report of the incident to Madrid. And when the *Princess Royal* arrived at San Blas a month later it was followed by a second report. Flores was on the point of being relieved as viceroy by Count Revilla Gigedo, who later released the Englishmen and restored their ships to them. Revilla Gigedo waited several months for instructions from Madrid and finally acted on his own initiative, since he felt that Martinez did not have sufficient grounds for seizing the ships. But it was not until the spring of 1790 that the ships were released, and meanwhile they were used by the Spaniards for gathering material for the reinforcement of Nootka. In the interim the two English captains went to Mexico City to lay their complaints personally before the viceroy, but Revilla Gigedo delayed acting while waiting for the expected instructions from Madrid. Eventually, and still without any word from Spain, early in May he released the two ships on the condition that they would not trade or try to establish themselves on the Spanish coast. Colnett sailed from San Blas in the *Argonaut* in July and went to Nootka, where he expected to receive the *Princess Royal*. She was not there when he arrived but was delivered to him at Hawaii several months later. While at Nootka he professed to have lost the passport given him by the viceroy because in it, he later explained, he "was expressly forbid trading on the Coast." [8] He intended to gather a cargo of furs on the northwest coast before returning to China and did so.

CRISIS IN EUROPE

The viceroy of Mexico's first dispatches on the seizure of the *Argonaut* reached Madrid in early January, 1790. At that time Spain had regained some of her lost prestige and was considered still a nation to be reckoned with in Europe. Charles III, the ablest of her Bourbon kings, had died only two years before; and his equally able minister, Count Florida Blanca, was still in office. In the Treaty of Paris of September, 1783, which formally closed the American Revolution, Spain failed to get her main desire of Gibraltar from England, but she did get Minorca and East Florida to add to her West Florida, in exchange for Providence Island, the Bahamas, and recognition of England's right to cut logwood in Honduras. On the whole she gained from that war and was still in a relatively strong position in 1790.

Soon after the dispatches from Mexico concerning Nootka reached Madrid, and, before Spain took any formal action on them, the British chargé d'affaires sent to London a garbled account of the incident, based on rumors. He was unable to get any amplification of those rumors. But in February, 1790, the Spanish ambassador in London handed the British Foreign Office a short note, which, after reciting the barest outline of the Nootka incident, asked the British government to restrain its subjects from violating Spanish territory. Pointedly, the Spanish note volunteered the information that the port of Nootka had been discovered by Martinez in 1774, four years before Captain Cook visited the place. Finally the note stated (in error) that the English prisoners had been released. Its tone was abrupt and demanding, with no hint of being conciliatory.

The British reply, handed to the ambassador two weeks later, was equally sharp, and subsequent events pointed up quite clearly that England did not intend to recognize Spain's claim to Nootka as Spanish territory. Her subjects had been trading on the northwest coast, and England was even then preparing to establish a permanent colony in that part of the world. The reply of the government of the younger Pitt demanded the immediate restoration of the seized vessel and suspended all discussion of Spanish pretensions to the territory until satisfaction was given for the seizure. Even while the first formal steps in the Nootka incident were being taken, Pitt was listening with some sympathy to the schemes of the South American agitator Colonel Miranda, who hoped to set up a new form of government in Spanish America. Further evidence that Pitt and his government were deeply interested in the American continents lay in a proposed scheme to found a convict colony on the northwest coast.

In 1788 Richard Cadman Etches, one of Meares's new partners, suggested to Sir Joseph Banks, who had been instrumental in the

establishment of the convict colony at Port Jackson (Sydney),
Australia, early in that year, that the government should found
a similar colony on the northwest coast. Sir Joseph was skeptical
of the costs, and Etches countered with another proposal on a
more modest scale. He also suggested that a survey of the coast
be made from Nootka Sound to Cook Inlet in Alaska. The latter
recommendation, in Judge Howay's opinion, may have been
the first for what was to become Vancouver's later expedition.[9]
Whatever the source of the idea, by the end of 1789 plans for
an expedition to the northwest coast, to include a detailed survey
of the coast and another search for the Northwest Passage, were
well advanced.

According to early plans, discussed in a draft of a letter dated
March, 1790, from Lord Grenville to Governor Philip of Australia, two ships were to be sent to the area. One, the *Gorgon,*
was to proceed to Australia, where it was to pick up about thirty
convicts and officers, and then to transport the men and supplies
to the northwest coast of the American continent. There the new
colony was to form "such a settlement as may be able to resist
any attacks from the natives, and lay the foundation of an establishment for the assistance of His Majesty's subjects in the prosecu-
tion of the fur trade from the N.W. coast of America." [10] The
other ship, the *Discovery,* was to be equipped to make a survey of
the northwest coast.

The letter from Grenville to Philip was apparently never sent,
and plans were altered subsequently, but the draft letter clearly
establishes that, before news of the seizure of Meares's ships at
Nootka reached England, plans for a permanent settlement on
the northwest coast had progressed almost to the point of execution. From the sequence of events following that seizure it is also
apparent that, confronted with the new situation, the British
government seized upon the Nootka incident as the vehicle for
gaining its objectives on the northwest coast. Although we cannot be certain, since the site of the proposed colony was not
named, it is probable that it was to be Nootka Sound. This was
the best-known harbor on the coast at that time, and it was
used as a base by most of the ships engaged in the fur trade.
It is of interest to note that one of the reasons given by Viceroy

37

Flores for ordering Martinez to occupy Nootka in 1789 was the potential threat from the new British colony in Australia.

The *Gorgon* sailed for Australia in March, 1790, after Sir Joseph Banks, indicating a personal interest in the project, had been instrumental in getting a Lieutenant Harvey assigned to command her, but she returned to England later in the same year.

The other ship selected for the expedition was obtained in the fall of 1789. Captain Henry Roberts, who was a lieutenant with Cook on his second voyage and with Clerke on the third voyage, was selected to command the ship. Lieutenant George Vancouver, who had returned from the West Indies in September, and who had served in the same ships with Roberts under Cook, was chosen as his first lieutenant. A ship of 340 tons, suitable for being rigged for surveying, was nearing completion at a shipyard on the Thames.[11] She was purchased by the Admiralty late in 1789, was named *Discovery* on being launched, and was commissioned as a sloop of war January 1, 1790. The following day she was moved to Deptford dockyard on the Thames between London and Greenwich. Near the end of April she was almost ready for sea and the voyage when developments in the Nootka incident caused the expedition to be canceled.

A few days after the *Discovery* was commissioned Lieutenant Vancouver reported on board, and for the next three months he was busily engaged in supervising the multitude of details that are a part of fitting out any ship for sea. Dockyard artificers were on board almost daily, setting, fitting, and testing masts, spars, rigging, and sails. There was a steady flow of equipment, supplies, and provisions to be received on board and stowed below— hundreds of items that would be needed on the long cruise. There were five anchors, three of them weighing over twenty-one hundred pounds each; coils of ropes and cables; rolls and bolts of canvas. Stowed on board were barrels, casks, hogsheads, and puncheons of salt beef, salt pork, peas, beer, and other provisions, including ample supplies of the antiscorbutics that Cook had used.[12] As executive assistant to the captain, Vancouver had to supervise all of this activity and insure that nothing was overlooked; a forgotten item might mean disaster when there was no dockyard to turn to later on.

While Vancouver was thus fully occupied with fitting out the ship, the Nootka Sound incident was being built into a major international crisis. The Spanish government took a month and a half to reply to the first British demand, and meanwhile it took steps to increase its active navy and prepare its Caribbean possessions for defense. These measures were ominous signs that Spain did not intend to yield and was preparing to fight for her position. Late in March the Spanish government directed the viceroy of Mexico to release Meares's ships, but that official had already done so before the order reached him. By early April the British chargé in Madrid observed the martial preparations and reported to London the rapid mobilization of the Spanish navy.

On April 20 the Spanish ambassador handed the British government a note reporting that Meares's ships had been released, reasserting Spain's claims to the northwest coast and advising that the incident was considered closed. It also renewed the Spanish demand that English subjects respect Spain's rights in that part of the world.

Then Meares arrived in London from China with his version of the affair. On April 30, writing as a lieutenant in the navy, Meares submitted a memorial to the House of Commons reporting the seizure of his land and ships by Spanish authorities at Nootka. In it he claimed that he had purchased land for his house from Indian chiefs in 1788, that he had built a breastwork and later made a deal with the local Indians for exclusive trade. Then, in 1789, Martinez seized Captain Douglas and the *Iphigenia* and Meares's land at Nootka, and later also seized the *North West America,* the *Argonaut,* and the *Princess Royal.* Martinez was reported to have claimed to the Englishmen that all land from Cape Horn to latitude 60° north was Spanish territory. He estimated his actual losses as 153,433 Spanish dollars and probable total losses as 500,000 dollars.

That memorial provided the ammunition the British ministers wanted. In the very evening of the day Meares submitted his memorial to Commons, the cabinet recommended to the king that a demand be presented to Spain for an "immediate and adequate satisfaction for the outrages committed by Monsieur de Martinez." [13] It also recommended fitting out a squadron of ships of the line to match the Spanish mobilization. The king approved the measures, and for the armament a general impressment of seamen was carried out suddenly during the night of May 4. The next day the English people, with no hint of developing trouble up to then, had a full-scale war scare.

The *Discovery,* nearing completion of her fitting out at Deptford, had her part in the general impressment. During the afternoon of May 4, Captain Sir Hyde Parker, later Nelson's superior at Copenhagen, came on board with a party of officers and men, and a pool of boats was assembled at the ship. Then, according to Joseph Whidbey, Vancouver's friend and now master of the ship: "AM 3 went with the Pool & began to Impress Men. 8 [A.M.] the pool returned—served grog (there being no Beer) to the Ships Compy & imprest Men." [14] Reporting an action repeated dozens of times at dozens of ports in England in the small hours of May 5, that brief and unimaginative entry in one officer's journal tells us eloquently what the impressment system for recruiting crews for British naval vessels was in that day. Without warning and late at night every able-bodied man that could be found was simply seized and herded aboard ship where he was hardly more than a prisoner, to be kept so until the national emergency was over. Only experienced seamen were supposed to be impressed, but press gangs seldom bothered to ask for seaman's credentials; live bodies were what counted. It was a cruel and brutal system, hard to appreciate in a more enlightened era, but it was the way England manned her ships for the many wars she fought in the eighteenth century.

On May 5 the king informed Parliament of the reason for the armament, outlined the state of negotiations with Spain to date, and revealed the Spanish claim to all the territory involved. It was this claim that stirred the British cabinet to action; the seizure of Meares's ships was made the excuse for a showdown on the point. On May 6 Pitt led the debate in Parliament stressing that acceptance of the Spanish claim would exclude England from the eastern Pacific. There was minor criticism from the opposition, but the address carried unanimously and the government's actions were confirmed. It was determined to make Spain acknowledge that she had no valid claim to any other part of

America than the territory she then occupied. Public feeling was incensed at the arrogance of the Spaniards; its support of the government's action was enthusiastic, and the naval rearmament went forward rapidly.

Vancouver's reaction to that rearmament was that "the uncommon celerity, and unparalleled despatch which attended the equipment of one of the noblest fleets that Great Britain ever saw, had probably its due influence upon the court of Madrid." [15] The Roberts expedition was canceled, and Vancouver joined his old friend Sir Alan Gardner in the ship of the line *Courageux*, captured from the French in 1761, and thirty years later still considered one of the finest 74's in the Royal Navy. He joined her late in May, 1790, as third lieutenant, and served in her through the mobilization—the Spanish Armament it was called at the time—until mid-December, 1790. The *Courageux* operated uneventfully with the Channel Fleet during that period. At the end of September Vancouver became first lieutenant upon the promotions of the former first and second lieutenants. The *Discovery* was used as a receiving ship for impressed seamen during the mobilization.

During these preparations, England asked for the support of Holland and Prussia under the alliance of 1788. The Dutch Republic responded openly by sending a fleet to join the English fleet, and Prussia also agreed to support England.

Spain also tried to line up allies. Her first choice and logical ally was France, with which she had been bound by the Family Alliance since the Seven Years' War. But Louis XVI was sitting on a tottering throne, and the National Assembly was in control of France in the early phases of the French Revolution. Spain's overtures were met by a partial mobilization of the French fleet, which precipitated the great debate in the National Assembly over whether the king or the people had the right to make war and peace. It was resolved by Mirabeau's compromise that only the legislative body could declare war after it had been formally proposed by the king. Spain could take some reassurance from the French rearmament, which was stated to be a precaution against the English mobilization, but she had no assurance that the French monarch could or would come to her assistance in case of war.

England sent one of her ablest diplomats, Alleyne Fitzherbert, as ambassador to Spain, and he carried out the remaining negotiations at Madrid.[16] England's military, or rather naval, strength was greater than Spain's, and her position with respect to allies was stronger. Under the circumstances Spain, with her own alliances shaky, yielded. The negotiations and diplomatic jockeying required to reach that result stretched over several months.

In the end Spain accepted the Nootka Sound Convention, an eight-article treaty that provided first for formal restoration of the buildings and land seized at Nootka in April, 1789, and for payment of reparations. The really important articles guaranteed that the nationals of both parties would not be disturbed in carrying out trade with the natives in the Pacific Ocean, except that British subjects would not engage in illicit trade with Spanish settlements. To insure that result it was agreed that British ships would not navigate within ten marine leagues of the coasts then occupied by Spain. North of that part of the coast actually occupied by Spain, wherever the subjects of either party had made settlements since April, 1789, the subjects of the other would have free access for trade. One article dealt with the temporary use of lands in South America southward of the existing Spanish settlements there. In a secret additional article it was agreed that that special article would no longer be in force should the subjects of a third power found settlements there. In the Nootka Sound Convention England got a foothold on the northwest coast of America, but the question of the northern limit of Spanish territory was left open. That omission was destined to play an important part in Vancouver's later negotiations and in the long-drawn-out Oregon Boundary Dispute many years later. The magnitude of the British diplomatic victory is indicated by the fact that in the Nootka Sound Convention, for the first time since the Treaty of Tordesillas of 1494, Spain formally conceded that another nation had rights in the Pacific.

A general war in Europe was averted by Spain's accession to the British demands. In England it was decided to send an officer to Nootka Sound at once to receive formal restitution of the lands seized by Martinez in 1789. Vancouver was chosen as that officer, and, at the same time, he was to command an expedition that would survey the western coast of North America from latitude 30° north to Cook Inlet in Alaska.

Up to this point Vancouver's name has not figured very prominently in this study, and necessarily so. There is little left in the records to tell us about his early life in the navy. He was a young officer who took part in historic events but had neither a voice nor a leading part in those events. In presenting the incidents and associations of his life thus far, the object has been to recreate, in some measure, the environment in which he grew up and in which he was being prepared to assume the responsibilities that were about to be given to him. In common with his fellows in the Royal Navy, he shared the prejudices, suspicions, and pride of the British people at that time in history. The Spanish Armament, and the martial spirit that went with it, illustrate the extent to which Britain was prepared to go to support her subjects and to maintain British prestige in the world. George Vancouver was a product of that environment, and how it influenced his future actions and attitudes will become more apparent as he now takes his rightful place as the central figure in this study.

4

Return to the Pacific
(1791-92)

AFTER AGREEMENT on the Nootka Sound Convention in Madrid in November, 1790, England made plans for taking under its flag the lands and property seized by Martinez at Nootka in 1789. The idea of the Roberts expedition was revived, and Lieutenant Vancouver was summoned to London from the *Courageux* in the middle of November to be offered command of the new expedition. Captain Roberts had resigned his commission in the *Discovery* to take command of another ship and was then in the Caribbean. Vancouver was promoted to master and commander, approximately equivalent to the modern naval rank of commander, and on December 15 he rejoined and assumed command of the *Discovery*.[1] Since the ship had been almost ready for sea in April when the Spanish Armament canceled the first expedition, less than a month was required for signing on a crew and completing taking on stores at Deptford. Two of her three lieutenants, Peter Puget and Joseph Baker, and Joseph Whidbey, the master, had been with Vancouver under Sir Alan Gardner and were his own choices for this voyage. Lieutenant Zachary Mudge was the first lieutenant. In addition to the four officers, the *Discovery* carried a surgeon, boatswain, gunner, carpenter, three master's mates, and twelve midshipmen. The balance of the *Discovery*'s company, her crew, was made up of various petty officer ratings, cooks, seamen, servants, and seventeen marines. Altogether there were 101 persons on board when the *Discovery* sailed from England.[2] Classed officially as a "sloop of war," she was a three-masted full-rigged ship.

On January 7, 1791, she made sail for the first time and stood down the Thames to Long Reach where she completed taking in her guns, ammunition, and other stores that had not been obtained at Deptford. Then she proceeded down the river and through the Channel to Falmouth, with calls en route at Spithead, Plymouth, and Guernsey. There she waited for her tender to join her.

Chosen as the consort for the *Discovery* was the armed tender *Chatham*, a two-masted brig of 130 tons.[3] She was built at Dover in 1788 and was used as a tender for impressed seamen during the Spanish Armament. She was to have accompanied the *Discovery* in the Roberts expedition and, being in need of repairs, was placed in drydock at Woolwich, on the Thames below Greenwich. There, on January 1, 1791, Lieutenant William R. Broughton placed her in commission and assumed command.[4] This sturdy little vessel, only about sixty feet long and broad for her length, was often criticized for her poor sailing qualities during the voyage, but she carried her crew of forty-five safely around the world in a voyage that was to last nearly five years. In addition to Broughton she had one lieutenant and a master, the usual warrant officers, and seven master's mates and midshipmen.[5] The *Chatham* completed her repairs in the middle of February, dropped down the river to complete her ordnance stores at Long Reach, and later joined the *Discovery* at Falmouth.

As was the case with every voyage of this nature, Sir Joseph Banks had a voice in the preparations. Before the *Discovery* left Long Reach she embarked a native Hawaiian Islander named Towereroo, who had been brought to England by a fur trader in 1789, and whose return passage had been arranged by Sir Joseph. In addition, Banks was instrumental in having Archibald Menzies, a surgeon in the navy who had made an earlier voyage to the Pacific in a fur-trading vessel, appointed naturalist of the Roberts expedition. When that expedition was revived under Vancouver's command Menzies asked to go as surgeon of the *Discovery* with

45

additional duty as naturalist of the expedition. Vancouver, who had definite ideas of his own on how this expedition was to be conducted, objected to this arrangement, and Menzies was assigned only as botanist of the expedition. A most unusual circumstance was that Lord Grenville, secretary of state for home affairs, whose department had a material interest in the expedition, had Sir Joseph Banks prepare the formal instructions for Menzies and his natural science work.[6] A small greenhouse for keeping botanical specimens, designed by Sir Joseph, was erected on the quarterdeck of the *Discovery.*

Banks had withdrawn from Cook's second voyage after Cook objected vigorously to the elaborate equipment that the former insisted on taking with him. Vancouver also strongly objected to Sir Joseph's interference with his own preparations. Shortly before the expedition sailed, Menzies wrote to Sir Joseph complaining of his messing arrangements and asking assistance in getting reimbursed for some extra charges made to him.[7] In a letter to Menzies the following August, Sir Joseph wrote these ominous words:

> How Captain Vancouver will behave to you is more than I can guess, unless I was to judge by his conduct toward me—which was such as I am not used to receive from one in his station. . . . As it would be highly imprudent in him to throw any obstacle in the way of your duty, I trust he will have too much good sense to obstruct it.[8]

It was unfortunate that Menzies should have to begin the voyage under such contentious circumstances, for he proved to be one of the most interesting and valuable members of the expedition. Later he became a distinguished physician and naturalist and ended his days as president of the Linnean Society. Vancouver's resentment in his case was directed at Sir Joseph Banks's interference in his plans for the voyage rather than at Menzies personally.

A further indication that Vancouver was lukewarm to having nonservice specialists with him was his belief that it was not necessary to take along an astronomer. He felt that, with their earlier experience in the Caribbean, he and Whidbey could handle all the required astronomical observations during the voyage. But he had a quick change of mind on that point, for after leaving England he took the first opportunity to write back from Tenerife asking that an astronomer be sent out in the storeship that would bring him supplies the following year.

Like Captain Cook, Vancouver had a great deal to say about the instructions issued to him. Before joining the *Discovery* he spent a month at the Admiralty during which the proposed voyage and its objects were outlined to him. While his ship was lying at Plymouth for final repairs in February he spent three weeks in London consulting further on the details. And in March at Falmouth, where he waited for the final draft of his instructions, he wrote a long letter to the Admiralty outlining his desires with respect to the rendezvous of the storeship and the supplies to be sent to him. As we shall have reason to refer to his instructions in some detail as we go along, they, together with the supplementary instructions sent to him in the storeship, are reproduced in full in the appendix. Once his instructions were in hand Vancouver waited impatiently for the *Chatham,* then working her way from the Thames to Falmouth, where she arrived on the last day of March.

In retelling the events of a long voyage of exploration, such as this one, reliance must be placed mainly upon the official account of the voyage, in this case Vancouver's own encyclopedic three-volume work, published under the auspices of the Admiralty in 1798. In addition there are the journals which the officers and midshipmen were required to keep and which were collected and delivered to the Admiralty at the end of the voyage. This kind of record is likely to be dull, lifeless, and of little value, for any critical or overly frank remark could be used against its author in the future. Nevertheless, many of the journals, notably the very detailed one of Lieutenant Peter Puget, contribute materially to our knowledge of this voyage. Three other journals, which escaped the chain of official channels, are invaluable in revealing details and incidents that are missing from the official accounts. These are the journals of Archibald Menzies and of Edward Bell, captain's clerk of the *Chatham,* and a private journal kept by Thomas Manby—midshipman, master's mate, lieutenant in the

Discovery, and for a time master of the *Chatham*—in the form of letters to a friend. Manby's formal journal, though less frank a narrative than the private one, is also useful.

AUSTRALIA AND NEW ZEALAND

With favorable winds, at dawn on April 1, 1791, the two ships got under way from Falmouth to begin what was to prove to be one of the longest continuous voyages in history. It began under circumstances not unlike those that marked the departure of Cook on his third voyage in 1776. Only the evening before, the king's proclamation ordering what came to be known as the Russian Armament reached Falmouth. This was a new mobilization of the fleet to back up Pitt's intervention in the Russo-Turkish War, then going against the Turks, to prevent Catherine the Great from expanding her territories too far. Less powerful than the Spanish Armament, it proved to be politically embarrassing to Pitt and was disbanded after the Russo-Turkish War ended in August.

Most of the journals kept by the officers and midshipmen followed a form prescribed in their navigational textbooks. Daily at sea for every hour was recorded the ship's speed in knots, the compass courses steered, the wind direction, and the state of the weather.[9] The right-hand side of the form had space for remarks and the recording of routine events on board such as changing sails, how the crew was employed, and so on. In those journals may be found, of almost daily occurrence and sometimes oftener, the entry, "Made the Chatham's signal to bend on more sail." [10] Experienced naval officers will recognize there, from their own watch-standing days, the sailing ship equivalent of the modern tactical signal, "Close up." Smartness in precise station-keeping in formation was and is a matter of pride—the outward sign of a good seaman. This was Vancouver's first command, and he was doubly fortunate in it, for he not only commanded his own ship, but also was "commodore" of a two-ship squadron. The frequent displays of concern for the station-keeping of the *Chatham,* annoying no doubt to her officers when so often repeated but otherwise rather harmless, were a sign of the autocratic powers inherent in a command such as his, and of his tendency to assert them. A strict disciplinarian and a real seaman, he was serving notice that his small force was expected to maintain the same high standards of performance that prevailed in the big ships and fleets. It will be seen, however, that, every time the two vessels became separated, in spite of her reputation for sluggishness the *Chatham* managed to reach the next port ahead of the *Discovery*.

Having his choice of routes to the Pacific, Vancouver followed Cook's precedent and chose the Cape of Good Hope route, planning to stop at the Madeiras en route for a supply of wine and fresh provisions. Unfavorable winds carried him past that group, and he then chose Tenerife, in the Canaries. Another reason for making a stop so early in the voyage was to shift ballast in the *Chatham* in an effort to improve her seaworthiness.

The ten-day stay at Tenerife was marred by what came near to being another international incident. On a Sunday afternoon Vancouver and several of the officers and midshipmen, and some of the crews, were on shore seeing the sights. As sailors do, several of them soon found the local equivalent of the Thames-side grog shops. When one of the midshipmen took the boats in to bring off the liberty party he found many of them brawling among themselves at the landing. As the midshipman was trying to herd them into the boats, a Spanish sentry, who was taking a look at the proceedings was disarmed by one of the men. The sentry ran to the sentry house and called out the guard. When Vancouver heard of the ruckus he rushed to the landing and in trying to break up the melee was pushed overboard, as were several of the others. Only one of the officers was in uniform and armed at the time. Whidbey, who was in Vancouver's party, was lunged at by a Spanish soldier with a bayonet and sidestepped just in time to see the bayonet shattered on a stone wall beside him. The whole English party finally got off with no more than a few bruises.[11] The next day Vancouver sent a strong letter of protest to the governor of the island. The latter answered regretting the incident and promising to punish the offenders. Vancouver gave two of his own offending sailors a taste of the lash for their part in the affair, and two seamen and a marine in the *Chatham* received the same.

49

From Tenerife Vancouver shaped his course to pass close to and westward of the Cape Verde Islands. Pushed on by the steady northeast trade winds, the ships made a fast and pleasant passage until soon after they passed the Cape Verdes, when they entered the doldrums, the belt of calm airs lying between the northeast and southeast trade winds. Vancouver chose to cross the doldrums considerably westward of the then generally accepted track for the Cape of Good Hope, correctly believing that the doldrum belt was narrower there than it was further east. He crossed the line in longitude 25° west; from there his southerly track leaned westward to within about 350 miles of Brazil and thence southward to the belt of prevailing westerly winds, which carried him in a great looping sweep to the Cape of Good Hope. His track from the Canaries to the Cape followed closely the modern recommended track for sailing vessels.

Irked at the fancied poor sailing of the *Chatham,* about ten days before he reached the Cape, Vancouver decided to make the rest of his way independently, leaving the *Chatham* to do the same. But on July 11 when the *Discovery* reached Simon's Bay, across a neck of land from Capetown itself, the *Chatham* was found quietly riding at anchor there, having arrived the day before. The 5,700-mile run from Tenerife to the Cape was made in sixty-three days, an average of just over ninety miles a day.

The Cape of Good Hope was a major crossroads of the world in that day of sail. No fewer than seventeen ships were there when the *Discovery* and *Chatham* arrived, British East Indiamen, Dutchmen, Danes, and Americans. Three of them were transports bearing convicts to Australia under convoy of the *Gorgon,* the ship that was to have been in the original Roberts expedition. The thrifty Dutch had a large and profitable trade at the Cape, supplying passing ships with meats, vegetables, and other supplies and services. The crews of the *Discovery* and *Chatham,* for example, had fresh meat, vegetables, and soft bread every day they were in port.[12]

If anything, Vancouver was even more meticulous than Cook in watching over his crew's health and in taking measures to prevent and treat scurvy. Since this was the last civilized place they expected to visit for an indefinite time, both ships took on all the provisions they could stow; eighteen months' supply for the *Discovery* and fifteen for the *Chatham*. Necessary voyage repairs were made, and the rate of error of the chronometers was determined on shore. Everything possible was done to prepare the ships for the long voyage ahead when they would be completely on their own resources. Four seamen who were in poor health were sent home from the *Discovery*. They were replaced from the transports and an East Indiaman. Unexpected and unwelcome was a severe epidemic of dysentery that broke out on both ships. It also appeared on shore and among the other ships present. Investigation traced the source to a Dutch ship that had brought many cases into port in a dying condition.[13] Since the outbreak occurred near the end of their stay, Vancouver felt it best to get clear of the port as soon as possible. The two ships sailed in the middle of August, after a stay of six weeks at Simon's Bay.

While at the Cape, Vancouver wrote to Lord Grenville of his intention to explore and survey the southwest coast of Australia, then mainly blank on the map. The subject had been under discussion before he left England, but no final decision had been reached. The leg of the voyage from the Cape of Good Hope to Australia was marked by alternating stormy and fine weather. It was the winter season in the southern hemisphere, and the track was near the fortieth parallel of south latitude, marking the edge of the fabled "Roaring Forties." On the seventh of September one of the marines died of dysentery contracted at the Cape, the first fatality since leaving England. Two days later the ships passed between St. Paul and Amsterdam islands, where Vancouver wanted to check the charted position of one of them, but stormy weather prevented observations. From there the track to Australia was laid between those of earlier voyages in case there might be an undiscovered island or two in those waters. There was not, and late in the month a landfall was made near the southwestern point of Australia; Point D'Entrecasteaux it is now called, but Vancouver named it Cape Chatham.

From that point he sailed close inshore and surveyed some 350 miles of the southern coast of Australia. The most important find was King George the Third's Sound, now shortened to King George Sound. The town of Albany now lies on an inner harbor of the sound, which was named Princess Royal Harbor by Vancouver. There he took formal possession of the country in the name of his king. It is worthy of note that, unlike Cook's instructions, Vancouver's omitted any order to take possession of new discoveries; but Vancouver did so regularly. He endowed many land features along this coast with the names of officers in the navy—a practice that he also followed later on the northwest coast of America. In late October, faced with threatening weather and a southerly wind, he gave up the survey of the Australian coast and headed for the southern cape of Tasmania. Rounding that cape four days later, and with a fair wind, Vancouver laid course for Dusky Bay, New Zealand. Although the dysentery had nearly disappeared, many of the crew were still weak, and Dusky Bay was the most accessible nearby place for them to recuperate.

The nine-hundred-mile run across the Tasman Sea was made in only six days, a splendid performance for both vessels. They reached Dusky Bay just ahead of a bad storm. While there the men were employed in fishing, brewing spruce beer, operating a portable observatory on shore for checking the rates of error of the chronometers and the geographical position of the bay, and general work about the ships. Many of the officers, including Captain Broughton of the *Chatham,* spent much of their time shooting, and they brought back geese, ducks, and indeed about anything else that came within range of their guns. Vancouver, more seriously inclined, spent his time surveying an inlet that Cook had indicated on his chart with the title "Nobody Knows What." "The heads of these arms, in conformity with Captain Cook's name of their entrance, I have called *Somebody Knows What,*" he recorded.[14]

After a three-week stay in Dusky Bay the two ships sailed for Tahiti, intending to pass southward of New Zealand.[15] Shortly after they left the port a violent storm made up just as six feet of water was found in the *Discovery*'s hold. With the wind increasing hourly this could have been a very serious development. Fortunately the wind was from the northwest, allowing the ship to run before it well clear of any land while the cause of the water in the hold was being sought. In short order it was found that the pumps were choked—since the daily tests of the pumps had

Portrait believed to be of Captain George Vancouver
(see chapter 5, note 13)

Mount Rainier, from a plate in Vancouver's *Voyage of Discovery*

shown no water it had been assumed that the hold was dry. Once the situation was corrected a few hours at the pumps cleared the hold of several weeks' accumulation of water, and all was well again.[16]

By then the storm had increased in fury, and during the night the *Chatham* lost touch with her consort. In the morning land was sighted from the *Discovery;* it proved to be a group of rocky islets, lying about sixty miles southwest of Stewart Island, the southernmost of the New Zealand chain. Vancouver named the group The Snares. The storm continued for another day, and when it abated the *Discovery* could shape a course northeastward for Tahiti. Much to Vancouver's disappointment, during that run the last of thirteen sheep, taken aboard at the Cape of Good Hope and intended as a present for the natives of Tahiti, died.

Just before Christmas, after the *Discovery* had been driven well to the east by contrary winds, an island was discovered in a part of the ocean where no known ship had been before. It was not a large island, nor did it appear to be productive of surplus food-stuffs, so Vancouver spent little time there. As nearly as he could understand from the natives its name was Oparo, but it is shown on modern charts as Rapa Island. The *Discovery* sailed on and anchored in Matavia Bay, on the northern side of the island of Tahiti, on December 30, to find that the *Chatham* had arrived there three days before.

The *Chatham* had been battered about severely by the storm. She had sighted The Snares the same day the *Discovery* did, but soon afterward was able to sail direct for Tahiti. En route Broughton spent several days exploring an extensive island. When he landed on one occasion the natives would not respond to friendly overtures, and he decided to re-embark rather than have possible trouble. Just as he was about to get his small party back into the boat some of the natives attacked them with spears. A marine shot one of them without waiting for Broughton's order to fire, and the others then withdrew. This was the first of only two fatal brushes with natives in the course of the entire voyage.

The island, lying about 450 miles east of South Island, New Zealand, received the name Chatham Island, honoring the second earl, then First Lord of the Admiralty, rather than the ship. An inscribed lead plate and a sealed bottle left a permanent record of Broughton's discovery. After leaving Chatham Island the little vessel had mixed weather and winds, but one day in mid-December she logged 150 miles, "which for our *Dung Barge* was reckon'd tolerable," according to her clerk.[17] She reached Matavia Bay without incident. Broughton was much surprised that the *Discovery* had not yet arrived, because of her "superiority in sailing"; and his surprise was matched by Vancouver's on finding that the *Chatham* had beaten him in again.

TAHITI

On a prolonged sea voyage such as this a feeling of boredom unavoidably develops in a small ship. The intimacy of life and the confines of the ship breed frayed nerves, irritations, and antipathies. Above all the captain's mind and method are laid open to minute examination. The *Discovery* was a mere one hundred feet long by thirty feet beam, by modern standards a very tubby little ship, with few sanitary facilities or comforts. There was no heat in cold weather, and candles provided the only light at night. Ventilation below decks was irregular, and with one hundred men crowded into such a small space the smells could become unbearable. That was why Cook, and his pupil Vancouver, periodically had smudge fires built below decks and the living spaces scrubbed down with vinegar. Life aboard such a small ship was much more confining and disagreeable than on any modern one, so it is not surprising to find that jealousies and tempers began to flare up. By the time the *Discovery* and the *Chatham* reached Tahiti the expedition was already nine months away from England—over six of them spent at sea.

Vancouver ran what is known as a "taut" ship. Strict and firm, he matched those qualities with wisdom and at times tact, and he was concerned with the health and welfare of his men. That concern was not always appreciated because of the way in which it was shown. At times he gave way to sudden outbursts of temper, a trait that the writer, after much reflection and study, believes to be derived from the malady that took his life at a relatively early age. This characteristic behavior will be considered more fully as it increases later in the voyage. It is at Tahiti that we find the early signs of the irritations and resentments, inevitable after the months of monotonous cruising.

Vancouver's first act at Tahiti was to issue an order forbidding trade with the natives until the ship's needs in provisions such as hogs, vegetables, and coconuts were filled. When trade was allowed no article could be exchanged that tended to depreciate the value of the iron and beads that were the standard articles of trade. An effort was to be made to cultivate the friendship of the natives, and they were to be treated with kindness and humanity. Men employed on shore would be especially alert to prevent thefts by the natives. Severe penalties were assured for violations of the order.[18]

Such orders were wise, for the friendly and easygoing Polynesians, swarming about the ships and anxious to trade, had their own culture and way of life, very different from the European way. Even the most watchful and conscientious of captains could not prevent some contacts with their inevitable impact on the natives, but Vancouver took firm action to correct abuses and to prevent their spread. The only members of the crews allowed on shore at Tahiti were those on duty, an arrangement that Bell, the clerk of the *Chatham,* thought very unjust. Nevertheless he believed that Vancouver's motive, to prevent possible quarrels between the sailors and natives, was a good one. "My opinion of the natives however is such that I think I would answer for their not being the agressors and as to the Sailors I am inclin'd to think that as there are no Grog-Shops ashore to stop at, they would be equally peacable." [19]

The observatory was sent ashore to keep a running check on the chronometers, and the ships began stocking hogs and other provisions in which the island abounded. By means of a special press that Vancouver had built, the *Discovery* was able to salt and preserve twenty to thirty hogs per day. Vancouver and Broughton, with some of the officers, spent much of their time exchanging visits and presents with the native king and the principal chiefs of the island. Many of those whom Vancouver had known fifteen years before were then dead, but he found new friends and was soon on the best of terms with them. An old acquaintance of his earlier visits, who professed to remember him well, was Pomurrey, a leading chief who was a frequent diner on board the *Discovery.*

One day, Vancouver relates, during and after dinner Pomurrey managed to down a whole bottle of brandy and fell into a stupor. After an hour's nap and a massage by some of his people he seemed to be completely sober and demanded more brandy. Vancouver tried to convince him of the evils of excessive drinking, but Pomurrey accused him of being stingy and a poor companion. With that Vancouver decided to let him have his way and allowed him to consume all the brandy and rum he wanted, hoping that in a few days the effects of the liquor would cure him of his excessive appetite. "In this I was not mistaken," wrote Vancouver; "before the week expired he ceased calling for spirits; and a few glasses of wine, at and after dinner, completely satisfied him; frequently saying, that all I had told him of the 'Ava Britarne' was perfectly true." [20]

One evening Vancouver had a display of fireworks set off on shore for the entertainment of the natives. Though this was received with both terror and admiration, he was well pleased with the results, since it helped to impress the natives with the power of their white visitors. He and his officers were frequently entertained by the chiefs, in turn, with native dances and singing.

Near the end of their stay two of the natives were caught stealing a hat from on board the *Discovery.* As some petty thefts had also occurred at the camp on shore, Vancouver decided to make an example of the culprits. He had them taken to the camp and, in the presence of their chiefs and other natives, had their heads shaved and then had each given "a slight manual correction," as he expressed it.[21] Though seemingly an unusual punishment, the head-shaving was actually a shrewd device that he had learned from Cook. The victims became marked men among their fellows, "lost face" with them, and were usually seen no more around the ships.

A few days after that incident a bag of Captain Broughton's linen was filched from the camp ashore. This was much more serious, and Vancouver demanded the immediate return of the stolen goods, threatened to recover them by force, and further threatened to burn all the houses and destroy all the canoes in Matavia if the linen was not returned promptly. Tension grew, and many of the natives fled from the place, but Vancouver continued to deal patiently with some of the leading chiefs. He managed to keep at least one of them, or one of their wives, with him either at the camp or on board the *Discovery*. Although not forcibly held, they were hostages for insuring that the promises he received on returning the linen would be carried out. One suspect was brought in and Vancouver had him taken on board the *Discovery* with a halter around his neck. There the man was confined in irons, and the chiefs were assured that he would be hanged if the goods were not returned. When a leading chief convinced him of the prisoner's innocence, however, Vancouver released him. It was at this time that Towereroo, the Hawaiian passenger, decided that he preferred Tahiti to his home island and disappeared from the ship. Although Vancouver had formed a rather low opinion of the man, he was determined to return him to Hawaii and insisted that the chiefs deliver him back along with Broughton's linen. As an inducement for greater effort on their part, he told them that he planned to give each of them a substantial present on his departure but that unless Towereroo and the linen were recovered they would get nothing. During the negotiations and search, the tents and observatory were taken down and returned to the ships, and preparations were made for sailing. Towereroo was eventually returned by one of the chiefs, and Vancouver was very much annoyed by his having delayed sailing for a day or two. Broughton's linen was never recovered, since it was established that the thief was from a distant village, and Vancouver did not want to delay sailing any longer to press the issue.

All accounts of early voyages to the Pacific, Vancouver's included, contain long and detailed descriptions of the natives of the various islands, their customs, and their way of life. From them the reader gets a picture of a carefree and happy people whose needs were few and who expended a minimum of effort to supply their needs on those lush islands. Their community life was ruled by a hierarchy of chiefs centering in a leading chief or king. It was more of a social hierarchy than a military one, although the military element was present, especially among the Hawaiians, who were much more warlike than the Tahitians. There was a primitive code of justice among them, and a form of religion expressed in certain ceremonial rites and punctuated by many taboos, strictly enforced. They had a very strong respect and reverence for their leading chiefs or kings.

In the time between Vancouver's earlier visits to Tahiti and the present one there had been a change of kings. One of the signs of the people's veneration was that on the accession of the new king the lesser chiefs changed their names, and a number of the commonest words in the language were also changed. Everyone was required to use the new forms. Vancouver was a victim of that custom, for one of the older and more friendly chiefs "would frequently correct me on my accidentally using the former mode of expression, saying, I knew it was wrong and ought not to practice it." [22] His ability to learn a native language quickly was a strong factor in Vancouver's general success in dealing with the native chiefs.

The reader of the early accounts is impressed also by the evident promiscuity of the women of the islands, for the European code of morals was completely foreign to those peoples. It was inevitable that the early European visitors, including seamen who were often recruited from the lowest strata of society, should introduce European vices and social diseases among them. The effect of such evils was already apparent to Vancouver on his later visit to Tahiti. Both he and Cook tried to prevent such contact, but there was little hope of success when it was then the practice in the navy to permit women to live on board men-of-war in home ports. With that standard recognized and condoned at home in the late eighteenth century, what chance would any commander have in trying to impose a higher standard at some remote island in the Pacific?

Vancouver had an uncanny faculty for sifting out the various ranks and relative importance of the native chiefs, and of treating each with the deference due his rank and position. The senior ones he would receive on board the *Discovery* with honors and gun salutes, a compliment that was duly appreciated by the chiefs since it enhanced their standing among their people. Vancouver called ceremoniously on the young king of Tahiti, a boy of about ten, and gave him a lavish present. The king could not return that visit, either to the tents on shore or on board ship, for in native eyes they would thereafter be under a taboo and none of the other chiefs could visit either place. Vancouver also easily recognized the petty fraud in some chief who claimed to be of higher rank or greater influence than he really was. In dealing with all the chiefs he was careful to be completely fair and honest with them. Judging by his account, he genuinely enjoyed the society of the native chieftains, and almost without exception he had their admiration and respect in return. With old Pomurrey, in particular, there was a bond of real friendship.

During the efforts to recover the stolen linen at Tahiti a high state of tension developed, but there was no violence. To be sure, after the linen was stolen Vancouver posted additional sentries and gave orders to shoot any native caught stealing, but this was to be done only in the presence of an officer, who in turn had orders to be very circumspect in such cases. In the end, when Towereroo was returned, Vancouver made his promised gifts, but he refused to give the natives another fireworks display, as he had promised earlier, in order to impress them with his disapproval of what had happened during the last days.

After a month among the people of Tahiti, the ships had been repaired and replenished, and the desired astronomical observations had been made. The health of the crew was fully restored by an abundance of fresh meat and vegetables, and both ships were ready for sea and the next leg of the voyage.

5

New Albion
(1792)

LATE IN JANUARY, 1792, the *Discovery* and the *Chatham* sailed from Tahiti for the Hawaiian Islands, where it was hoped a storeship might be waiting for them, as promised in Vancouver's instructions. En route Vancouver intended to stop at Christmas Island for a supply of turtles, but when he reached the latitude of that island his ships were 150 miles too far east. By then also the ships were nearly a month behind schedule. As events developed that made no difference, for the storeship had not yet arrived and Vancouver went on to the northwest coast of America without waiting for it.

On that uneventful leg of the voyage, as well as on all the others, Vancouver himself and many of the officers and midshipmen took many lunar observations for the longitude. In most ships of that day the observations were made only by the master and his mates, but in the *Discovery* the work was part of a training program for the forthcoming survey of the northwest coast, a project that was foremost in Vancouver's mind from the start. The observations were faithfully checked with the chronometers, and precision in navigation was the rule during the entire voyage. When the two ships made a landfall on the island of Hawaii on March 1, it was found that the difference between the longitude by observation and that by reckoning was over 5°, the true longitude being that much west of the one found by dead reckoning.

The first landfall in the Hawaiian Islands was near the southwestern point of Hawaii, from which point the ships cruised slowly up the leeward or west coast of that island. Two days later they were off Kealakekua Bay where, thirteen years earlier, Vancouver had played a part in the exciting and dangerous conflict at the time of Cook's death. Now, concerned with his current problems, he seemed more interested in checking the accuracy of his chronometers than in recalling the past.

Several natives came off to meet the ships with a supply of pigs and vegetables and some very welcome watermelons, grown from seeds left on the island earlier by one of the trading captains. Vancouver thought the prices the natives demanded for their produce exorbitant, and he noticed that they did not appear very anxious to trade. He was not long in learning the reason: they wanted firearms, one item that he would not barter with them.

Vancouver's first important visitor was Kaiana, a chief from the island of Kauai who had been to China with Meares. On returning to the islands he had cast his lot with Kamehameha, a rising chief of Hawaii, destined to become Hawaii's great Kamehameha I.[1] At that time Kamehameha was just beginning his rise to power by bringing all of the island of Hawaii under firm control.

Kaiana told Vancouver of the civil war then going on in the islands and of the rising power of Kamehameha which he, Kaiana, had helped in no small measure. He reported that the only ships that had visited the islands recently were four American brigs and Captain Colnett in the *Argonaut*. There was no report of a storeship's having called at any of the islands. When Kaiana learned that Vancouver planned to touch at the other islands in the chain, including Kauai, he asked if he and his retinue could take passage to that island, to which request Vancouver agreed. Kaiana then spent a night on board the *Discovery* during which it was noticed that he was very curious about the total number of the crew, and how many were on deck during the night. The next morning the routine weekly formal muster of the crew was held. Each man, as his name was called out, presented himself before the captain for a personal inspection in his best uniform.

Kaiana and his party watched that ceremony closely and were very much impressed by it. They planned to embark that same afternoon, but after much private consultation among them Kaiana decided not to go to Kauai after all.

Kaiana offered to provide Towereroo with a house and land, and, since Towereroo's home island of Molokai was held by enemies of Kamehameha, he preferred to stay on Hawaii. He was not sure of the treatment he would receive and, knowing that the ships expected to return in a few months, asked Vancouver to keep his remaining belongings for him. Vancouver decided that it was "advisable to fix him with *Tianna* for the present, that, on my return in the winter, I might be enabled to form some judgment of his treatment." [2] Other members of the expedition apparently did not understand that arrangement. At least one of them felt that putting Towereroo ashore without a large supply of clothing, tools, and trade items was like casting him "ashore like a Convict to his place of transportation." [3] Vancouver left a letter with Towereroo for the commander of the storeship, should the latter call at Hawaii.

While cruising along the coast of Hawaii soon after leaving Kealakekua Bay, the *Discovery* was boarded by a native who spoke broken English and who had been to Boston in an American trader. He boasted of the name "Jack," and when he asked to go along to the northwest coast Vancouver decided that he might be useful as an interpreter and signed him on. He was also visited by another important chief, Keeaumoku, who gave him a somewhat different version of the recent wars and the rise of Kamehameha from the one he had received from Kaiana.

It becomes obvious to the reader of his *Voyage of Discovery* that Vancouver from the first showed a keen interest in the internal politics of the Hawaiian Islands and in the status and fortunes of the various chiefs. The reason for this does not become apparent until his later visits to the islands. His instructions told him only to complete a survey of them, and to spend the following winter there. He was also to cultivate the friendship of the natives. But he sensed the strategic importance of the chain and formed in his own mind the idea of annexing them to Great Britain. There is no indication of that purpose in his first rather

fast reconnaissance of the major islands, except that by the time
he left for the northwest coast of America he had collected a clear
picture of the alliances of the various chiefs and the extent of the
civil wars then in progress. He did not meet Kamehameha until
the following year, but he was much impressed by his reputation
among the other natives.

After leaving Hawaii the two ships coasted along the lee side
of the chain until they anchored in Waikiki Bay, on the south
coast of Oahu, at the end of the first week in March. There Vancouver wanted to replenish his fresh water while minor repairs
were made to both ships.[4] On landing he found the large villages
almost deserted because Kahekili and Kaeo, kings of Oahu and
Kauai, and many of the men were away on Molokai preparing
to resist an expected invasion by Kamehameha. The remaining
natives appeared to be quite docile and reserved and extremely
unlike the friendly natives of Tahiti. The only suitable fresh
water available had to be brought to the beach from a considerable distance inland. Since it would be a difficult and tedious
process to get enough on board for their needs Vancouver decided
to "proceed immediately to Attowai [Kauai];[5] where I was assured
we should have that necessary article completely within our reach
and power." A day later found the ships anchored off Waimea,
on the southwestern side of Kauai.

To get ashore there it was necessary to go through surf to reach
an open beach. Shortly after anchoring Vancouver and several
of the officers landed in three of the boats to make arrangements
for water and to see something of the countryside. He found the
same reserve among the natives that he had noticed on Oahu, but
a minor chief, on learning of his wants, placed a taboo on some
houses near the beach for the use of the watering parties. Arrangements were then made for filling the water casks from a
stream; the work, together with trading for fresh provisions, was
carried out by an armed party under Lieutenant Puget. Since
several days would be required to finish the work, and the natives
seemed peaceful enough, many of the officers spent a good part
of their time ashore, hunting and sightseeing.

It was reported that three Englishmen were living on the island,
and the day after the ships arrived one of them appeared on

board the *Discovery* with two of the native chiefs. It developed that they were from the crew of the American trader *Lady Washington,* Captain Kendrick. They had been left on neighboring Niihau six months before with instructions to return to Kauai to collect sandalwood and pearls for the China market. They were to be picked up when the ship returned from Boston after stopping in China to dispose of a cargo of furs.

This is one of the earliest instances on record of the beginning of the rich sandalwood trade in the Hawaiian Islands, which did not reach its peak until about 1810.[6] It is an excellent example of how the enterprising Yankee traders were able to develop a trade in which British traders, hampered by their license restrictions, could not compete successfully. Having disposed of his furs from the northwest at a profit, the Boston captain could then ship a cargo of China goods for Boston which would bring another large profit in due course. Starting from home again with a fresh supply of trade goods he would have still another valuable cargo waiting for him when he touched at Kauai from the northwest coast.

Kendrick's man warned Vancouver to be very alert with the natives, since they had captured the American schooner *Fair American* at Hawaii some time before and had tried to capture a brig at Maui. Kaiana was accused of having been the instigator of the capture of the schooner. When told that Kaiana would have been killed instantly if he had returned to Kauai, and recalling that chief's suspicious interest in his ship at Hawaii, Vancouver concluded that Kaiana's actions "were not dictated by motives of the most friendly and disinterested nature." [7] Others, more bluntly, saw in Kaiana's wanting passage to Kauai a scheme to capture the two English ships.

The two chiefs told Vancouver that Kaumualii, the young son of the absent king, Kaeo, and the regent of the island would visit him in a day or two. Since he expected to remain only long enough to fill his water casks, Vancouver sent a message to the prince asking him to make his visit very soon. One of the chiefs produced four letters from captains of various trading vessels, cautioning future visitors to be very careful in dealing with the natives. Telling the chief that the letters were much in his favor,

Vancouver advised him to be sure to show them to any future captain who might stop there.[8]

Considering his first-hand experience with the natives at the time of Cook's death, it is not surprising that Vancouver was suspicious of them this time. Their apparent docility and reserve puzzled him. While ashore on a Sunday afternoon he noticed fires burning in the hills eastward of the landing point. He suspected that they were a signal calling in large numbers of natives, and his suspicion was confirmed by conflicting explanations received at the beach. Mr. Johnstone, master of the *Chatham*, and Menzies, the naturalist, had been in the islands before in trading vessels, and they tried to convince him that there was no special significance in the grass fires. They were commonly used in clearing the land and harvesting sugar cane. But "Captain Vancouver thought proper to torture his mind with ill founded suspicion; on observing a large fire burning in the distant hills, he construed it to be the flaming signal for War," wrote Master's Mate Manby about the situation.[9] The surf was running too high for the ships' boats to beach, and in going through the surf in a native canoe Vancouver was upset and spilled into the surf. He was convinced that the natives had designs on his life and that the spilling was deliberate, although the same natives rescued a midshipman who nearly drowned in the same accident.

Warning Puget, who had about twenty armed men with him, to be especially alert for trouble, Vancouver refused to try the surf in another canoe and swam off to the waiting boat. On returning to the *Discovery* he ordered two heavily armed boats to spend the night as close to the beach as they could get. Chiefs near the camp on shore were puzzled by all the excitement and wanted to know what caused it. Nothing at all happened during the night, but the next day Vancouver's suspicions were aroused again by new fires in the hills and the fact that the prince had not yet appeared. In the late afternoon he ordered the party on shore to re-embark. Puget sent word that the surf was running so high that it would be dangerous to come off after dark and suggested that he wait until the next morning. In reply to this seemingly reasonable request he received peremptory orders to come off immediately.[10] Some muskets, tools, and other articles were lost from a spilled canoe in the surf, and several of the officers' personal effects were left on the beach. Puget was confident that those articles were safe with the chief, who had placed a taboo on them, but Vancouver remained skeptical and suspicious.

The following morning Puget was sent in to recover the articles left on the beach. Everything, including the muskets and other articles lost in the surf, was recovered. On the beach he also found the young prince of the island with his guardian. By then native suspicions were also aroused, and the chiefs would not allow the prince to go off to the ships unless hostages were left on the beach. Two midshipmen were detailed for that purpose, and the guardian went aboard the *Discovery* first to see if it would be safe for the prince to follow. He professed to remember Vancouver well from the time of Cook and reminded him of his having given Kaeo a lock of his hair at the time, but Vancouver had no recollection of the incident. The chief's visit and his anecdote restored Vancouver's good humor, and after a suitable exchange of presents the old chief left, to be followed on board soon afterward by the prince. Much impressed by the conduct and carriage of the youth, and with his confidence in the natives apparently fully restored, in the evening Vancouver had a fireworks display set off for their entertainment. His earlier attitude of suspicion disappeared, and he expressed himself as convinced of the honesty and fair dealing of the natives of Kauai.

Vancouver has been described as a commander of great accomplishments but one who was unduly harsh with his midshipmen and officers.[11] His suspicion of the natives' intentions at Kauai and the precautions he took to insure the safety of his men ashore could be considered the act of a prudent leader guarding against a surprise attack. But what proved to be an unjustified conviction that the natives tried to kill him by deliberately spilling him into the surf from a canoe, and the burst of impatience and temper in recalling his men from the beach under dangerous circumstances, were hardly displays of normal prudence. That display of impatience was an early manifestation of a pattern of Vancouver's behavior that became more pronounced as time passed. During the voyage he continued to have violent bursts of temper over apparently trivial incidents, and he occasionally showed tremendous spurts of physical energy. He was from time to time forced to bed by physical exhaustion. His nervous energy was reflected in his impatience and drive. In themselves those characteristics might not have had any special significance. Bligh, his contemporary, had somewhat comparable traits and lived to see high rank and relative old age after surviving the well-known mutiny on the *Bounty* and two lesser known ones later in 1797 and while he was governor of New South Wales.

Vancouver lived but a very few years after the completion of this voyage, and toward the end of his life he was an invalid. The pattern of his failing health suggests that he suffered from a chronic malady that started on the voyage and reached an advanced stage before the trip was completed. Menzies, becoming surgeon of the *Discovery* when the assigned surgeon was invalided home, recorded that he had "constantly prescribed for Capt. Vancouver himself since we left England." [12] Unfortunately, he left no details of the nature of Vancouver's illnesses.

The course of his ailment appears to fit the gradual development of a hyperthyroid condition known as Graves's disease. The cause and proper treatment of that condition, with its attendant goiter, were not known in Vancouver's time. Without proper treatment its symptoms grow more and more severe. The available records give us some of the most obvious symptoms in Vancouver's case: irritability, bursts of energy, unexpected loss of temper, and fatigue. In the only existing portrait of Vancouver, the artist has treated the coat and scarf as if to conceal a goiter; and the right eye, especially, has the puffiness of lids that goes with a hyperthyroid condition.[13] If we assume from accounts of the voyage and from his appearance in the portrait that Vancouver suffered from a chronic hyperthyroid condition, some of his later actions have a plausible explanation that goes far to clarify his character.

After leaving Kauai, the ships spent a few days at the island of Niihau taking on a supply of yams, and they sailed for the American coast on March 16. On taking leave of the Hawaiian Islands after that brief visit Vancouver reviewed the great changes that had taken place since his earlier visits. The relatively small supply of provisions his ships obtained were paid for in trade articles that had been in the greatest demand earlier, but were then little wanted. Kaiana, returning to the islands after his trip to China with Meares, brought back a supply of firearms that excited the jealousy of all the other chiefs. In a very short time firearms and ammunition were in universal demand among them, and they became the standard, if not the only, item of trade that would purchase the islands' products. Vancouver had strong convictions on that development:

> The evil of this trade will be materially felt by vessels that may have occasion to resort to this country, unequipped with military stores, for the inhuman purpose of barter with these people; and it is much to be apprehended the mischief will extend considerably further, as we have been acquainted, by the late adventurers in the fur trade, that these islanders have tried various schemes to destroy the crews, and to gain possession of some of the trading vessels. . . . Neither the conviction of their own security being wholly dependent on these powerful means of defence, nor the common principles of humanity, seem to have had sufficient influence to restrain a traffic, encouraged by avaricious pursuits in defiance of all moral obligation.[14]

Vancouver found every chief he met, from Hawaii to Kauai, disappointed with his standard presents of blue coats and pieces of red cloth. All made it clear that they preferred firearms and ammunition. He refused all requests for these items and was able to placate the chiefs in each case by explaining that his weapons belonged to King George, who had placed a taboo on giving them as presents. By dealing only with the leading chiefs, and by giving them liberal personal presents, in many cases he was able to supply his needs in food by having it delivered as return presents from those chiefs.

Vancouver found the various islands of the chain at war with each other, and the great crowds of curious natives of his earlier visits were missing. The villages seemed smaller, and he thought the population of all the islands had been reduced as a result of the wars then in progress.

START OF THE CONTINENTAL SURVEY

Shortly after the *Discovery* left Niihau the foretopgallant yardarm carried away from the mast. It was taken down and found to be beyond repair, and Vancouver had the carpenter make a new one. He was not satisfied with the product, and this roused the ire of the carpenter, Mr. Phillips. Phillips' heated remarks to the captain resulted in his being relieved from his duties and confined under arrest, and his berth was given to one of his mates.[15] He was later sent home in the storeship under arrest to await a court-martial for insolence and disrespect—a court-martial that was held more than three and one-half years after the incident took place.

About three weeks out from Niihau an incident occurred that conflicts with the superstition used by Coleridge in 1798 as the central theme of *The Rime of the Ancient Mariner:*

> And I had done a hellish thing,
> And it would work 'em woe:
> For all averred I had killed the bird
> That made the Breeze to blow.

Almost daily during those weeks one or two large birds had been seen, which some on board believed to be albatrosses. On a fine Sunday morning in a dead calm Menzies settled the point by shooting and recovering a brown albatross—better known as the gooney bird of the North Pacific. In the description of the bird, with its seven-foot wingspread, there was no hint of the superstition that killing an albatross brought bad luck; rather the feeling was one of satisfaction in finally identifying it. And more than once Cook had mentioned the shooting of an albatross on his second voyage.[16]

Killing the albatross from the *Discovery* brought no misfortune on that occasion, for the winds picked up and steady progress was made until the two ships approached the coast, when the weather thickened. In the afternoon of April 18 the coast of New Albion was sighted—all English sailors at that time clung to the name Drake had given to that part of the world. The land sighted was a point on the California coast about 110 miles north of San Francisco Bay. From there began the remarkable hydrographic survey, unique in its scope, thoroughness, and accuracy, that is Vancouver's greatest and most enduring accomplishment. Traces of that original survey may still be found on some charts of the northwest coast.

Vancouver's instructions directed him to examine the coast between latitudes 60° and 30° north, and the first object of that survey was:

> The acquiring accurate information with respect to the nature and extent of any water-communication which may tend, in any considerable degree, to facilitate an intercourse, for the purposes of commerce, between the north-west coast, and the country upon the opposite side of the continent, which are inhabited or occupied by His Majesty's subjects.[17]

In short, he was to search for a Northwest Passage, and it should be a British passage. Even if such a passage were not found:

> It would be of great importance if it should be found that, by means of any considerable inlets of the sea, or even large rivers, communicating with the lakes in the interior of the continent, such intercourse could be established . . . The survey should be so conducted, as not only to ascertain the general line of the sea coast; but also the direction and extent of all such considerable inlets, whether made by arms of the sea, or by the mouths of large rivers. . . .[18]

A glance at the map of the Pacific coast from northern California to the head of the Gulf of Alaska shows what a huge order that really was. The only descriptions of that intricate coast at the time were the general chart made on Cook's third voyage and a few fragmentary charts made by British traders showing parts of British Columbia and Alaska; these indicated a shore line greatly indented and backed by mountains. There was also a fanciful chart in Meares's account of his voyages, in which he implied a knowledge of the Strait of Juan de Fuca. This chart showed the strait to be a deep inlet with a large islandlike land mass on the northern side around which the American Captain Gray had sailed in the *Lady Washington*. The Spaniards had done considerable surveying along the coast before Vancouver's arrival, but they did not publish their charts. For all practical purposes the northwest coast was new territory.

In starting his survey Vancouver must have reasoned that, if a Northwest Passage existed, he would be bound to find it if he made a landfall at a place he was sure was part of the continent and then followed the continental shore line carefully until he either came to the passage or found that it did not exist. That is the procedure he followed, and it took him three summer seasons of phenomenally hard work to carry out this great project.[19]

It will be of value here to review briefly the state of hydrography in Vancouver's time. It has already been noted that the Admiralty directed that harbor surveys be made in the Caribbean in 1786, and that Vancouver and Whidbey made detailed surveys of Kingston Harbor and its approaches. But it was not until 1795 that the Admiralty recognized the need for and established a hydrographer's department for the purpose of organizing the large volume of hydrographic information in its files. Until then the making of new surveys and the writing of sailing directions were largely a matter of individual initiative, chiefly among the masters of the ships in the fleets.

The production of charts and sailing directions in England was done by private firms of chart makers. The East India Company had its own hydrographer and published a large number of charts and sailing directions for the use of its ships. In 1778 there was published, under the Admiralty's direction, a four-volume *Atlantic Neptune,* an atlas of charts covering the Atlantic coast of North America from the St. Lawrence River to the West Indies. There were also numerous charts for European and Mediterranean waters, and other maritime nations published and exchanged charts and nautical information. By 1790 the well-known and traveled waters and seacoasts of the world were reasonably well surveyed and charted. The notable exception was Spain's secrecy with respect to the Pacific Ocean.

Textbooks on hydrographic surveying were in existence from the 1770's. At the same time textbooks of general navigation began to appear. The most popular of these was John Hamilton Moore's *The Practical Navigator and Seaman's Daily Assistant,* first published in 1772 and in its thirteenth edition by 1798. It contained explanations for making the required astronomical observations, and instructions for the care and adjustment of instruments and for keeping a journal of each day's navigational work at sea. It also contained a section on hydrographic surveying and the construction of charts in the field. In the eighth edition of *The Practical Navigator* (1784), the one used by

Vancouver's officers and midshipmen, we are first told that "it is a general Complaint among Seamen, that few Sea Charts are found correct." Then Moore gives instructions for conducting a survey of a coast and constructing a chart, a procedure very similar to the "running survey" described in modern textbooks.

First, with the ship in a convenient position to observe the seacoast, Moore directs:

> . . . take with the Azimuth Compass, the Bearings, in Degrees, of such Points of the Coast as form the most material Projections or Hollows; write down these Bearings, and make a rough Sketch of the Coasts. . . . Then let the ship run in a direct line, which must be carefully measured by the Log or otherwise for one, two, or three miles. . . .

Then the compass bearings of the same land features were to be recorded again, and new bearings taken of new headlands or features that showed up ahead. An eight-column form was recommended for keeping accurate records, for as the ship sailed along the coast a large mass of data would accumulate. To handle the task properly a qualified team of four was required, working constantly. One member took the necessary compass bearings. (The sextant could also be used for measuring angles between headlands.) Another member of the team checked the chip log used for measuring the speed through the water and kept a careful track of the ship's run. A third supervised the leadline for sounding the depth of water as the ship ran along, and the fourth kept a running plot of the observations to scale on a sheet of plotting paper. When the bearings of a given headland were plotted on the sheet from successive positions of the ship, the point at which the bearing lines intersected fixed the position of the headland with respect to the ship's track.[20] By sketching a shore line between the land features as it appeared from the ship, the surveyor produced a map of the coast. To assist in describing and identifying the coast it was customary to make sketches of important headlands, rocks, or other distinctive features, which were incorporated on the margins of the finished chart.

The accuracy of a map or chart built up in such a manner depended directly upon the accuracy of the navigation, and this accounts for the large number of astronomical observations that Vancouver and his officers took at every opportunity. That Vancouver used the system outlined by Moore or one very similar to it is indicated by the way his own survey was conducted, although he sought greater accuracy than most captains required. This meant the taking of hundreds of compass bearings and other observations, extremely careful navigation, and the keeping of voluminous records. For example, in the three weeks before making the first landfall of the California coast, he and other officers and midshipmen took eighty-five sets of lunar observations to establish accurately the starting point for the survey.[21]

During darkness the ships plied offshore; they returned inshore at daylight to resume the survey at the point reached the evening before, running along two to five miles offshore. At times, as happened off Cape Mendocino, California, a storm might hold them up for two or three days before they could continue. Rather than rely upon the results of Cook's and Meares's explorations Vancouver, in his determination to make his own survey as complete and accurate as possible, used his own observations and positions throughout. In many places his account points out discrepancies between his own and Cook's work.

One case of such a discrepancy occurred off present-day Cape Arago, on the Oregon coast. From Cook's description Vancouver believed the headland was his Cape Gregory, although there was a disagreement in latitude. He also thought it might be the Cape Blanco of Martin d'Aguilar, who was supposed to have made a voyage to that vicinity in 1603, even though its appearance did not justify that name. Near there d'Aguilar reported a large river for which Vancouver was on the lookout but of which he saw no trace. Yet he described accurately how, a few miles northeast of Cape Arago, the rocky coast line changes direction northward and gives way to a long sandy beach. The modern seaman approaching that point sometimes needs the assurance of his chart to confirm that he is making for the entrance to Coos Bay, an important lumber port. Even with the help of its modern breakwaters and improvements it is not always easy to recognize from seaward, especially in hazy or thick weather. It need not be wondered at that Vancouver missed it on this occasion, for just inside the entrance the bay turns sharply north and runs parallel to the outer coast. It is actually the tidal part of the Coos River.

Two days after passing Coos Bay he was off a prominent headland which he recognized as Meares's Cape Disappointment. He was not impressed by what he then saw:

> The sea had changed from its natural, to river colored water; the probable consequences of some streams falling into the bay, or into the ocean to the north of it, through the low land. Not considering the opening worthy of more attention, I continued our pursuit to the N.W. being desirous to embrace the advantages of the now prevailing breeze and pleasant weather.[22]

Vancouver's failure to recognize this spot as the mouth of the Columbia River has been emphasized many times by American writers on the Oregon Boundary Dispute, and it is still pointed to as one of his major failures. Miss it he did on that occasion, but as one who is familiar with the Columbia River entrance on that coast, under a variety of weather conditions, the writer feels he should come to the defense of his fellow seaman; for even today, with the entrance to the river well marked and improved, ships treat it with deep respect when a heavy swell is running.

Vancouver's account indicates fair weather while the ships were off the river's mouth, but Puget and others give us a more complete pattern of the weather just before and at the time. The afternoon before had been squally with fresh winds and hail and rain, and a swell from the west. By morning the weather had moderated considerably, but it was still cloudy and a westerly swell was still running. On the opposite side of the entrance from Cape Disappointment is a five-mile sand spit, and the surf was breaking heavily all along the spit on that day. Mist rising from the surf under such conditions tends to obscure the view up the Columbia River from seaward. On a clear day the wide breach between the mountains inland, through which the river flows, can readily be seen over the spit, and this is an unmistakable sign of a large river. When Vancouver passed the spot mist obscured his view, and the stormy weather passing inland from over the sea also probably obscured the mountains. From the masthead Menzies saw what appeared to be a river or inlet running inland to the south of Cape Disappointment. Bell also saw what appeared to be an opening there, but the surf seemed to break entirely across it. Manby noted at the time that it might prove to be a river, but that it was decided not to wait for the weather to moderate enough to investigate further, since it was the intention to examine the opening in detail later.[23] While Vancouver dismissed the opening as of little consequence at the time, there was enough doubt in the expedition about the extent of the opening to reserve final judgment until later.

Just how much importance should be given to Vancouver's failure to investigate the mouth of the Columbia River at that time is not easy to assess. In a dramatic meeting only two days later he was to learn of its existence from the man who is given credit for its discovery, Captain Robert Gray of the *Columbia,* out of Boston. His discovery gave the United States a wedge for a claim to a vast territory by right of first discovery in the long and involved Oregon Boundary Dispute of the nineteenth century. Had Vancouver entered the river he would have been the first to do so and might have established a similar claim for England. Earlier than that Gray had been prevented from entering the river for nine days by adverse currents. There remains the fact of Gray's actual discovery, which he clinched by entering the river two weeks after his meeting with Vancouver.[24] Later Vancouver, very much disturbed by Gray's report of the river and his own failure to recognize it as such, had it surveyed for a considerable distance inland.

6

Puget Sound
(1792)

ONE OF THE specific tasks given to Vancouver on this voyage was to investigate the little known Strait of Juan de Fuca on the northwest coast. It was "said to be situated between 48° and 49° north latitude, and to lead to an opening through which the sloop Washington is reported to have passed in 1789, and to have come out again to the northward of Nootka." [1]

When Cook sailed along the coast in 1778 he named a headland Cape Flattery because its appearance from a distance suggested that a good harbor might be found behind it. "It is in this very latitude where we now were," Cook wrote, "that geographers have placed the pretended strait of Juan de Fuca. But we saw nothing like it; nor is there the least probability that any such thing existed." [2] What makes that statement so noteworthy is that the Cape Flattery he named actually marks the southern entrance to the fifteen-mile-wide arm of the sea that leads to Puget Sound and is now known as the Strait of Juan de Fuca. Cook was just ahead of a storm and was driven offshore soon after sighting the cape, and the next morning it was blowing a hard gale with rain and sleet. It is probable that the evening before it was misty or drizzling, with poor visibility, so that what lay beyond Cape Flattery was indistinct. But Cook was obviously

76

skeptical, and he clearly ranged himself with those who, even in that day, refused to accept the legend of Juan de Fuca, a legend that persists in some degree to the present.

The story was first published by Samuel Purchas in *Purchas— His Pilgrimes* in 1625. Juan de Fuca, a Greek pilot in Spanish employ, claimed that he was sent from Acapulco, Mexico, in 1592 to search for the Straits of Anian, supposed to connect the Atlantic and Pacific oceans north of the then known North America. Between latitudes 47° and 48° north, de Fuca reported, he found a broad inlet into which he sailed for twenty days and reached the Atlantic, whereupon, his task completed, he returned to Acapulco. He also reported that in the Pacific entrance to his inlet there was a great stone pillar. The fact that a smaller but still important inlet, the present Strait of Juan de Fuca, was found about where de Fuca claimed to have made his discovery has helped to keep the tale alive. Hubert H. Bancroft, in his *History of the Northwest Coast,* gives a full account of the story and his reasons for believing it to be pure fiction. Neither any record of such a voyage nor any evidence to support de Fuca's story could be found; the sole source was the account in Purchas' book.

Recently Henry R. Wagner has made a more thorough study of the tale and found that, while there is a basis for some parts of it, the body of the story is an old sailor's yarn based on legend.[3] The theory of the existence of a Northwest Passage grew out of legends of a Portuguese voyage through it to China and back in about 1540. From these grew the legend of the Straits of Anian, which was seized upon by several theoretical geographers in the middle of the eighteenth century to support their theories. Besides de Fuca's claim there was another story of an Admiral de Fonté's discovery in 1640 of a great River Los Reyes in latitude 53° north. De Fonté's claim was in the form of a letter, but there is no record of an Admiral de Fonté who existed at that time. These tales attracted little attention when they first appeared, but they were revived after the discovery of Bering Strait in 1728.

Wagner's studies convinced him that de Fuca was in Mexico from 1588 to 1594. He was captured by Cavendish in 1587 and may have been the Greek pilot "Juan" captured by Drake in 1577. There is no record of any voyage such as that claimed by de Fuca in his story, and probably all he could have known of was a voyage up the Gulf of California about the time he claimed to have made his discovery. Speculation about the Straits of Anian was commonplace among the pilots of that time, and it is likely that de Fuca's story was compounded from his own local knowledge and the earlier theories concerning the Straits of Anian.

What revived interest in the tales of de Fuca and de Fonté, according to Wagner, were theories expressed by Nicholas Delisle in Paris in 1750, superimposing the supposed discoveries of the two men upon the real discoveries of Bering and Chirikof. They were supported by a map prepared by Phillippe Bauche, a mapmaker in the Department of Marine, on which were shown the discoveries of de Fuca and de Fonté as Bauche imagined them. This was a typical bit of the geographical theorizing so popular in that era. In 1753 Delisle published a set of *Nouvelles Cartes,* which included a map showing de Fonté's discoveries. The charts inspired a wave of criticism in England, France, and Spain, but they also had supporters in England. In the same year John Green, an English cartographer and one of Delisle's sharpest critics, pronounced the stories of de Fuca and de Fonté either forgeries or fictitious. From that time there continued a lively interest and divided opinion about the supposed discoveries among English seamen and geographers that extended throughout the period of this study. As late as 1790 Alexander Dalrymple, who was never very far from the middle of any geographical argument, expressed his faith in de Fuca and de Fonté, although he had available Spanish denials of their tales dating back to 1757. It should be recalled, however, that until Cook's third voyage the only information about the northwest coast of America available outside of Spain came from fragmentary reports supplied by Russian explorers in the upper Gulf of Alaska and the Bering Sea. Geographical speculation, under the circumstances, was an open game, and the truth could be established only by painstaking exploration.

Vancouver was given special instructions concerning the Strait of Juan de Fuca because of reports shortly before he sailed of its actual discovery. Meares, in the account of his voyages published in 1790, implied his own discovery of the strait. He also asserted that the American Captain Gray, in the *Lady Washington,* had entered the strait in 1789 and returned to the ocean around a large land mass north of the entrance to the strait. Meares's book even had a chart showing the track of that alleged cruise.

PUGET SOUND

Early in the morning of the second day after the *Discovery* and the *Chatham* passed the mouth of the Columbia River, while most eyes were scanning the coast for possible signs of the Strait of Juan de Fuca, a sail was sighted in the west standing inshore. It was the first strange sail the expedition had seen since leaving the Cape of Good Hope eight months before. She proved to be the *Columbia,* a trading vessel out of Boston, Captain Robert Gray commanding. To Vancouver, with his thoughts fixed on the Strait of Juan de Fuca, Captain Gray's name raised a question. Could this be the same American Captain Gray whose voyage into that strait Meares had described? Puget and Menzies were soon aboard the *Columbia* to confirm the story. It proved to be the same Gray, but he was astonished to hear what he had been given credit for doing. He had entered the strait in the *Lady Washington* in 1789 but had gone in only about fifty miles and returned to the ocean by the same route. By coincidence this chance meeting took place only a few miles from the entrance to the strait.

Thus one of Meares's major statements was discredited before Vancouver's expedition reached the strait. Vancouver's reaction was that Gray's story "differed very materially from that published in England." [4] Puget felt that "Mr. Mears must have trusted to bad Information in that Respect." [5] But to Menzies that meeting with Gray "enables us to detect to the world a fallacy in this author which no excuse can justify." [6] The most plausible explanation of how Meares got the story is given us by Thomas Manby, as he heard it from a mate of the *Columbia.* Gray and Meares were rivals in the fur trade and were wary of exchanging accurate information. After Meares had boasted of great success in trading for sea otter skins, "the cunning Yanky in retaliation, knowing the Northwest Passage to be the Hobby horse of his

opponent in Commerce, reports his discovery of it—which is believed with greedy avidity." [7] Manby was very scornful of Meares
and his misstatements.

This one example is a good illustration of the general untrust-
worthiness of Meares's account of his voyages—and of the events
at Nootka in 1789. As a curiosity of eighteenth-century maritime
adventure Meares's book is of interest, but it contains so many
inaccuracies throughout that his statements must be supported by
other sources before they can be accepted at full value. To support
his implied discovery of the Strait of Juan de Fuca in 1788 Meares
included a plate in his book that gives a good view of the entrance
from a point near Tatoosh Island. In it, however, the engraver
has inserted a huge nonexistent stone pillar in the center, presumably to support the legend of Juan de Fuca.

It is probable that Meares got his first information about the
strait from Captain Barkley, of the *Loudon* (or *Imperial Eagle,* as
she was more commonly known), an English trader sailing under
Austrian colors to evade the license requirements. Barkley is
generally credited with the discovery of the Strait of Juan de
Fuca in 1787.[8] It may have been seen as early as 1774 by the
Spaniard Martinez, who later, while governor at Nootka in 1789,
sent a ship to reconnoiter the opening. After 1789, under the
energetic direction of Viceroy Revilla Gigedo, the Spaniards took
the lead in exploring the strait. In 1790 Quimper examined the
waterway as far as New Dungeness on the Washington side and
Rosario Strait on the opposite side, taking possession of the country for Spain in the process. Eliza, in 1791, continued the exploration begun by Quimper. When Vancouver entered the strait late
in April, 1792, several had preceded him, although the only positive information he had of it came from Gray.

Keeping to the southern, or continental, shore, the *Discovery*
and the *Chatham* anchored the first night a few miles inside the
entrance to the strait.[9] The next day, still keeping to the continental shore, the ships worked their way up the strait. Late in the
afternoon they came abreast of a low spit of land behind which
there appeared to be a good harbor; Vancouver called it New
Dungeness. There they anchored for the night. Some time before the ships reached the harbor, land began to show behind the

eastern horizon, and a snow-capped mountain peak was seen in the northeast. It was named Mount Baker, in honor of the third lieutenant of the *Discovery,* who first saw it. Vancouver then erroneously thought that he was farther into the strait than any European had yet been.

The first concern was to find a secure harbor where the observatory could be set up, water and wood obtained, and the ships repaired. Only emergency work had been done on either of the ships since they were at Tahiti. Wooden ships twist and strain at sea under the impact of sea and wind, resulting in opened seams and wear and tear on all the rigging of the masts and yards. To keep a ship seaworthy it was necessary to calk leaky seams and overhaul the standing rigging at regular intervals.

May 1 dawned bright and clear, and Whidbey set out in a boat to find a fresh-water stream, but without result. Vancouver himself then took three boats to explore the coast eastward in search of a better harbor. Only a few miles east of New Dungeness was found a fine harbor that suited all their purposes and had an entrance protected by an island. The next day both ships moved into that harbor and prepared for an extended stay. A camp was established ashore, and the men were set at the many urgent tasks at hand, not the least of which was operating the brewery for the production of spruce beer. Whidbey, the master, was placed in charge of the camp with the additional task of surveying the harbor. Vancouver was deeply impressed with the harbor and gave it the name of his ship, Port Discovery. Later, when it was learned that the Spaniard Eliza had been there the year before, some of the officers began to refer to it by Eliza's name of Port Quadra, but Vancouver retained his own name for the harbor.

When everything was organized and running smoothly at Port Discovery, Vancouver set out to continue the survey of the coast by boat leaving the large ships at anchor. The exploring party consisted of Vancouver and Menzies in the *Discovery's* yawl, Puget in her launch, and the master of the *Chatham,* Mr. Johnstone, in that vessel's cutter, all with five days' provisions. In the many similar expeditions that followed this one at least two boats formed each party, for safety in case of accident and for better protection against possible hostile Indians.

81

Only about five miles east of Port Discovery the magnitude of the job ahead began to suggest itself. The shore line took a sharp turn to the right, and extensive openings showed up in the distance. At that point the party was looking into what we now call Puget Sound. That inland sea, with its intricate shore line, was traced in its entirety by the boats of Vancouver's expedition in just one month.

The technique of surveying with the boats differed in some respects from that of coastal surveying from the ships. Moore's *Practical Navigator* helps us again to understand how it was done. His boat method presupposed a relatively small harbor around the shores of which were placed easily recognized markers at prominent features. On a suitable flat section of the shore a base line was laid out, half a mile or more long, and its length was carefully measured. Corrected compass bearings from each end of the base line were then taken of the several markers. Those bearings, plotted on a suitable sheet of paper, fixed the positions of the markers relative to the base line and each other, and the shore line between them was sketched in from an examination on the spot. This method was used by Whidbey in surveying Port Discovery. Vancouver's problem was much more difficult than making a single harbor survey in the same manner. Although working in restricted waters much like harbors, he was tracing out a whole shore line rather than a series of harbors, and his method was modified accordingly.

A careful record of the boat's tracks was kept as the shore line was followed from one point of land to the next. At each prominent point the officers landed and took compass bearings of all the other prominent points in sight. Making supplementary sketches and notes as they went along, they accumulated data from which a map could be constructed, much as for a coastal run by the ships. Whenever possible, observations of the sun were made at noon for the latitude. After the boats returned to the ships a smooth map was made from the observations and was tied into the mapping that had been done before; adjustments and corrections of past results were made as the new observations required. It was a slow and laborious process, but through it the trend and shape of the continental shore line were gradually and carefully developed and later adjusted to positions obtained by astronomical means at the observatory.

In this first of Vancouver's boat expeditions the shore was traced through present-day Port Townsend and all of Hood Canal, a western arm of Puget Sound. When winds were favorable the boats were under sail, but much of the time there was no wind, and that meant long hours at the oars. The boats were kept on the move from daylight to dark except for the periodic stops to take compass bearings and for the noon meal. With provisions for only five days, Vancouver's first boat expedition was stretched out to eight in order to make sure that Hood Canal was not a channel around an island.

Meanwhile at Port Discovery workers at the observatory were busy fixing the latitude and longitude of the place, finding the variation of the compass (i.e., the difference between the compass north and true north), and determining the rate of error of the chronometers. All the other work kept pace, and in two and a half weeks the ships were ready to move forward. From the top of the island guarding the entrance to the port Vancouver saw a cluster of islands on the northern horizon, and Broughton was sent with the *Chatham* to examine them.[10] With the *Discovery* Vancouver moved up to the first fork in the channel beyond the limits of the map developed on his boat trip. It proved to be near Restoration Point, opposite Seattle, where the main channel, running southward, appeared to branch into two arms.

From there a two-boat expedition under Lieutenant Puget and Whidbey, with two weeks' provisions, set off to extend the survey. Continuing the practice of always keeping to the right-hand or continental shore, Puget traced the whole of the upper part of Puget Sound in eight days, and for this feat Vancouver gave Puget's name to that part of it.[11]

Aside from that noteworthy accomplishment there occurred one of the few instances of trouble or near trouble with the Indians. In one of the many arms that form the upper part of Puget Sound, Puget tried by friendly signs to call some Indians in a canoe alongside his boat, but they held back. He then tied some presents of sheet copper, looking-glasses, and trinkets to a piece of wood and left it floating in the water while the boats pulled away. The Indians recovered the presents, and after two or three repetitions of the procedure they did come alongside Puget's boat, although they remained shy and distrustful. After showing his friendly intentions in this manner Puget had the boats pull along the shore for about four miles and then beach for the noon meal. There, as the men were about to run a seine for salmon, six canoes filled with Indians were seen approaching.

Part of Puget's party had climbed a low bluff a few yards from the beach and boats. Fortunately, he had taken the precaution to have three or four muskets with the group. When the Indians landed nearby, a line was drawn on the sand beyond which, by sign language, they were told to stay. In a little while they re-embarked in their canoes and paddled offshore where they were seen talking among themselves and frequently pointing to the two parties. Other canoes joined them, swelling the total number of Indians to about thirty, and suddenly the whole party landed again, stringing their bows as they did. By then Puget had his party armed and alert for an attack. One Indian approached to within four yards of the party on the hill with drawn bow and arrow, but he was induced to withdraw. Feeling confident of his position but not wishing to have an open fight, Puget then had one of the boats' swivel guns, loaded with grapeshot, fired over the water.[12] While this did not seem to impress the Indians very much, during the excitement Puget got his party reunited at the boats and prepared to embark and pull off. Quite suddenly the Indians changed their attitude completely and began to barter their bows and arrows. By his alert and coolheaded action Puget succeeded in changing what might have been a fatal incident into another friendly if somewhat strained meeting with the natives.

While Puget's party was away from the ship the survey was being refined from the *Discovery*. During a walk along the beach one afternoon Henry M. Orchard, the ship's clerk, discovered an arm leading to the north and west a few miles west of the anchorage. Vancouver sent boats to survey the arm, to which he gave the name Port Orchard. On its shores now stands one of the United States Navy's largest shipyards at Bremerton, Washington.

The *Chatham* rejoined the *Discovery* at the anchorage, and Broughton reported that he had examined an archipelago of

The *Discovery* on the rocks, from a plate in Vancouver's *Voyage of Discovery*

Nootka, from a plate in Vancouver's *Voyage of Discovery*

islands beyond which there was an unbroken horizon to the northwest. By then Vancouver was convinced that most of the survey would have to be done from the boats. Becoming restless at the long absence of Puget and Whidbey, he set out himself with two boats to examine the arm southeast of the anchorage. Before leaving he told Broughton to take the *Discovery*'s boats when they returned and with the *Chatham* survey an arm that could be seen northeastward of the anchorage.

By noon of the first day away from the ship Vancouver and his party pulled into the entrance of Commencement Bay, at the head of which now lies the city of Tacoma. It must have been a fine clear day toward the end of May, for the engraving in his *Voyage of Discovery* gives a striking if somewhat distorted view of Mount Rainier towering behind the head of the bay. He gave it the name of one of the officers whom he had known in the Caribbean, Captain Peter Rainier, afterward rear admiral. Continuing on in the boats Vancouver spent several days exploring the same waters that Puget had already covered and then returned to the ship. By that time the *Chatham* was gone with Whidbey and a *Discovery* boat to examine the northeastern arm. Elliott Bay, on which stands the city of Seattle, is clearly shown on Vancouver's chart, but the explorer was not enough impressed by it to give it a name.

It was near the end of May when the *Discovery* moved up to join the *Chatham,* from which two boats were out surveying to the north. The passages they surveyed apparently led to dead ends, and so, having completed the survey of what is now known as Puget Sound, Vancouver decided it was time to formalize his discoveries thus far. Landing at a point near the present city of Everett he took formal possession of the land he had already surveyed for Great Britain, giving it the name of his sovereign, New Georgia.[13] On his growing chart he named a great many natural features; most of these names are retained in some form today. The majority of them honor contemporaries of his in the navy; Mount Rainier as we have noted, and Hood Canal for the renowned Admiral Lord Hood, are examples. The names of most of his own officers were given to some prominent feature; Puget Sound, Port Orchard, Mount Baker, and Whidbey Island were thus named. Many names, such as Foulweather Bluff, Birch Bay, and Possession Sound explain themselves. Admiralty Inlet, as Vancouver named it, extended from Port Townsend to Tacoma, but today it is only the channel off Port Townsend connecting Puget Sound and the Strait of Juan de Fuca. Usage has expanded Puget Sound, originally designating only the part south of Tacoma, to include most of Vancouver's Admiralty Inlet. To all of the inland sea he had already explored he gave the name Gulf of Georgia, but all that remains of that name is Georgia Strait, lying mainly in British Columbia.

Most residents of the Puget Sound country will readily agree that Vancouver himself was a prophet as well as a eulogist when he wrote:

> To describe the beauties of this region, will on some future occasion, be a very grateful task to the pen of a skilful panegyrist. The serenity of the climate, the innumerable pleasing landscapes, and the abundant fertility that unassisted nature puts forth, require only to be enriched by the industry of man with villages, mansions, cottages, and other buildings, to render it the most lovely country that can be imagined; whilst the labour of the inhabitants would be amply rewarded, in the bounties which nature seems ready to bestow on cultivation.[14]

Other members of the expedition shared Vancouver's enthusiasm for the country as they saw it in May and June. Menzies, the botanist, after a stroll in the flat lands near Everett, was inspired to a most flowery tribute:

> A Traveller wandering over these unfrequented Plains is regaled with a salubrious and revivifying air impregnated with the balsamic fragrance of the surrounding Pinery, while his mind is eagerly occupied every moment on new objects & his senses rivetted on the enchanting variety of the surrounding scenery where the softer beauties of landscape are harmoniously blended in majestic grandeur with the wild & romantic to form an interesting & picturesque prospect on every side.[15]

In a more practical vein Joseph Whidbey a few months later wrote to an unidentified friend suggesting the formation of a trading company with headquarters on Barclay Sound, on Vancouver Island, and with posts extending from the Queen Charlotte Islands to the Columbia River. Having heard that the Australian convict colony had not met expectations, he proposed, for con victs who had served their time, that "instead of returning to England to become a fresh prey on the Publick . . . [they] be sent to this country and settled at the Head of Fuca Straights— where there is country equal to any in the world." [16]

VANCOUVER ISLAND

After tracing several hundred miles of continental shore line in just over a month, Vancouver found himself landlocked and had to return to the Strait of Juan de Fuca.[17] Once through Admiralty Inlet he sent off two boats under Whidbey to continue tracing the continental shore while he took the two ships to an anchorage in the San Juan Islands. The boats took only two days to bring the survey forward to the anchorage, after which the ships moved further north to Birch Bay, just south of the present British Columbia border. There the observatory was sent ashore again, Whidbey was sent back to bring the survey forward, and Vancouver himself set out with Puget in two boats to extend the survey to the northwest.

In the course of the first afternoon away from the ship he was forced well offshore by an extensive shoal with several small streams running through it. This was the delta of the Fraser River, one of the large rivers of the Pacific watershed but not very impressive when its mouth is viewed from seaward, and certainly not navigable for ships. Anyone searching for a ship passage would, as Vancouver did, pay little attention to the delta.

The next day was spent in tracing the shore line of Burrard Inlet, which he named for an old shipmate of *Europa* and *Expedition* days in the Caribbean, Sir Harry Burrard of the navy.[18] The inlet merits special notice because it was selected by the Canadian Pacific Railroad for its Pacific terminus in 1885. There it founded and named the now bustling modern city of Vancouver for the man who gave the inlet its name.

The boats left the ship with only a week's provisions, but it was not until they had been away for eight days that Vancouver decided to return. He might have stayed out even longer had it not been for an incident that occurred the evening before he turned back. Manby, who had been with Puget in his earlier boat

87

expeditions, was left in charge of the boat while Puget joined Vancouver to discuss the next day's work. At dusk Manby headed up a channel thinking he was following his commander, but Vancouver had taken another channel. Realizing that he was separated from the other boat, and low in provisions, Manby made his way back to the *Discovery,* which he reached the day before Vancouver returned. When Vancouver realized that the cutter was missing, and that he was left with only one boat, he cut the survey short and also returned to the ship. There, angered by the interruption to the work, he gave Manby a tongue-lashing. Manby's journal records, ". . . His salutation I can never forget, his language I will never forgive unless he withdraws his words by a satisfactory apology." [19]

When Vancouver was almost back to Birch Bay he was disturbed to see two strange sails anchored near Burrard's Inlet. They proved to be the small Spanish brigs *Sutil,* Dionesio Galiano commanding, and *Mexicana,* Cayatano Valdes commanding, employed as Vancouver was in surveying that inland sea. They had been sent from Mexico by order of the viceroy of Mexico for that purpose and to continue the surveys made earlier by Eliza and Quimper. Both small vessels arrived at Nootka in May and entered the strait only about two weeks before the meeting with Vancouver in the latter part of June. They reported also that Don Juan Francisco de la Bodega y Quadra, naval commandant of San Blas and California, and the Spanish commissioner appointed to deliver the lands at Nootka to Vancouver, was at that port awaiting his arrival. Vancouver's instructions required that he was to give every assistance he could to any Spanish vessels engaged in similar service to his own and exchange information and charts with them. In the spirit of those instructions he was soon on friendly terms with the Spanish commanders, and his meeting with them ended with his suggestion that the two expeditions join forces and continue the survey together.[20]

As yet Vancouver had no specific instructions concerning the transactions with Quadra[21] at Nootka; detailed orders for making the exchange of property were being sent to him in the storeship. Until she arrived, therefore, nothing could be accomplished at

Nootka, and the survey continued to absorb Vancouver's attention.

The *Discovery* and the *Chatham* got under way from Birch Bay and joined the two Spanish vessels. Then the little fleet worked its way up to a bight near the head of Georgia Strait, where an anchorage was selected from which extensive boat work could be carried out. Puget and Whidbey dropped back with their boats to bring the survey forward from the point where Vancouver and Puget had stopped earlier. Johnstone, of the *Chatham,* took two boats to explore openings to the northwest, and Valdes undertook the survey of another inlet in between. The coast of British Columbia is deeply indented with winding fiords dipping back deeply into the coastal mountain ranges, and the coastal waters are complicated by a maze of off-lying islands. To untangle the geography of the shore and reduce it to map form required patient and detailed work by the boat parties.

It was not long before the entente with the Spaniards lost some of its cordiality. Shortly after entering one of the several arms of the sea, Puget met Valdes, who told him that the arm was closed a few miles farther inland. Puget, feeling that he had no choice but to follow his orders, proceeded to examine the arm himself. The Spaniards, annoyed at the suggestion of distrust of their work, protested to Vancouver that mutual confidence was essential for best results. He replied that he had full confidence in them but felt it necessary that his own people examine everything having to do with the continental shore. This controversy, developing so early in the joint effort, was perhaps based less on a lack of confidence than on the contrast between the drive and thoroughness of the Englishmen and the leisurely methods of the Spaniards. At any rate, the joint survey work was given up at the first opportunity.

After the various boat expeditions had left the ships, Vancouver himself set out to learn more of the main channel of Georgia Strait, but a heavy rain storm drove him back. Since rain had not stopped him before, this incident may be an indication of his failing health.

When Puget and Whidbey had completed their first assignment they were sent off to survey the main channel and the southern shore of the strait that Vancouver had started to explore. John-stone and his assistant, Spelman Swaine, a master's mate, returned for more provisions and were off to continue their part of the survey. Puget and Whidbey returned to report a deep channel along the southern shore through which the flood, or rising, tide came from the northwest, a strong indication of some connection with the ocean in that direction.[22] Johnstone was away nine days instead of his allotted week, having eked out his provisions with berries, clams, and fish picked up along the way. But he brought back electrifying news—he had discovered a clear channel lead-ing to the ocean, proving all the land that lay to the west to be a large island mass.

To reach the point from which he had a clear view of the ocean Johnstone had traveled about 120 miles from the ship and had passed by several openings on the continental shore that would have to be investigated later. Before he reached the wide and deep channels to the west he had had to work his boats through strong tidal currents in a narrow, rock-studded channel not far from the ships; this is Cordero Channel on modern charts. To Vancouver, studying the information then at hand, it seemed that the channel Puget had found probably joined the one Johnstone had discovered. A combination of the two should pro-duce a better access to the ocean from the anchorage than the channel Johnstone had used. When he suggested the idea to the Spaniards they insisted that they must continue along the con-tinental shore. Thus, in less than a month, the joint expedition separated, after the leaders had exchanged copies of all their surveys to date. All accounts of the short-lived association agree that socially the relations were most harmonious and friendly, but that the little Spanish vessels were not equal to keeping up with the strenuous schedules of the Englishmen.

It is a tribute to Vancouver's thoroughness and vision that the route he selected to the open sea is the only safe navigable passage from Georgia Strait to the sea; it is the one used today by all ships running the Inside Passage to Alaska. Hugging the Van-couver Island shore, it is a scenic and clear passage with but one real hazard near its southern end—Seymour Narrows, where tidal currents reach as high as twelve knots. Boiling and swirling through the narrows, those currents render it necessary that all but the most powerful ships make the passage at or near the periodic slack-water periods. Discovery Strait, named for Vancouver's ship, forms the southeastern part of the passage, and Johnstone Strait, named for the man who discovered it, makes up the rest of the route.

The *Discovery* and the *Chatham* made the first recorded passage through these channels mainly by using the favorable ebbing tidal currents. When they reached the inlets on the continental shore that Johnstone had passed by, boat expeditions were sent to continue the survey. A little later the *Chatham* was sent over for the same purpose while Vancouver went on to a large Indian village Johnstone had described. There he hoped to meet Maquinna, chief of an extensive region on Vancouver Island that included Nootka. Maquinna was not in the village, but Vancouver left some letters with one of the lower chiefs to be delivered overland to Quadra at Nootka. Then he doubled back to the continental shore to join the *Chatham* and continue the survey.

7

Quadra and Nootka
(1792)

On leaving the main channel and holding to the continental shore north of Johnstone Strait, Vancouver's ships found themselves among small islands and rocks through which it was difficult and dangerous to make their way. More than ever the brunt of the survey fell on the boats while the captains were fully occupied with working their ships through the southeastern part of Queen Charlotte Strait in rainy and foggy weather. Shortly before they reached the relatively clear waters of Queen Charlotte Sound, in the present Walker Group of small islets and rocks, a near disaster occurred. In the foggy afternoon of August 6 the *Discovery* ran aground on a ledge of submerged rock at almost the highest stage of the tide.

She grounded only under the bows but hard and fast. When the rapidly ebbing tide gave her a sharp list to starboard, the yards and upper masts were taken down and spare yards were put over the sides as shores, or braces, to prevent her from capsizing altogether. For seven hours her crew sat helplessly on the ship's side waiting for high tide to return. The *Chatham,* anchored nearby and ready to help with her boats, was a welcome and reassuring sight to those on the *Discovery* wondering what moment might be her last. About an hour before low water she took a sudden lurch and for an instant it was feared she would capsize, but the shores held. Her main deck was within only two inches of the water, which, fortunately, was calm at the time. At low tide the depth of the water under the bow was only three and one-half feet while under the stern it was twenty-four feet, a precarious situation indeed for a ship normally drawing about fifteen feet of water. A stern anchor was carried out, and with the return of high water at about two o'clock in the morning the ship was pulled off into deep water apparently undamaged.

This was one of the first groundings in the Inside Passage of which we have record, but it is a common experience in the history of the route to Alaska. Many ships have grounded in those deceptive waters, often with far more serious results than in this case. The range of tides between high and low water reaches twelve feet and more. Small ships have been known to ground on a rocky ledge at high tide and be completely out of water at low tide. Anyone who has sailed through these passages with the benefit of modern aids to navigation can only marvel at the courage and tenacity of Vancouver, probing his way through them and learning their secrets for the first time. By following the mainland shore so closely, rather than sailing along the Vancouver Island shore, he missed the clear channel that would have carried him from Johnstone Strait into Queen Charlotte Sound without trouble.

As if to match the *Discovery*'s performance, the *Chatham,* on the following afternoon, also grounded on a submerged rock. It was at about half ebb tide, and, while she pounded on the rocks in the light swells running at the time, she too came off with the returning high tide during the night without serious damage. Both vessels grounded in constricted waters several times later, but this first time was the most serious for each.

To the relief of all hands, shortly after these trying experiences the ships sailed into the open waters of Queen Charlotte Sound. It was a short respite for them, however, for after a few miles of open sea they came to a new chain of islands offshore forming another series of inland passages. The continental shore continued to be deeply indented with arms of the sea. Parts of the inland waters in that vicinity had been visited by fur traders, and Vancouver headed for a Port Safety, which had been described by Captain Duncan, an English trader. Anchoring in what he believed to be that cove, he resumed the survey with the boats. Puget and Whidbey set out with two boats on their tenth expedition of the season to return and trace the part of the continent that the ships had passed en route to the anchorage. Vancouver, with Johnstone and Mr. Humphreys, a master's mate of the *Chatham,* headed north in three boats to trace the continental shore in that direction. After four days of rainy and disagreeable weather Vancouver himself had to turn back, leaving Johnstone and Humphreys to continue the survey.

While Vancouver was waiting at the anchorage for the boats to return, an English trading vessel, the *Venus* of Bengal, arrived in the cove. Her captain reported that the long awaited storeship *Daedalus* was then at Nootka, and that Quadra was waiting impatiently to deliver the disputed land to Vancouver. A sad note was a letter from the master of the *Daedalus* reporting that her captain, Lieutenant Hergest, and Mr. Gooch, the astronomer sent to join Vancouver's expedition, had been murdered by natives on the island of Oahu, in the Hawaiian group. Hergest, Vancouver wrote, had been his most intimate friend for many years. He had been a midshipman under Cook and had been second lieutenant of the *Discovery* before the Spanish Armament.

The news caused Vancouver to discontinue the survey for the season as soon as the boats returned. On the nineteenth of August, with the boats safely on board, the *Discovery* and the *Chatham* sailed for Nootka, by then known to lie on the outer coast of a large island. The decision to give up the survey for the season was received with a feeling of relief by the officers and men who had done the heavy work of the survey in the boats. Menzies, who had spent most of his time during the season in one of the boats studying the natural history of the region, paid a well-earned tribute to those men:

> . . . it will readily be allowed that such an intricate & laborious examination could not have been accomplished in so short a time without the co-operating exertions of both men and officers whose greatest pleasure seemed to be in performing their duty with alacrity & encountering the dangers & difficulties incidental to such service with a persevering intrepidity & manly steadiness.[1]

94

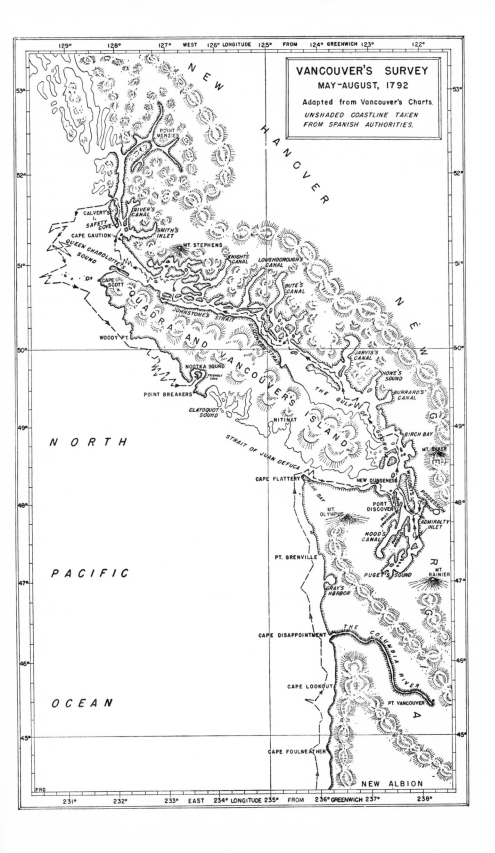

VANCOUVER'S SURVEY
MAY–AUGUST, 1792

Adapted from Vancouver's Charts.
UNSHADED COASTLINE TAKEN
FROM SPANISH AUTHORITIES.

NEW HANOVER

POINT MENZIES

CALVERT'S I.
SAFETY COVE
CAPE CAUTION
QUEEN CHAROLOTTE'S SOUND
CAPE SCOTT
WOODY PT.

RIVER'S CANAL
SMITH'S INLET
MT. STEPHENS
KNIGHT'S CANAL
LOUGHBOROUGH'S CANAL
BUTE'S CANAL

QUADRA AND VANCOUVER'S ISLAND

JOHNSTONE'S STRAIT
DISCOVERY PASS

JARVIS'S CANAL
HOWE'S SOUND
BURRARD'S CANAL
THE GULF W
BIRCH BAY
MT. BAKER

NEW G

NOOTKA SOUND
FRIENDLY CVE
POINT BREAKERS
CLAYOQUOT SOUND
NITINAT

STRAIT OF JUAN DEFUCA

CAPE FLATTERY
NEW DUNGENESS
WHIDBEY'S

NORTH

BAY
MT. OLYMPUS
PORT DISCOVERY
ADMIRALTY INLET
HOOD'S CANAL

PACIFIC

PT. GRENVILLE
PUGET'S SOUND
MT. RAINIER

GRAY'S HARBOR

G

CAPE DISAPPOINTMENT
THE COLUMBIA RIVER

OCEAN

CAPE LOOKOUT
PT. VANCOUVER

A

CAPE FOULWEATHER

NEW ALBION

PRG

The total number of miles the boats covered in following the shore line and tracing out each fiord and inlet during the season cannot be computed accurately. Working from dawn to dark and sometimes pulling at the oars all night, in all kinds of weather, the men performed remarkably by any standard. Yet none suffered from it—a broken arm from a fall while the *Discovery* was on the rocks was the most serious accident. Whenever the ships anchored for any considerable length of time spruce beer was brewed and served freely. Berries, clams, fish, and occasional fresh game added variety to the ration and helped to keep scurvy from breaking out.

From the first of May to the nineteenth of August, 1792, the period in which the boats were used for most of the survey work, the two ships themselves traveled through about 475 miles of inland and constricted waters. During those months the continental shore line, with all its indentations and irregularities, was traced from the Strait of Juan de Fuca to a point in northern British Columbia not far from the Alaskan boundary. In three comparable seasons Spanish explorations covered only a fraction of the survey made by Vancouver in that one season. Galiano and Valdes, following Vancouver at a slower pace, also circumnavigated Vancouver Island in the summer of 1792, adding considerably to the maps of Quimper and Eliza, but none of them had even looked into Puget Sound.

Henry R. Wagner, who has devoted much study to the Spanish explorations in that region, considers Galiano's maps superior to Vancouver's for the inlets of the mainland of British Columbia.[2] In assessing Vancouver's work in detail it is necessary to recall that he was searching primarily for a Northwest Passage. While each of the meandering inlets had to be traced to its head, once it was determined to be a dead end as far as navigation was concerned, further interest in it was lost. The great barrier of the coastal ranges of mountains was recognized for what it was, yet no opening that might possibly be a passage through it was overlooked.

Outstanding in the record of the summer's achievements are the vision, courage, and perseverance of the man who led the expedition. In so far as his health permitted, Vancouver drove himself as hard as any of his officers and men, and he shared the hardships of exposure in the boats. As the professional navigators the two masters, Whidbey and Johnstone, shared the heaviest part of the boat work. Puget also had a full share, and Lieutenant Baker, in the *Discovery*, was hard pressed to keep abreast of the survey by plotting the results on master charts. We shall see the same driving energy displayed throughout the remainder of the voyage.

QUADRA

Vancouver planned to include the southwestern coast of Vancouver Island in his survey, but the weather interfered. The *Chatham* lost touch with her consort and anchored in Friendly Cove, Nootka Sound, during the morning of August 28. The *Discovery* came in that afternoon. To a Spanish pilot boat that met her off the entrance the *Chatham* was a most welcome sight. The *Chatham*'s clerk reported that the Spanish crewmen were "ready to leap overboard for joy, for it seems that we were so long expected, that they had now given up all hope of seeing us at all this season." [3]

Shortly after the *Discovery* anchored, Vancouver sent Puget ashore to announce his arrival to the governor and to offer to salute the Spanish flag, provided the salute was returned gun for gun. Compliance assured, a thirteen-gun exchange of salutes opened the formalities at Nootka, according to an international custom still followed by the navies of the world.

The trading vessels on the northwest coast, as well as the naval vessels, regularly exchanged gun salutes whenever they fell in with each other. Just what purpose was served by such a display in that wild and remote part of the world is not apparent, but Menzies has left us an amusing glimpse of the extremes to which saluting was practiced at Nootka:

. . . saluting was so common among the Trading Vessels that visited the cove that there was scarcely a day past without puffings of this kind from some vessel or other, & we too followed the example, & puffed it away as well as any of them, till at last we were become so scarce of ammunition to defend ourselves from the treacherous Indians, that we were obliged to get supplies of Powder from both the Spaniards and Traders before we left the coast. [4]

97

If that was literally true it was very much out of character for the usually careful and thorough Vancouver. But at Nootka two years later he begged off salutes, pleading a powder shortage, and when he arrived at Monterey, California, in November, 1794, he sent an officer ashore to apologize for not saluting. These instances may have been due to a powder shortage, as Menzies suggests, or they may have been a display of Vancouver's pique at his reception at Monterey in 1793; Vancouver, of course, does not tell us. It is not easy to believe that any prudent commander, and Vancouver certainly was that, would fritter away his gunpowder needlessly when he was so dependent upon his own resources for defense. No doubt Menzies exaggerated the situation.

With the saluting formality out of the way, Vancouver landed to pay his respects to Señor Quadra. From that first meeting between the two men grew quickly a most cordial and friendly relationship. Quadra was a most interesting and colorful personality, but, unfortunately, most of what we know of him comes from records of his meetings with Vancouver during this voyage. Edmond S. Meany, in *Vancouver's Discovery of Puget Sound*, devoted a chapter to Quadra, including all the information he could assemble.[5] Born of noble parents about 1740, in Lima, Peru, Quadra was approximately seventeen years older than Vancouver. He first appeared in the history of the northwest coast as the energetic second in command of a Spanish exploring expedition in 1775 that reached well into the Gulf of Alaska. At the time of his meetings with Vancouver he was a captain in the Spanish navy and was serving as the naval commander of San Blas, Mexico, and California. Neither Vancouver nor Quadra spoke the other's language, but Mr. Dobson, a master's mate in the *Daedalus*, who spoke fluent Spanish, was transferred to the *Discovery* to become the interpreter.

Every log and journal covering this period at Nootka singles out Quadra for special attention, and his hospitality, consideration, and friendliness are mentioned only in the most glowing terms. One action is typical of his generosity: he provided all vessels in the cove, warship and trader alike, a daily supply of hot rolls, fresh milk, and vegetables from the shore. Above all Quadra enjoyed company and liked to entertain. Officers from all the vessels in port were regular guests at his dinner table. The day after he arrived Vancouver and as many of his officers as could be spared sat down to a five-course dinner with Quadra. It was a meal, Vancouver reported, such as "we had lately been little accustomed to." [6]

If Vancouver was somewhat restrained in describing this affair at Quadra's quarters, Mr. Boit, a mate of Captain Gray's in the American ship *Columbia,* found an earlier similar experience almost unbelievable:

> . . . [Quadra] gave us a grand entertainment at his house, at which all the Officers of the Fleet partook, fifty four persons sat down to Dinner, and the plates, which was *solid silver,* was shifted five times, which was 270 plates, the Dishes, Knifes and Forks, and indeed everything else, was of Silver and always replaced with spare ones. There could be no mistake in this as they never carried the dirty plates or Dishes from the Hall where we dined. . . .[7]

Who would not be impressed by such a display of luxury and lavishness in that remote wilderness settlement?

Among those present at Vancouver's first dinner with Quadra was Maquinna, the Indian chief of the region. Earlier in the day Maquinna had tried to board the *Discovery* but, not being recognized as a chief, was turned away. His dignity and feelings were deeply wounded by the apparent snub. Quadra did his best to explain the oversight and to placate the chief but had little success. A few days later Quadra suggested to Vancouver that the two of them pay a formal call on Maquinna at his home village, twenty miles up the sound. Vancouver agreed that this would offer an excellent chance to regain his prestige and suggested that they set out the next morning.

Four boats carried a large party of English and Spanish officers to visit Maquinna. The chief was flattered by the gesture, and the Englishmen were fully restored to his good graces. He arranged an impressive entertainment of warrior maneuvers and native dances for his visitors, to which Vancouver responded by having the sailors do some English reels and country dances. Quadra provided a sumptuous dinner served on his silver plate. It proved to be a pleasant excursion for all concerned, and during the trip Quadra asked Vancouver to commemorate their meeting and friendly relations by giving their names jointly to some headland or island. Vancouver selected the large island they were then on, naming it Quadra and Vancouver Island. That unwieldly name remained on the maps until about the middle of the nineteenth century, when usage gradually reduced it to its present form, Vancouver Island. Quadra's name is still preserved in the region; Quadra Island, less prominent than Vancouver Island, lies on the opposite side of Discovery Strait in the upper part of Georgia Strait.

Work was not neglected during these early social activities. The observatory crew was sent ashore to work up necessary astronomical observations for the survey. It was suspected that the *Chatham* had suffered some underwater damage when she grounded in Queen Charlotte Strait, and she was hauled out onto the beach for examination. First her rigging and masts were stripped out of her and her stores were taken out and sent ashore. At a favorable high tide she was hauled as high up on the beach as possible. In that position, when the tide went out, most of her underwater body was exposed and could be worked on at low tide. Some hull damage was found that needed immediate repair, and part of her copper sheathing had been torn away.

STALEMATE

Apart from the social and scientific activities and ship repair was the serious business between Vancouver and Quadra that brought them together at Nootka. Before Quadra was sent north from Mexico on the mission to deliver the lands at Nootka to Vancouver, Spain's position in that part of the world had been given careful study in Mexico City. To appreciate the scope and significance of that study we should return for a moment to Martinez at Nootka in 1789.

Complying with an order of the viceroy, Martinez practically abandoned Nootka in October, 1789, when he returned to San Blas. A new viceroy, Revilla Gigedo, the outstanding viceroy in Spanish America of that era, assumed office in October with a keen and vigorous interest in Nootka and its environs. He reported to Madrid that he planned to send a new expedition to Nootka and that Spanish possession of that port would be vigorously upheld against any foreign power that challenged it. Eliza, the new commander sent to Nootka, was directed to fortify the port, erect permanent buildings, and be prepared to defend them. He was also directed to send ships to survey the coast as far north as Cook Inlet, Alaska, and to survey the Strait of Juan de Fuca. These measures ordered by Revilla Gigedo reveal his determination to retain Spain's claim to Nootka, at least until more specific instructions were received from Madrid. They were taken, of course, long before the conclusion of the Nootka Sound Convention. Meanwhile they insured permanent possession of the port for Spain.

Below is a review of the terms of the Nootka Sound Convention, since what took place at Nootka in 1792 is of course directly concerned with them. The first and the fifth articles, which are the most important, are quoted directly. The remaining articles are summarized.

(I) . . . The buildings and tracts of land situated on the Northwest Coast of the continent of North America, or on islands adjacent to that continent, of which the subjects of His Britannic Majesty were dispossessed about the month of April, 1789, by a Spanish officer, shall be restored to the said British subjects.

(II) Reparations and restitution for any act of violence by the subjects of either power after April, 1789, are provided for.

(III) The subjects of both powers are to be free to navigate the Pacific Ocean and South Seas, to trade with the natives, and to make establishments in places not already occupied, subject to the restrictions of the following articles.

(IV) British subjects will not conduct illicit trade with the Spanish settlements in the Pacific. British subjects will not navigate within ten marine leagues of any part of the coasts then occupied by Spain.

(V) It is agreed that as well in the places which are to be restored to British subjects by virtue of the first article as in all other parts of the Northwest Coasts of North America or of the islands adjacent, situated to the north of the parts of the said coast already occupied by Spain, wherever the subjects of either of the two powers shall have made settlements since the month of April, 1789, or shall hereafter make any, the subjects of the other shall have free access and shall carry on their commerce without disturbance or molestation.[8]

Royal orders for carrying out the provisions of the Nootka Sound Convention reached the viceroy of Mexico in the spring of

1791. They recommended that the boundaries of exclusive Spanish possessions be fixed at latitude 48° north, and that Nootka should be divided between England and Spain. The convention did not define the northern limit of Spanish territory other than by the vague "coast already occupied by Spain." In effect, the Spanish government directed renewed negotiation of that feature of the treaty, with the hope that the English commissioner would accept Spanish terms. Understanding that point helps in a recognition of Vancouver's later predicament. The Spanish royal orders also suggested that Captain Quadra be named the Spanish commissioner at Nootka.

Quimper's explorations gave Revilla Gigedo better information on the geography of that region than was available in Spain. The viceroy thought it would be better to make the Strait of Juan de Fuca the boundary, since a limit of latitude at 48° north would exclude the strait from Spanish territory. He also believed that the strait might extend into New Mexico, and for that reason an even better boundary would run due north from the entrance of the strait to latitude 60° north. Without discussing the full merits of his proposal, the Spanish government implied that it would approve the change.

Quadra's instructions, contained in a letter from Revilla Gigedo sent in October, 1791, outlined the viceroy's views on the subject. The best port in the Strait of Juan de Fuca must be occupied at once, and it should have a garrison as strong as the expected English garrison at Nootka. Such a fortified post was contrary to the spirit of Article V of the convention if it was intended to offset the English post at Nootka, as implied. Quadra was alert to the need for such an arrangement from the Spanish point of view, for just before he sailed for Nootka at the end of February, 1792, he reported to Revilla Gigedo that he had seen an English map, dated 1790, which placed the boundary between English and Spanish territory just north of San Francisco. Just one month after Vancouver entered the Strait of Juan de Fuca Lieutenant Salvador Fidalgo, in the *Princessa,* arrived at Neah Bay. This is a sheltered cove, the site of an Indian village, lying about five miles east of Cape Flattery on the Washington side of the strait. There Fidalgo formed a settlement that was named Nunez Gaona.

Nunez Gaona pinpoints the final act of the expansion of the old Spanish Empire, 1492-1792. Nootka, occupied in 1789, was farther away from Mexico; but Nunez Gaona was intended to be the barrier port, extending the limits of Spanish territory to the Strait of Juan de Fuca. Ironically, the abandonment of that port a few months later was the first step in the contraction and later collapse of the Spanish Empire.

These preliminary discussions and steps tell us eloquently of the plan evolved by Spanish officials to minimize any gains the British might derive from the Nootka Sound Convention. Through Quadra they were prepared to negotiate a new agreement with the British commissioner when he arrived at Nootka, aimed at fixing a boundary as far north as possible. In his report to the viceroy, announcing that he was waiting for Vancouver's arrival, Quadra stated that he intended to negotiate a boundary between the two establishments at Nootka, leaving the entrance free for both nations. The viceroy approved this idea.

While he waited at Nootka for Vancouver to complete his survey work, Quadra assembled more information to support the Spanish position. From Captain de Viana of the *Iphigenia,* one of Meares's ships that had been involved in the incident of 1789, he obtained a statement that he had been well treated by Martinez during the time he was detained at Nootka. De Viana also stated that there were no English buildings of any kind in the port when Martinez arrived there. Two American captains, Gray of the *Columbia* and Ingraham of the *Lady Washington,* both of whom had been present when Martinez arrested Colnett, gave Quadra a joint statement recounting their version of the incident. It agreed closely with Martinez' report and was very different from Meares's claims in his book and *Memorial* to the House of Commons. Gray and Ingraham further stated that they had traded with the Indians in the vicinity for nine months and never heard them mention that Meares had purchased any land from them. Thus, when Vancouver arrived at Nootka, Quadra was well prepared with eyewitness statements supporting Martinez' version of the incident.

Vancouver received, in the *Daedalus,* a letter of instructions from the Admiralty, dated August 20, 1791, over a year before it reached him. Enclosed with the instructions was a copy of an order from Count Florida Blanca to the Spanish commissioner at Nootka to deliver to the English the buildings and districts or parcels of land in Nootka Sound and Port Cox (Clayoquot Sound) that were occupied by British subjects in April, 1789. Specifically, Vancouver's instructions with respect to Nootka were these:

> . . . you are to deliver to the Spanish officer, commanding at that port, the above-mentioned letter from Count Florida Blanca, and to receive from him, conformably thereto, on the part of His Britannic Majesty, possession of the buildings and districts, and parcels of land, of which His Majesty's subjects were possessed at the above-mentioned period.[9]

The balance of his instructions dealt with other matters, mainly with sending the *Daedalus* to Port Jackson, Australia, after his ships had been supplied from her. That the Admiralty considered the restitution of the buildings and lands a mere formality is also apparent from the fact that Lieutenant Hergest, should he reach Nootka before Vancouver did, was authorized to receive the property in Vancouver's place. With Hergest dead, Thomas New, master of the *Daedalus,* wisely waited for Vancouver's arrival when Quadra notified him that he was prepared to deliver the designated lands.

Two days after his arrival Vancouver received a formal letter from Quadra enclosing copies of the statements of de Viana and of Gray and Ingraham. Quadra's own letter reviewed the history of Nootka, beginning with its discovery in 1774 by Spanish explorers. It dealt at some length with the Martinez-Colnett affair according to Martinez' version of it. Quadra offered to demonstrate that Captain Meares's claims were "chimerical," as Vancouver expressed it, and were almost entirely without merit. Therefore, said Quadra, Spain had nothing to deliver nor any damages to make good. In the interest of a solid and permanent peace, however, he was willing to cede to England, *"without prejudice to the legitimate right of Spain,"* the buildings and gardens that the Spaniards had built and occupied at Nootka, after which he would retire to Nunez Gaona.[10] The northern boundary of Spanish lands should be fixed at Nootka, he argued, and English ships should not pass to the south of the Strait of Juan de Fuca.

Quadra's proposals were in furtherance of the viceroy's idea of including the strait within the limits of Spanish territory.

Vancouver was disturbed by Quadra's letter and its implications. Nothing in his year-old instructions authorized him to reopen negotiations concerning the provisions of the Nootka Sound Convention. He was not even told what to do with the place after it was delivered to him, although he was familiar with the earlier plans to found a convict colony on the northwest coast. A copy of Lord Grenville's draft letter to Governor Phillip concerning that colony had been furnished to him. He later intimated, in his *Voyage of Discovery,* that he expected a permanent English settlement to be made at Nootka,[11] and, until he received more specific instructions, he planned to leave the *Chatham* there with Broughton in charge of the port.

In reply to Quadra's unexpected proposals Vancouver stated that he was not authorized to discuss the rights or pretensions of the courts of Spain and Great Britain north of California, as they had been fully reviewed in negotiating the Nootka Sound Convention. He was empowered only to receive the buildings and territories in accordance with that convention and Count Florida Blanca's order. Further, it was his understanding that the Spanish settlement at Neah Bay was open to vessels of both countries, since in April, 1789, the northernmost permanent Spanish settlement on the coast was San Francisco. Therefore, all settlements north of that port, including Neah Bay, should be open to the joint use of both nations in accordance with the fifth article of the convention. He expected full restitution of the port of Nootka and concluded by offering Quadra every assistance after he received it and the continued use of its facilities until Quadra was ready to leave.

The next day, when Vancouver landed to go to the observatory, he met Quadra, who told him how pleased he was to be dealing with a man of Vancouver's character and suggested that the two of them tour the settlement. The Englishman was well pleased and impressed by what he saw. The buildings were in good repair; there was a new oven built especially for the new owners; and the gardens were well kept and productive. Except for what his ships would need for the passage south, Quadra planned to leave the remaining fowl, cattle, and swine with Broughton, together with a large supply of garden seeds. The storehouses had been ordered cleared so that the supplies in the *Daedalus* could be unloaded and stored ashore. Vancouver set the English crews to that task. With all the necessary work in the port arranged for and proceeding smoothly the two leaders set off on their visit to Maquinna. As a result a second letter that Vancouver had received from Quadra the evening before did not get translated until after their return.

In this letter Quadra again stated that his evidence showed that there were no buildings at Nootka when Martinez arrived there, and that the Spanish buildings were on a different site from that where Meares's hut had been. If Vancouver did not feel free to accept his first proposal Quadra was willing to leave him in full possession of the spot where Meares's building had been. He would place the rest of the settlement under Vancouver's command until the whole matter could be referred to their respective governments for final agreement. Meanwhile Quadra would retire from the port. Vancouver's reply accepted the suggestion to make a full report of the local transactions to his government and to ask for further instructions. Not yielding his position, he remained ready to receive the buildings and lands at issue in accordance with the terms of the Nootka Sound Convention and the order of Florida Blanca.

While the formal letters showing basic disagreement were being exchanged the social relations between the two men remained most cordial and friendly. Nearly every day Vancouver and his officers dined with Quadra on shore. After dinner one day Quadra asked for a personal discussion of the questions at issue. Vancouver and Broughton, with Dobson, the interpreter, then reviewed the main points with Quadra and one of his officers. According to Vancouver's version of the discussion, they agreed to refer the whole matter to their respective governments. Quadra would leave him in full possession of the port; the Spanish flag would be struck, and the British flag hoisted over the port. Quadra would salute the British flag, and the salute would be returned gun for gun.[12] But the next morning brought another letter from Quadra in which he agreed to deliver only the land that Meares had occupied, while the Spanish settlement would remain at Nootka pending the decision of the two governments. This proposal drew an immediate rejection from Vancouver. He would not even consider hoisting the British flag on the small plot of ground indicated, a triangular section of beach shingle about one hundred yards on each side, hemmed in on the shoreward sides by steep bluffs.[13] It had access to the Spanish buildings by land only at low tide. British pride and dignity could not accept a situation in which its flag flew over such a small plot while the flag of Castile flew over a more spacious settlement on higher ground nearby.

After another exchange of letters in a similar vein, Vancouver brought the discussion to a head by asking for a categorical statement of Quadra's willingness to restore the port of Nootka to him. Quadra's reply reiterated his former position, whereupon Vancouver advised him that he would consider Nootka to be a Spanish port henceforth, and he requested Quadra's formal permission to remain there. That Quadra readily granted, and he cordially offered to continue every assistance and service as before. So ended the negotiations after a two-week exchange of correspondence.

Bancroft felt that Vancouver was wrong not to enter into a discussion of the events of 1789, although he conceded that Vancouver was probably right in refusing to accept anything but surrender of the entire port if he had reason to believe his government expected that.[14] Henry R. Wagner held that Vancouver's stubbornness blocked a plan that would have saved much grief later.[15] These views, which place the onus of failure to reach agreement on Vancouver, do not consider the realities of his position at the time. He had already taken possession for England of all the land he had surveyed during the past summer, starting with the point where he first sighted California, near Cape Mendocino. Regardless of the validity of that act, it alone would have made him reluctant to enter into negotiations recognizing the Strait of Juan de Fuca as Spanish territory; but there are other reasons not so obvious.

It has already been noted that Vancouver was aware of the plan to found a convict colony on the northwest coast. Apart from this specific plan for using the area, the British government had throughout the controversy made clear its strong sense of ownership of the lands in the American Northwest. When news of the 1789 incident at Nootka reached Europe, England mobilized for and was prepared to go to war to exact satisfaction for that "outrage" from Spain. Neither the British government nor Vancouver knew that Meares's account of the incident, on which the somewhat vague Nootka Sound Convention was based, was colored, misleading, and in some respects false. Therefore, Vancouver was completely unprepared for the questions now being raised by Quadra. When presented with the carefully organized Spanish version, differing in every essential from Meares's, of what had happened in 1789, Vancouver, as the English commissioner, had to stand by the English account.

His dilemma was aggravated by his inability to consult with his government and the knowledge that a year would elapse before he could receive further instructions. That inability to communicate rapidly placed a heavy burden of responsibility on his own conduct and judgment. To some extent the same was true of Quadra, although he had the advantage of being fully informed of the viceroy's ideas and desires while Vancouver had only the most general instructions and no guidance for proceeding in case events did not develop as expected. This situation affords an excellent example of the freedom of action, and the accompanying need for good judgment, on the part of naval officers representing their countries in remote regions in the days before the cable and radio brought every decision of this nature within immediate control of the home government.

Vancouver suspected that Quadra was trying to maneuver him into an agreement that would either weaken or set aside the spirit of the Nootka Sound Convention. Expecting to carry out only a formality that had been settled conclusively in Europe, he very wisely refused to be drawn into the trap. He was deeply worried about the reaction in England to his conduct of negotiations and his decisions at Nootka. The Home Office, which had cognizance of the convict colony in Australia, as well as the Admiralty, had a material interest in his expedition, a further indication of the future plans for Nootka, and thus he sent long reports to both.

He wrote a personal letter to Evan Nepean, secretary of the Home Office, which was to be produced only if his conduct at Nootka came under censure. In it he mentioned other personal letters to the Earl of Chatham at the Admiralty and to Lord Grenville, secretary of state for home affairs when Vancouver left England, but by then foreign minister. His purpose in writing to Nepean was to explain in detail his reasons for acting as he did. He complained that, despite a promise from Nepean before he left England that he would be sent detailed instructions about the restitution of Nootka, he had received neither official nor personal letters from the Home Office. The instructions he had received from the Admiralty told him only to accept the buildings and lands involved but said nothing of what he was to do with them. He even worried about his decision to leave Broughton in charge at Nootka while he continued the search for the Northwest Passage, rather than remaining there himself.[16] This letter clearly shows that Vancouver expected to receive detailed instructions concerning the future development of Nootka after it had been placed under the British flag. Failing to receive them he was completely in the dark as to what was expected of him, and he prudently parried the efforts of Quadra to make a local agreement.

If, as is probable, a fortified British colony was to be established at Nootka after its restitution, Quadra's proposal blocked that plan. On the other hand Vancouver's obstinate refusal to negotiate at all checked Revilla Gigedo's scheme to extend the boundary of Spanish territory to the Strait of Juan de Fuca. If his conduct of the affair should be censured at home, Vancouver confided to his journal, the cause would be "a want of sufficient diplomatic skill, which a life wholly devoted to my profession has denied me the opportunity of acquiring." [17] That may be so, but, recalling the sharp official differences that developed between Vancouver and Quadra—that the desires of each were checked by the attitude and position of the other—and that during those tense negotiations a warm personal friendship and mutual regard grew between the two men, both must be termed skilled and expert diplomats.

The Columbia River and San Francisco
(1792)

V ANCOUVER's decision to consider Nootka a Spanish port meant that all the supplies landed from the *Daedalus* must be reloaded into her hold. When the order for that work was issued, rumors began to fly through the little squadron. With characteristic British humor the small patch of beach shingle that Quadra offered to cede to Vancouver was dubbed with the facetious but impressive title of "The British Territories," [1] More seriously, an atmosphere of depression developed in the ships when it was realized that Nootka was not to become a British port and that there would be a long period of waiting and suspense before new instructions could arrive from England.

On the day Vancouver stopped negotiations with Quadra, the *Fenis and St. Joseph,* a trading vessel under Portuguese colors, entered the harbor. On board as supercargo was a Mr. Duffin, who had been with Meares at Nootka in 1788 and was in the *Argonaut* when she was seized in 1789. He gave Vancouver a sworn statement of the occurrences at Nootka in those years, which supported the Meares account for the year 1788. Upon his return in 1789, Duffin continued, the Spaniards were already in possession of the port, and he then saw no sign of the house that Meares had built the year before. Some Americans from the *Columbia* had their tents pitched on the site, and Duffin observed that the Americans were not molested by the Spaniards in their trade with the Indians.

The apparent favoritism shown by the Spaniards toward Americans was a sore point with the Englishmen. Vancouver and his officers believed that Captain Gray and Captain Ingraham, in their statement to Quadra, deliberately distorted their account in order to discredit Englishmen and to curry favor for themselves with the Spaniards. After he returned to England Vancouver had several conversations with Captain Colnett which confirmed and strengthened that belief in his mind. Manby believed that Ingraham, who arrived at Nootka on September 11, was responsible for Quadra's refusal to transfer the port to Vancouver;[2] actually, as we have seen, Quadra was following a carefully prepared plan to enlarge Spanish holdings.

The continuing friction and rivalry between British and American traders on the northwest coast is illustrated by an incident that occurred during this visit of Vancouver to Nootka. After the British ships had been in port for some time it was discovered that a Mr. Magee, captain of the *Margaret* of Boston, was carrying on a surreptitious but profitable trade with Spanish and British seamen. He was "generously charging four dollars a Gallon for Yankee Rum that cost him probably about 2s or half a Crown a gallon." [3] Quadra stopped that traffic at Vancouver's instigation. Magee, however, had the last word. Just before he left the port he delivered to Vancouver a formal complaint against the English captains Brown, of the *Butterworth,* and Baker, of the *Jenny,* charging them with piracy and being accessory to piracy. More specifically, they were accused of having fired at Indians in Clayoquot Sound, a few weeks before, in a wanton and barbarous manner.[4] Puget, the source for this, did not know what answer Brown and Baker made to the charges, but he felt that the conduct of Magee and the *Margaret* toward the Indians at the same time was also blameworthy. More details of the incident that provoked the charges were revealed by Puget when he returned to Nootka in 1793.

On that occasion he again noted that the Americans were selling rum more or less openly at a dollar a quart. But Puget was most bitter because the Americans were trading muskets and gunpowder to the Indians. After the Nootka incident of 1789, according to his journal, American traders promised the Indian chiefs an annual payment of weapons if in the future they would trade only with Americans. When the *Butterworth* and the *Jenny* went into Clayoquot Sound in 1792, they found the Indians hostile and unwilling to trade because of that agreement. According to an American version of the affair, Magee came to the rescue of the English vessels and drove the Indians off.[5]

Puget obtained the story from his own countrymen, and it is, no doubt, colored by prejudice. He singled out Captain Kendrick, of the *Lady Washington,* as one who gave the Indians large quantities of arms. Most of the Americans did trade weapons to the Indians, and the practice was general with the English traders as well. Meares was one of the first to engage in that traffic. Vancouver and his officers recognized the danger inherent in arming the Indians, and they commented frequently and strongly in their journals on the evils of the trade in weapons. The arms traffic was the direct cause of many bloody fights between the traders and the Indians; the latter, as to be expected, were the ultimate victims and the real sufferers from the practice.

One result of Vancouver's insistence on recognizing Nootka as a Spanish port was that Quadra sent word to Fidalgo at Neah Bay to re-embark everything on shore there and to prepare to abandon Nunez Gaona. This step was the first recessive move in the breakup of the Spanish Empire, and Vancouver unwittingly was its architect. After arranging a future meeting with Vancouver at Monterey, in California, Quadra sailed from Nootka. He called at Neah Bay to direct Fidalgo to return to Nootka as acting governor, and then sailed south to California.

Before Vancouver could follow Quadra there remained much to be done at Nootka. First, a full report of the events and negotiations in that port must be sent to London as soon as possible. For one channel Vancouver directed his first lieutenant, Zachary Mudge, to proceed to Canton, China, in the *Fenis and St. Joseph.* From there Mudge was to make the best of his way to England in an East India Company ship. Once in England he would be available to amplify Vancouver's reports and return to him with new instructions. Mudge arrived in China at the end of December and was given passage to England in an East Indiaman.

It had been necessary for Vancouver to make several changes among the officers of his ships during the weeks at Nootka. To the vacant captaincy of the *Daedalus* he appointed Lieutenant Hanson, first lieutenant of the *Chatham*. Johnstone, the master, was promoted to first lieutenant of the *Chatham;* and Spelman Swaine, a master's mate in the *Discovery,* was given Johnstone's berth as master of the smaller ship. When Vancouver decided to send Mudge home with dispatches, Puget and Baker were advanced to first and second lieutenants of the *Discovery* and Swaine was brought back from the *Chatham* as third lieutenant. His berth in the *Chatham* was given to Thomas Manby, another master's mate in the *Discovery.* This was a welcome assignment for Manby, still smarting from the tongue-lashing he had received earlier in the season. In the *Chatham* he would no longer be under Vancouver's immediate command. Alexander Cranstoun, surgeon of the *Discovery,* had been sick since the ships had left the Cape of Good Hope, and he was transferred to the *Daedalus* to be invalided home by way of Australia. Phillips, the former carpenter of the *Discovery,* was also placed in the *Daedalus* under arrest to be sent home to await his court-martial. Menzies, who originally volunteered to serve as both botanist and surgeon and was refused that dual assignment, was now given Cranstoun's post as surgeon and thus became a regular member of the *Discovery*'s company. He objected at first, but Vancouver told him that if he refused the appointment he must state his refusal in writing. Not knowing how that might affect his standing at the Admiralty in the future, Menzies reluctantly accepted the post.[6]

The great survey was not neglected in all the other activity at Nootka during those busy weeks. The *Sutil* and the *Mexicana,* brief companions of the British ships in Georgia Strait earlier in the season, also circumnavigated Vancouver Island and arrived at Nootka a few days behind the *Discovery* and the *Chatham.* A week later Señor Caamano, another Spanish explorer, in the *Aranzazu,* arrived after a season of surveying farther north in the vicinity of the Queen Charlotte Islands. Vancouver gave Quadra copies of all of his surveys and received in return copies of those made by the Spanish vessels. At the observatory Vancouver himself found time to take 49 of the 106 sets of lunar observations made for the longitude. He found that his result differed by one third of a degree from the longitude found by Cook, but he believed that his own was more accurate.[7] He adopted the meridian of Nootka as the basic longitude for the survey.

The end of the fair weather season at Nootka was approaching before the *Daedalus* was reloaded and all the other preparations for putting to sea were completed. Fidalgo arrived from Neah Bay early in October and assumed the post of acting governor. A few days before Vancouver sailed, the *Jenny*, Captain Baker, against whom Magee had lodged his charges, arrived at Nootka. He wanted to sail directly to England, but he had on board two young Hawaiian girls, natives of Niihau. He asked Vancouver to return them to their native island, a request the latter was happy to grant for he was sure that they were on board the *Jenny* only because they had been kidnaped.

After six busy and eventful weeks at Nootka, the *Discovery*, the *Daedalus,* and the *Chatham* sailed for California in the middle of October; but, before they reached the Spanish ports there, other important tasks were to be accomplished.

GRAY'S HARBOR AND THE COLUMBIA RIVER

After his chance meeting with Vancouver near the Strait of Juan de Fuca in April, Captain Gray, of the American trader *Columbia,* sailed southward along the coast from Cape Flattery. He discovered Gray's Harbor, on the Washington coast, and in May he succeeded in crossing the Columbia River bar; he was the first to negotiate that difficult entrance and actually enter the river.[8] While he was trading in the river Gray reached a point about twenty miles up the river from the entrance. Near the end of the season he was in Nootka for a day while Vancouver was lying there late in September. Through Quadra Vancouver obtained a sketch of Gray's discoveries.

En route to California Vancouver planned to re-examine the coast and check his earlier work, to extend his survey along the

California coast, and to survey in detail Gray's Harbor and the Columbia River. At the beginning the weather smiled on his design. The three ships approached Gray's Harbor on one of the crystal clear and pleasant days that sometimes occur off that coast in October. Mount Rainier, ninety miles inland, was clearly visible for several hours. Off Gray's Harbor Vancouver sent the *Daedalus,* with Whidbey and one of the *Discovery*'s boats, to survey the harbor while the *Discovery* and the *Chatham* went on to the Columbia River. The *Daedalus* was to rejoin them there, but in case she missed the other ships Monterey was fixed as the next rendezvous.

Gray's Harbor is an extensive body of water on the outer coast of the state of Washington, but it is choked with sand banks and shoals. It has marshy shores and only one narrow channel deep enough for seagoing shipping. The *Daedalus* took three days to work her way inside the harbor because of the shoals and adverse winds, and Whidbey spent six more days making the survey of the harbor. He considered the port of little value or importance, especially since the two essentials of wood and water were too far away from possible anchorages to be obtained easily. With dredged and well-buoyed channels it is today an important lumber port. After completing the survey and leaving Gray's Harbor, the *Daedalus* made her way to Monterey, where she joined the other ships.

As the *Discovery* and the *Chatham* approached the Columbia River entrance heavy seas were breaking all along the shore and across the entrance. Undaunted by the seas, Vancouver was determined to get inside the river if possible. He directed the shallower-draft *Chatham* to lead the way toward and through the entrance, and the *Discovery* followed. As the larger ship approached the entrance the depth of water shoaled to only four fathoms and soon to three, just three feet more than her draft. That was too narrow a margin to continue the effort safely, and, seeing breakers all around and even to seaward of his position, Vancouver hauled out to sea and withdrew. The *Chatham* managed to work her way about a mile inside the entrance, where she anchored; she was still not out of danger for the seas broke ahead of her on a large shoal that lies in the lower part of the river.⁹ The next morning was calm but hazy. A boat was sent from the *Discovery* to sound the depths of water between the two ships, but a rising easterly breeze and an ebbing tide prevented the boat from entering the river. Vancouver then signaled to the *Chatham* to send an officer out to report to him. In a short time Johnstone arrived on board the *Discovery* to report that the *Chatham* had had a very bad night in the breakers. Her clerk, in describing that experience, admitted that he had never been so frightened in his life.

The *Discovery* spent the afternoon trying to work her way through the entrance, but shifting winds and tides blocked the effort. The following morning a southeast storm ended all hope of getting her inside the river for several days. Driven offshore by the blow, Vancouver decided to give up the effort and proceed down the coast toward California, leaving the survey of the river to Broughton.

When Broughton realized that the *Discovery* had left the vicinity he set about surveying the river. He worked the *Chatham* about fifteen miles upriver from the entrance, but he found the shoals so extensive and the channels so intricate that he decided to anchor the ship and make the rest of the survey in the ship's boats. Setting out with a week's provisions, Broughton reached a point several miles above the present city of Vancouver, Washington, about one hundred miles from the sea and not far from the Columbia River Gorge. There, already a week away from the ship and with his provisions running low, he turned back.¹⁰ For some time it had been apparent to him that the river was not navigable for seagoing ships and not therefore a Northwest Passage. By sign language Indians indicated to him that there were waterfalls a short distance upstream.

Broughton named the farthest prominent point of land that could be seen from his turning-back point for his commander— Point Vancouver.¹¹ Before starting down the river he landed and took possession of the river and countryside for England, believing himself to be the first European to have seen it, as in fact he was. In commenting on Broughton's action Vancouver drew a very fine distinction between the river proper and its tidal estuary, for, from Gray's sketch, "it does not appear that Mr. Gray either saw, or was ever within 5 leagues of, its entrance." [12] Vancouver did give Gray credit for the discovery of the estuary, but he used the division of estuary from river proper to justify Broughton's work and his claim to the country upriver.

Broughton named many other land features along the river, mostly for the officers and midshipmen of the expedition, and nearly all these names are retained today. To one of the most striking and beautiful landmarks of the Pacific Northwest, which he could see from near Point Vancouver, he gave the name Mount Hood for one of England's greatest naval leaders, Admiral Lord Hood.

Manby, the sportsman of the expedition, was left in the *Chatham* while the survey party was away. He added welcome fresh meat, in the form of a deer and numerous ducks and geese, to the otherwise plain fare of salt meat. When the boat party returned to the ship Broughton had to wait several days before he could take her through the entrance because of heavy seas running continuously across the entrance. The *Jenny* was also in the river and was anchored just inside Cape Disappointment. There the two ships waited out the stormy weather. Friendly Indians in the neighborhood provided the *Chatham* with enough "moose deer," probably elk, to give her entire crew fresh meat. Manby's gun also brought in more geese and ducks.

As it always does eventually on the Columbia River bar, the weather moderated enough for an attempt to be made to put to sea. Captain Baker, of the *Jenny*, had been in the river earlier in the year, and he offered to lead out. The *Chatham* had several seas break over her deck, but she weathered it, stood out into the open sea, and headed for San Francisco. It was then the tenth of November, late in the season indeed for such a small vessel to be crossing the Columbia River bar. The bar has been the graveyard of many a sound ship and is still a place to be highly respected at any season of the year. The danger is in losing control of the ship in the short but heavy seas that build up across the entrance and having her driven aground on the shoals outside the channel where the seas can pound her to pieces.

While the *Chatham* was lying in the Columbia River and Broughton was surveying the river, the *Discovery* was having a full share of heavy weather and troubles. In the early part of her passage to San Francisco—for Vancouver planned to stop there before going on to Monterey—she had a succession of storms. In one of them a seaman was washed overboard by a heavy sea. A jolly boat, swung on davits over the stern, was promptly lowered and succeeded in recovering the man. The practice of carrying a small boat swung over the stern for just such an emergency was not usual in the navy of that day. Menzies, now the *Discovery*'s surgeon, believed that this foresight alone saved the man's life. He would have been hopelessly lost in the time that would have been required to unlash and swing out a boat from its normal midships stowage. Menzies noted that, although it was rare in the navy, it was then general practice to carry such a boat over the stern in the East India Company's ships.[13] The fact that Vancouver had the boat rigged there is further evidence of his progressive ideas.

South of Cape Mendocino Vancouver kept close to the coast in order to extend his continental survey southward. From then on the weather was much improved, but new troubles developed to bedevil him. Symptoms of scurvy appeared in six members of the crew. Both Vancouver and his surgeon attributed that outbreak to the general lack of fresh provisions and to the hard service the men had experienced since the beginning of the summer. Sauerkraut had been served regularly throughout the season as the standard antiscorbutic and preventive, but when active symptoms appeared the victims were served orange and lemon juice. Some of the men responded rapidly to the treatment, and the others grew no worse. Vancouver expected to obtain fresh provisions that would prevent further outbreaks of scurvy at San Francisco, but he was so intent upon making his survey of the coast complete that he would not drop any part of it for the sake of gaining a few days in reaching port. It was after dark on November 14 when the *Discovery* anchored in San Francisco Bay, about two miles in from the outer entrance.

At daybreak nothing was in sight except herds of cattle and sheep grazing on the hills, but soon several people appeared on the shore and signaled for a boat. A Spanish sergeant and a Franciscan missionary appeared on board to welcome the visitors and to offer them every assistance the port afforded. The *Discovery* had anchored much farther inside the bay than Spanish vessels usually did, and the Englishmen had passed the presidio the evening before without seeing it. In the afternoon Sr. Heamegildo Sal, commandant of the presidio, and the principal of the Mission of San Francisco came on board and repeated the welcome and offers of assistance. The viceroy had issued instructions that Vancouver's ships were to be well received and supplied, an exception to the normal practice of excluding all foreign vessels from the California ports. Sal suggested that the *Discovery* move closer to the presidio, and the men were set to the task of restocking the ship with wood and water, neither of which was considered to be of good quality.

As with Quadra and his officers at Nootka, Vancouver was soon on most cordial terms with Sal, his wife, and the other Spaniards of the small garrison. He found the presidio only partly completed, small, barren, lacking in comforts, and almost totally without defenses. That finding is most revealing in showing the Spanish lack of industry in protecting their missions, for the presidio of San Francisco had been founded fourteen years earlier. Its weakness was all the more surprising to Vancouver since he considered the port to be the key barrier for the protection of the Spanish mission settlements to the south.

At the invitation of one of the fathers, on a Sunday he visited the nearby mission. He was very much impressed with the kindliness and devotion of the missionaries toward their charges, but of the Indians themselves he formed a low opinion because of their general indolence and slovenliness. During his conversations at the mission Vancouver expressed a desire to visit the mission of Santa Clara, near the southern end of San Francisco Bay and about fifty-five miles from the presidio at San Francisco. Sal acceded to the request with enthusiasm and promised that guides and horses would be ready the next morning. Vancouver and several of his officers set out early, escorted by six Spanish soldiers, and the party reached Santa Clara that evening. It was one of the few excursions on shore that the botanist Menzies missed, for he was sick with a cold. All day on horseback, mostly at a gallop, was too much for some of the men, and Baker and Johnstone had to go to bed immediately because of soreness and fatigue. Saddle-sore and weary, the others were probably kept from doing the same thing by pride alone, for sailors have never been noted as horsemen.

Vancouver and his party were the first foreigners to be so far inland since the founding of the California missions. Just as at the mission of San Francisco, the visitors were warmly welcomed by the mission fathers, and two very pleasant days were spent at Santa Clara. The soil was the best Vancouver had seen, the gardens were lush, and the mission produced more grain than it could use. The Indians, however, had the same undesirable qualities of those at San Francisco. The technique and skill shown by mounted Spanish soldiers in lassoing half-wild cattle for slaughter made a deep impression on Vancouver and the rest of his party.

On returning to San Francisco, Vancouver found that the *Chatham* had arrived from the Columbia River. The *Discovery* was then nearly ready to sail, and preparations were made to move on to Monterey, eighty miles southward. Cattle, vegetables, and eggs were received from the settlement at San Francisco, but, when Vancouver offered to pay for them, much to his surprise Sal refused to accept any payment. He explained that Quadra's orders were that all financial matters would be arranged by himself with Vancouver at Monterey. Struck by that display of generosity and by the general poverty of the place, Vancouver left with Sal a gift of kitchen and table utensils, and hogsheads of rum and wine, to be distributed equally among the presidio and the two missions.

His custom of distributing generous presents was certainly one of the reasons that Vancouver was received so cordially at other California ports and missions in the future. With his obvious interest in and sympathy with the missionary work he would have been welcome in any case. He proved that his interest was sincere in a material way, for it has been estimated that the total value of the presents he gave during his three visits to California was ten thousand Spanish dollars.[14] The mission at Santa Cruz alone received about one thousand dollars' worth of material, with which it built a mill. Gifts of such magnitude were windfalls to the missions, which otherwise usually had to do without items they could not manufacture themselves; the priests were only human in being grateful. The presents came from a stock supplied to Vancouver for gift purposes by the government, but he was also put to considerable personal expense in entertaining the Spaniards.

9

The Islands of Los Majos

(1793)

THE *Discovery* and the *Chatham* reached Monterey, then the capital of California, near the end of November and found that the *Daedalus* had arrived four days before. After the usual formalities and exchanges of salutes, Vancouver resumed his cordial relations with Quadra, who had been awaiting his arrival for about a month. Quadra told him that he had just received orders to arrest all vessels found trading on the coast except those belonging to England and Spain. That order convinced them that their governments had reached final agreement on all points concerning Nootka. It made Vancouver more anxious than ever to get a full report of his failure to obtain possession of that port to England as soon as possible. He also wanted to send home copies of his own and the recent Spanish surveys of the northwest coast.

From Nootka, Vancouver had reported to the Admiralty his intention of sending Broughton home with the *Chatham* after a visit to California. At the same time he had asked for Broughton's return with instructions for himself in a better ship than the *Chatham*, preferably a forty-four-gun ship. At Monterey it occurred to him that if he could send an officer home through Mexico much time would be saved and he could keep the *Chatham* for further service. His choice for the journey through Mexico was Broughton, who had been a party to all his meetings with Quadra, and who would still be able to bring back the new ship. When the idea was suggested to Quadra, that ever accommodating officer offered to take Broughton to San Blas and provide him with money and every other assistance in crossing Mexico.

The arrangement was concluded at the first meeting, during which Quadra also gave his permission to land the observatory and offered to provide the assistance of his own people. Both the *Discovery* and the *Chatham* were to load to capacity with stores and provisions from the *Daedalus,* and there was the always necessary calking of seams and repairs to the rigging. Only when that work was organized and going ahead smoothly was Vancouver willing to turn to the social side of life at Monterey. One of his first ventures in that field was a visit with Quadra and a group of Spanish and English officers to the mission of San Carlos, about two miles from the presidio of Monterey. There they were warmly greeted by the Father President of the California missions, the Reverend Fermin Francisco de Lasuen.

Quadra made horses available, and the officers took frequent excursions through the countryside. Thomas Manby recorded his impressions:

We frequently made parties for the day, carried out provisions, and being well mounted took large sweeps through the Country. The Great beauties of this part of California certainly exceed any in the known World, few of our Noblemans [estates?] can equal the plains Woods and Lawns here to be met with. . . .[1]

At Monterey itself there was a great deal of reciprocal entertaining, during which Vancouver's efforts to be a genial host suffered some minor setbacks. Once, when a party of Spanish officers and their wives were on board the *Discovery* for dinner, the affair was cut short by the motion of the ship, which made some of the ladies seasick. Thereafter Vancouver entertained his guests at the observatory on shore.

Most of the Spanish officers and their wives were present at another party he gave soon afterward. In the evening he had a fireworks display set off, and, as he described it, "The evening was concluded by a dance and a supper, which was not ended until a late hour." [2] Menzies gives us an interesting sidelight to that particular party. During the evening's festivities one of the features was a fandango, danced by the Spanish ladies. Not to be outdone Vancouver asked the two Hawaiian girls embarked from the *Jenny* at Nootka to sing their native songs and give some of their native dances. The Spanish ladies were not pleased with what they saw, feeling that the purpose of the Hawaiian dances was to ridicule their own, and they left the party in a huff.

After the *Daedalus* delivered her stores to the *Discovery* and the *Chatham* she was to proceed to Australia for service under the governor of New South Wales, to return the following year to Vancouver if he requested. On the way to Australia she was to call at various islands in the Pacific to pick up livestock for the use of the convict colony. Vancouver arranged with Quadra to obtain some cattle and sheep, potentially much more valuable additions to the colony than the swine that would be collected in the islands. The hold of the *Daedalus* was fitted with stalls for thirty-six animals which Quadra contributed. Vancouver thought they should do well in Australia, since animals of the same breeds had thrived at Nootka with little attention.[3] The *Daedalus* sailed late in December with orders to stop at several islands. She made a good passage to Australia, but only four of the sheep survived the four-month voyage.[4]

After the *Daedalus* sailed, the main task left for the Englishmen at Monterey was to complete Vancouver's report and the charts that were to be taken to England by Broughton. When Vancouver spoke to Quadra about paying for the cattle and other foodstuffs his ships had received at Monterey, Quadra refused even to discuss the matter. Vancouver insisted that it was public business and that an accounting should be made, but he recorded that Quadra declared:

. . . the only settlement in which he could possibly engage, was that of seeing we were accommodated to the extent of our wishes, with every supply the country could bestow; adding, that repayment would most amply be made, by the promising success attending every creature and production, that we had either received for our own use, or that were destined for other purposes.[5]

Small wonder that Vancouver and his officers could find no adequate words in praise of Quadra! After Quadra had so freely given the cattle for the *Daedalus,* Vancouver asked him for four cows, four ewes, two bulls, and two rams, all that the *Discovery* could carry, to be taken to the Hawaiian Islands, where he would spend the rest of the winter. Those too were given. Vancouver matched Quadra's generosity with his presents, although there were reports of complaints that the missions served by Monterey were not treated as generously as had been those at San Francisco.

Monterey proved to have attractions for some of the English sailors as well as for the officers. The *Discovery* and the *Chatham* were ready to sail the first week of January, 1793, and it was planned to sail in company with Quadra for the first few days at sea. The ships were delayed for another week by the desertion from the *Chatham* of two men, the armorer, who was a key man, and a marine. Earlier, in December, a seaman had deserted from the *Discovery*, and a party of marines sent in search of him had returned empty-handed. Some time later it was learned that the man had made his way to the Carmel mission and there sought the protection of the mission fathers. Some of the fathers called on Vancouver to plead for the man's pardon, but all that he would promise was that the man would not be punished while the ship remained at Monterey. Another party of marines was sent to the mission to bring the man back to the ship, where he was kept in irons until the ship was at sea. Then, on two different occasions, he was punished with six dozen lashes, the most severe punishment Vancouver awarded during the voyage.[6] Menzies felt that on that occasion

. . . a mitigation of this severe punishment at the instigation of the Worthy Fathers would have been [an] equally efficacious & more conditional procedure, especially as we did not find that the severity of treatment in this case had prevented others from deserting before our departure.[7]

Three men had also deserted from the *Daedalus*, and Quadra had loaned her three of his own seamen for her passage to Australia. When the two men from the *Chatham* were missed, Vancouver offered a reward of twenty-five dollars to the Spanish soldiers at the presidio for the recovery of each of them. That offer was matched by Quadra and by the commandant of the presidio. Soldiers scoured the countryside for several days but could find no trace of the men. Menzies and others suspected that the men from the *Daedalus* were being shielded and hidden by the soldiers themselves. It was also suspected that the armorer of the *Chatham* had been enticed away from his ship by Spanish officers; one report was that he had been offered forty dollars a month. Whatever may have been the cause of the desertions, a little more than two months later the governor reported to the viceroy that all five of the Englishmen were being held at Monterey. He stated that three of them had deserted because they were Catholics and were not permitted to attend mass, and that the other two wanted to become Catholics. The viceroy instructed him to deliver the men to Vancouver's ships upon receiving payment for their expenses. The two non-Catholics should not be admitted to the Catholic faith unless they were in danger of death.

These were the only desertions that occurred on the voyage. The most plausible explanation for their occurrence all at one time is that the first visit to Monterey was an extremely pleasant one for the seamen as well as the officers. The men preferred to risk the consequences of desertion and remain there, even under Spanish rule, rather than continue the voyage and eventually return home. By ordering them held and delivered to Vancouver's ships, Viceroy Revilla Gigedo showed that he disapproved and discouraged further desertions in California. The succeeding visits of Vancouver's ships to California were less cordial than the first, and the atmosphere that might encourage desertion was lacking.

After six days of fruitless search Vancouver gave up his efforts to recover the *Chatham*'s men. He entrusted his dispatches to Broughton, who boarded the *Activa* with Quadra, and assigned his own first lieutenant, Puget, to command the *Chatham* in Broughton's absence. The loss of the armorer was serious, as he was the only smith on board. To meet the emergency Quadra offered to lend the *Chatham* the one smith then at Monterey. Vancouver recorded in his account that he was reluctant to accept the offer and was induced to do so only by the urgency of the problem. Puget, as the new captain of the *Chatham,* clarifies this reluctance for us. The man was not a volunteer and did not want to serve in the ship; he was brought aboard forcibly under guard.[8] Puget added that the idea was Quadra's and that Vancouver considered his action proof that none of the Spanish officers knew of or had encouraged the deserters. Aside from the disregard for the man's wishes, which after all was in keeping with the times, Quadra's act shows how genuine was his regard for the Englishmen. It is all the more remarkable when we recall that Spain and England were traditional enemies in war, and that the religious schism between Catholic and Protestant was usually sufficient to keep individual Spaniards and Englishmen cool toward each other.

Such an extraordinary relationship had to be two-sided. There is no doubt that Vancouver had a deep affection for Quadra, and that his officers shared that feeling. There is no record in any of the journals of the expedition of fights or disturbances between the English and Spanish sailors or soldiers, either at Nootka or at Monterey. Of the fathers at the missions Vancouver wrote with admiration and warmth; and to all the Spaniards he showed a high degree of personal charm and magnetism that contrasts with his handling of his own ships and crews, in which he was strict, somewhat aloof, and inclined to be cold and businesslike. He did have a motive for keeping on the best of terms with the Spaniards, for the second purpose of his voyage, according to his instructions, was to learn as precisely as possible "the number, extent, and situation of any settlements within the limits [between latitudes 30° and 60° north] by any European nation, and the time when such settlement was first made." [9]

As he did for every place that he visited, Vancouver left us a detailed description of life and conditions in California. He was the first to lift the curtain of secrecy from the presidios and missions, and in his *Voyage of Discovery* he revealed the military weakness of the entire chain. The Spaniards were not traders, and their small garrisons existed at that time to protect the missions rather than as guarded outposts for trade and commerce. Except for Nootka and Nunez Gaona, which were occupied as outposts to prevent foreign encroachments toward California, the central theme of the California settlements by the time of Vancouver's visits was to spread the Christian faith among the Indians. Vancouver recognized and admired that motive, and his descriptions of the missions show his interest and admiration for their spiritual accomplishments as well as their physical layouts.

After a stay of nearly two months at Monterey, the *Discovery* and the *Chatham* sailed in company with Quadra's *Activa* and *Aranzazu* in mid-January, 1793. For the first few days the course was southerly until they reached the point where Quadra must sail southeastward for San Blas and Vancouver southwestward toward Hawaii. There Vancouver invited Quadra on board the *Discovery* for a farewell dinner. It was a sentimental occasion. With an appeal to his readers to think of their own feelings under similar circumstances, Vancouver expressed his own feelings on parting with Quadra in this manner:

> [He] was the main spring of a society that had produced us so much happiness, who had rendered us so many essential benefits, and whose benevolence and disinterested conduct had impressed our minds with the highest esteem and veneration. On reaching the Active our friends took their leave; we saluted them with three cheers, which they cordially returned; and we each pursued our respective voyages with all sails set.[10]

A few days later one of the carpenter's mates disappeared through a gunroom port of the *Discovery;* he was the second man lost to the expedition since the ships had left England nearly two years before. He was presumed to have let himself into the sea and taken his own life, for he was a good swimmer and the sea was smooth with a light breeze at the time. If he had fallen overboard that fact would have been observed on deck. He was last seen about fifteen minutes before he was missed, and it was near sunset when his absence was noticed.

THE ISLANDS OF LOS MAJOS

Aside from staying with Quadra as long as he could, Vancouver had another reason for heading south from Monterey rather than shaping a course direct to Hawaii. He planned to search for the islands of Los Majos, shown on old Spanish charts of the Pacific about 10° eastward of the Hawaiian Islands. The names of the islands vary in different accounts of them, but Vancouver called them Los Majos, and that name is used here. After Cook's third voyage, on which he sighted and named the Sandwich (Hawaiian) Islands, there was much speculation that the islands of Los Majos and the Hawaiian Islands were the same, and a close study of the records of the Vancouver expedition shows that there was a conviction within that expedition that the Spanish islands of Los Majos were the same as the Hawaiian Islands. For that reason it is desirable to trace the history of Los Majos in some detail.

The French explorer La Pérouse, in the account of his voyage of 1785-88, was the first to suggest that the islands of Los Majos were the same as Cook's Sandwich Islands. While sailing northward in the Pacific in 1786, he and his pilots noted a difference, caused by ocean currents, between the longitude found by reckoning and that obtained by lunar distances and the chronometer. His observations were careful and accurate, for he noted successively what we now call the westerly setting South Equatorial Current, next the narrower belt of the easterly setting Equatorial Counter Current, and finally, in about latitude 7° north, the westerly setting North Equatorial Current. When he reached the Hawaiian Islands he observed that if, "like the ancient navigators, we had no means of ascertaining the longitude by observation, we should have placed the Sandwich Islands 5° more to the eastward." [11] By then La Pérouse had already made a systematic search for the islands of Los Majos. Starting from a position well to the east of the charted position of those islands, he sailed westward through their indicated positions until he sighted the island of Maui. It was this search that convinced him that Los Majos and the Sandwich Islands were the same. The earlier galleon pilots who placed the islands on their charts had no way of finding the longitude accurately or of knowing of and allowing for the ocean currents that bore their ships along to the west. La Pérouse suggested that Gaytan, in an expedition sent from Mexico in 1542, had made the first discovery of the Hawaiian Islands. In presenting these ideas and theories La Pérouse was seriously trying to improve geographical knowledge, not to discredit Cook, whom he called the "true Columbus of this country, of the coasts of Alaska, and of almost all the islands of the South Sea." [12]

Included in an account of George Anson's raiding voyage to the Pacific in 1740-44 was a replica of a chart of the Pacific Ocean captured from a Spanish galleon. On that chart was shown a group of islands roughly similar in shape to the eastern part of the Hawaiian Islands. They lay in the same latitudes as the eastern part of the Hawaiian group, but their longitudes were about midway between Hawaii and Mexico on the modern chart. Captain James Burney, a lieutenant in Cook's third expedition in 1778, published in the early nineteenth century his *Chronological History of the Voyages and Discoveries in the South Sea,* in which he reported a major error found in the Anson chart. The original Spanish chart of the Pacific was on two sheets, and in reproducing it on a single sheet for the Anson book the engravers placed all the longitudes on the land features on the eastern half 10° too far to the east. Burney also had a copy of a set of sailing directions prepared for the use of the galleon pilots and written by a pilot major in the galleon trade. These directions, published in Manila in 1754, gave the position of the group of Los Majos as about 10° east of Hawaii. In addition, Burney had two other old Spanish charts that showed Los Majos to be slightly farther to the west. By correcting the error of the Anson chart Burney found all his sources in substantial agreement with respect to Los Majos. He concluded, supporting La Pérouse, that the longitude error in them was due to ocean currents about which the galleon pilots knew nothing, and that the islands of Los Majos were the same as Cook's Sandwich Islands.

This opinion was widely accepted until 1916, when E. W. Dahlgren, a Swedish geographer, published a monograph entitled *Were the Hawaiian Islands Discovered by the Spaniards before Their Discovery by Captain Cook in 1778?* Dahlgren's answer to his own question was an emphatic negative. He searched the Spanish archives for records of any voyage that might have made the discovery but could find nothing that he could associate with the Hawaiian Islands. It is not necessary to follow all Dahlgren's reasoning, and he presents a strong case, to support his conclusion that nothing that could be identified with Hawaii was found in the records he examined. He felt that the evidence drawn from maps was untenable and that "no historical fact proves, nor is there any probability that the Hawaiian Islands were ever visited, or even seen, by the Spaniards before their discovery by Captain Cook in 1778." [13] Dahlgren's conclusion has since been accepted as the final word on the matter.

He made one questionable assumption, however. Although he recognized that the Spanish galleon pilots had no way of finding the longitude at sea, he assumed that, since the pattern of the ocean currents follows that of the trade winds, the Spanish pilots were familiar with those currents. Yet there is ample evidence in his own study that they did not know of the currents and that they did not allow for them in their reckoning of distances traveled from Acapulco to Manila. In several instances errors in distance given on the early charts are readily accounted for by the influence of the North Equatorial Current, of which the Spaniards were unaware. The group of Los Majos was placed on the Spanish charts exactly where the island of Hawaii would be found by a galleon pilot unaware of the westerly setting current, that is, about six hundred miles east of the correct location of Hawaii. The coincidence is so remarkably accurate that it must be conceded that the early Spanish pilots knew something of the island group later found by Cook although there is no record of their visiting that group.

In 1778 Cook was surprised to find that the Hawaiian natives were familiar with the use of iron, and that knives were the most valuable single item of trade with them. He speculated that pieces of iron might have been recovered from flotsam of shipwrecks or from casks that had drifted to the island from the east, and that the use of iron had developed from that source. Dahlgren and others have accepted Cook's speculation as the probable explanation for the islanders' familiarity with the use of iron. The weakness of that explanation is in the fact that any iron of this period that had been exposed to salt water for even a short time would have been so badly corroded that it could not have been readily converted to human use in any form. Any such treatment would have been particularly difficult for native islanders who had never seen iron before.

Cook also reflected that, if the Spaniards had discovered the Hawaiian Islands, they would have made regular use of them on their westbound passages to replenish their wood, water, and provisions. This is a plausible and strong argument to support the position that the Spaniards did not know of the Hawaiian Islands before Cook's time. But the conditions of the westbound galleon passage provide a reasonable explanation for this failure to use the islands, assuming that the Spaniards did know of their existence. Sailing toward Manila the galleons carried treasure, mainly silver received in Mexico for their cargoes of Oriental silks and goods. They were potentially the richest prizes afloat for pirate or privateer. The passage from Acapulco to Guam was made under ideal weather conditions and required only two months. The galleons normally passed three or four hundred miles south of Hawaii, about a month after leaving Acapulco, at a time when their provisions and other supplies were still adequate. The route was rigidly specified for each voyage, and any variations from it were discouraged and suppressed.

It is possible that a pilot, the only man on board who knew how to navigate, could have been far enough off his track to see and make note of the Hawaiian Islands. No firm claim is made here that such a trip was ever made. Yet it cannot be dismissed as imagination or chance that a group of islands roughly similar to the eastern part of the Hawaiian group was placed on old Spanish charts and in sailing directions just where it would have been placed had a discovery of which we have record been made. It should not be surprising if some future researcher finds an old document, hitherto unknown, that will clear away the mystery of Los Majos. It may be significant also that the Spaniards rarely called at the Hawaiian Islands after Cook's time. Although the question of whether or not the Spaniards were the first Europeans to see the islands may still have political and academic interest, there is no doubt that for Cook the group was a real discovery, and the history of Hawaii, insofar as its relations with Europeans are concerned, dates from his discovery in 1778. A possible connection between his Sandwich Islands and Los Majos presumably did not occur to the officers of his expedition. The Spanish islands are shown in addition to the Sandwich Islands on the general chart that was published with the account of Cook's third voyage in 1784.

When Vancouver began his search for Los Majos early in 1793, they were still shown on charts of the Pacific Ocean about 10° in longitude eastward of the Hawaiian Islands. The account of La Pérouse's voyage was not published until 1797, and the English translation was not published until 1798. Vancouver's search duplicated that of La Pérouse, but it was made independently and without the knowledge that a similar search had been made seven years before.

At Monterey Quadra gave Vancouver a chart prepared by one of the oldest Spanish pilots on the coast. The pilot knew of no authority for showing Los Majos on the chart, but he understood that the islands had been discovered by some vessels coming from China to Mexico many years before. Menzies rightly thought this explanation unlikely, for the eastward track of the galleons was far to the north, in the belt of favorable easterly winds.[14] Vancouver recorded that the Spanish officers had no faith in the existence of Los Majos, although they had first appeared many years before on a chart constructed by a pilot who enjoyed an excellent reputation.

In January and February, 1793, the *Discovery* and the *Chatham* spent ten days sailing west along the twentieth parallel of latitude on the lookout for Los Majos, in fine and clear trade-wind weather. Nothing was seen that remotely suggested the existence of land, such as seaweed or shore birds. It was that fruitless search by Vancouver, together with an earlier one by Portlock and Dixon, that Dahlgren used to support his contention that the islands of Los Majos were imaginary and could not be the Hawaiian Islands. Vancouver himself, by dismissing the islands with the statement that the Spanish officers had no faith in their existence, seems to support that viewpoint.

There was actually a great deal of speculation about Los Majos on board the *Discovery*. Menzies, as a botanist and surgeon, probably did not know how to navigate, but he suggested that an examination of the old Spanish records might show that Los Majos

. . . may own out to be the Sandwich Islands from their being placed in the same parallel of latitude, & from the uncertain mode Navigators formerly had of ascertaining their longitude in distant voyages, when the errors of reckoning with the influence of currents &c might in a long and tedious voyage increase to a very considerable amount, for were we to settle the Sandwich islands by our reckoning this time from California . . . we should place them at least three degrees & a half to the Eastward of their real situation; we ought not therefore to be surprised at finding much greater errors in the reckoning of former times. . . .[15]

This is almost identical with the reasoning used by La Pérouse in 1786. There can be no connection between the two because nothing was known in Vancouver's expedition of La Pérouse's voyage. That the surgeon presented the idea meant that he got it from someone who was well versed in the art of navigation and knew the significance of the new methods of finding the longitude at sea and of the effect of currents on reckoning. In reality Vancouver evaded expressing his own opinion on the subject by quoting the Spanish officers, and with good reason. Admitting that the Spaniards, rather than Cook, might have been the first discoverers of the Hawaiian Islands would have undermined his own significant work in those islands later in this voyage. He undoubtedly knew of the speculation going on in the ship about Los Majos and conceivably could have privately accepted the theory offered by Menzies.

Manby, the master of the *Chatham* and a qualified navigator, had definite ideas on the problem. He wrote, "I assure myself the Sandwich Islands are the Los Majos of the Spaniards." [16] In 1794 the two ships again searched for Los Majos a few miles south of the 1793 track, and on that occasion Puget expressed his opinion on the question. Without identifying the islands directly with the Hawaiian Islands, he suggested that the position of Los Majos might be in error through errors in copying or locating their position. Puget was familiar with Vancouver's designs on the Hawaiian Islands and had reason for not openly supporting their identity with Los Majos. On the whole, however, the Vancouver expedition did hold the view that the two groups were really one.

The search for Los Majos carried the ships to within sight of the island of Hawaii just two days less than a month after they cleared Monterey. Vancouver then had the two ships separate. The *Chatham* was sent around the southern coast of the island to Kealakekua Bay, surveying the coast en route. The *Discovery* rounded the northern coast for the same purpose.

Nothing of note occurred during those movements except that Vancouver anchored for a few days off Kawaihea, in a bight on the western side of the island near its northern point. There he again met Keeaumoku, father-in-law of Kamehameha, king of the island. He was still disturbed to find that the natives would trade produce only for arms and ammunition. Vancouver convinced Keeaumoku that trade in arms was strictly tabooed for his ships, and soon cloth and others of his trade items were being accepted. Keeaumoku and his wife embarked in the *Discovery* for the passage to Kealakekua Bay, which was made very slow by light winds and calms off the western coast of Hawaii. Two days before the *Discovery* reached Kealakekua Bay, the *Chatham* joined her, and the two ships continued together.

10

Kamehameha
(1793)

KAMEHAMEHA WELCOMES THE EXPEDITION

THE DAY BEFORE the two ships reached Kealakekua Bay, Kamehameha, king of the island of Hawaii, came on board the *Discovery*. After the death in 1782 of his uncle, the former king, Kamehameha had made himself master of the island through intrigue, leadership, and generalship of a high order. In recent years, while trying to extend his conquests to the neighboring islands of Maui and Molokai, he had found it necessary to return to his home island to suppress rebellious elements. From the summer of 1791 until Vancouver's arrival was a period of truce during which Kahekili and Kaeo, the kings of Oahu and Kauai, were preparing to challenge Kamehameha for power, and the latter was preparing to resume his conquests of the other islands. Vancouver met him now at a mid-point in Kamehameha's career when he was about forty years old.

From his earlier visit with Cook, Vancouver remembered the king as a young and physically powerful chief, with a strikingly savage face, who was even then standing out as a leader of his people. Fifteen years later his savage features had softened somewhat, as had his general disposition.

Kamehameha's purpose in boarding the ship was to invite Vancouver to anchor his ships in Kealakekua Bay, on which was situated his home village. It was a harmonious meeting, but as Vancouver was still suspicious of possible native designs on his vessels he would not permit Kamehameha to remain on board overnight.

As the *Discovery* and the *Chatham* approached the anchorage the next morning, they were surrounded by large numbers of canoes filled with friendly natives in a holiday mood, a preliminary setting for a state visit by Kamehameha.[1] Just after the ships anchored, a procession of eleven large canoes was seen putting off from the shore in a V formation. At the point was the largest, with thirty-six paddlers, bearing Kamehameha clad in a magnificent yellow-feathered cloak and wearing a large helmet on his head. The procession circled the ships in perfect order while the spectators in the smaller canoes got well clear. Then, with a flourish, ten of the king's escorting canoes lined up under the stern of the *Discovery* as the large one paddled furiously to the starboard gangway. With a sudden backing of the paddles the canoe stopped precisely in position for Kamehameha to step onto the gangway. On board, he made an impassioned speech of welcome, expressions of friendship were exchanged, and the ceremony was concluded with a final salute of touching noses with Vancouver. It was a grand and impressive spectacle, fully in keeping with the personality of the man who was to become Hawaii's greatest king.

Kamehameha presented Vancouver with some feathered helmets and a profusion of hogs and vegetables, too many for the *Discovery* to take on board at one time. Such regal generosity may have been inspired in part by Vancouver's introduction of cattle into the islands. He had given a few of the animals he had brought from California, those in the poorest condition, to Keeaumoku; but he purposely reserved most of them for Kamehameha. When he had asked Quadra for the cattle to be taken to Hawaii he had had in mind not only supplying the natives of the island, but also building up herds for the supply of future European visitors. He believed that placed under the immediate care of the king the little herd would have the best chance to survive and grow. He was pleased to see that Kamehameha took a keen interest in the animals, which he called "large hogs," and personally supervised loading them into large canoes in which they were taken ashore.[2]

Keeaumoku was a witness to these exchanges and complained that he and the other chiefs should have a greater share in the cattle. Kaiana, whose visit the year before had excited so much suspicion, came on board while Kamehameha was there, also bringing a present of fine hogs which Vancouver had to decline for the time being, as he had no room for them. Vancouver realized that receiving lavish presents from Kamehameha while deferring acceptance of those from lower chiefs would make it a delicate task to keep in the good graces of everyone, but he was determined to pay his principal attention to Kamehameha, as the leader and king of the entire island. When Kaiana entered the cabin, Vancouver saw in Kamehameha's face the same savage look that he remembered from fifteen years before. The king was sullen while Kaiana and Keeaumoku argued with Vancouver about his refusal to take the hogs. Kamehameha suddenly announced that it was not necessary for Vancouver to receive hogs or any other produce from Keeaumoku, Kaiana, or any other chief, as he had plenty more to give when the present supply was exhausted. That ended the argument and cleared the air for future relations.

Kamehameha had two white men in his service. One, Isaac Davis, was the sole survivor of the American schooner *Fair American,* captured by one of the chiefs in northern Hawaii in 1790. It had been commanded by the son of Captain Metcalfe, of the *Eleanora,* at the time of the capture lying in Kealakekua Bay. John Young, the English boatswain of the *Eleanora,* was ashore a short time later and was detained by order of Kamehameha, who feared that through him Metcalfe might learn of the capture of the *Fair American* and take revenge.[3] Both Young and Davis were later taken into Kamehameha's service and, although partly prisoners, they ranked as chiefs and were important advisers to the king by the time of Vancouver's visit. Young was usually at Kamehameha's side in his visits to the *Discovery* and the *Chatham,* and both were the king's agents on board the ships to regulate trade and to keep order among the natives.

Kamehameha offered Vancouver the use of some tabooed land

for the erection of the observatory. To preserve the friendly atmosphere that arose from their first meeting, they mutually agreed to measures regulating the conduct of affairs in the port. Kamehameha asked that the Englishmen should be ordered not to enter native *morais,* as consecrated places were called; that they should not stray about the countryside; and that Vancouver should permit none but the principal chiefs on board the vessels. Kamehameha would provide guides and porters for parties wishing to travel into the country. Vancouver thought his requests were sound and reasonable, and he added some rules of his own. Knowing the native craving for firearms, and aware that some of the officers might carelessly entrust their pieces to a native bearer on a hot day, he feared that an incident might occur if the native took to the bush with the weapon. He ordered that no firearms could be taken ashore except pocket pistols, which were to be kept concealed unless needed for self-defense, and that midshipmen were to be allowed on shore only in the company of officers. He was not entirely confident of the sincerity of all the apparent friendliness about him, and he landed an armed party of marines as a guard at the observatory. The ships were also anchored in positions from which their guns could cover the observatory in the event of trouble.

The restricting orders were bitterly resented among the officers in the ships. Puget recorded that he received these orders verbally and that Kamehameha was strongly of the opinion that parties ashore should be armed for there were many disaffected people about who would be glad to cause trouble. "All arguments were ineffectual," Puget wrote; "I must own myself so very dull of Comprehension as not at present to see [the order's] utility." [4] Puget's clerk Bell left some additional details. A few days after the order was issued, a midshipman from the *Chatham* tried to visit some of his friends on board the *Discovery*. He was told that by order of Captain Vancouver all communication between the midshipmen of the two vessels was forbidden unless they were on duty.

That afternoon Bell was ashore with two of the *Chatham*'s midshipmen. They met Puget, who told them that he was sorry to send the midshipmen back to the ship but he had just received verbal orders from Vancouver forbidding all persons except the officers to go ashore, unless in a duty status. Bell noticed that the clerk of the *Discovery,* Mr. Orchard, did not seem bound by the order. He took his own cue from Orchard, and Puget did not extend the order to him. Bell's journal expresses deep sympathy for the midshipmen of the *Discovery,* all of whom, he felt, were being made to suffer for some inattention to duty on the part of one or two of them. In what is the most critical passage that appears in the journals of the expedition, he wrote:

I cannot help observing that Captn Vancouver has rendered himself universally obnoxious by his orders—not only in this present instance to the Young Gentlemen but at various times to all ranks of officers in the Vessels under his command.[5]

Strong words indeed were these, especially to be confided to a journal being kept on board one of those vessels. They must be considered as indicative of two developments. First, friction among members of the ships' companies grew as the length of the voyage increased. Second, Vancouver was apparently still giving vent to his irritability in sudden actions that reflected his moods but defied ready explanation. After a season of very hard work in the wilderness of the northwest coast of America, and with another similar season in prospect, restrictions on relaxation in the lush subtropical climate of Hawaii would quite naturally be resented, regardless of the essential soundness of the restrictions. To impose further restrictions on all the midshipmen because of the offenses of one or two seems capricious, unless Vancouver had reason to believe that the offenses were the result of some concerted action on the part of all the midshipmen. His own account says nothing of the incident, so we must assume that it was just another example of a sudden burst of temper over some obscure incident, and a reflection of his physical condition.

In a very different mood was another incident that occurred about the same time, one that illustrates how diligently Kamehameha kept his agreements with Vancouver. He failed to appear for his daily visit one morning but sent off word that an axe and some other articles had been stolen from the *Chatham* by one of the women, who had a more or less free run of the ships. Kamehameha promised to return the articles as soon as he recovered them. The theft was reported before anything was missed in the *Chatham,* and in a short time Kamehameha made good his promise and spent the remainder of the day with Vancouver as usual.

THE PEACEMAKER

About ten days after their arrival Vancouver and several of his officers visited the spot where Captain Cook was killed. There Kamehameha described to them the details of that incident as he recalled them. Vancouver mentioned in his account that some native priests had foretold Cook's death at the time, but Puget's journal has more details of the prophecy. A high priest explained to him that while Cook's crews were gathering firewood ashore they had taken some pieces from the fence of a *morai.* This action had been sanctioned by one of the chiefs, but the general populace was incensed at the sacrilege. It was the act of taking the wood from the fence that had led the priests to predict Cook's death. Puget was convinced that Cook's death was not due entirely to the events of the morning on which he was killed, but rather that the people were ready to take advantage of the first chance that offered to fulfill the priests' prophecy.[6] Whatever the details or motives, the death of Cook was still a great event in the lives of the natives. He was still referred to by them as a god, and his death was used as a measure of time in their historical reckoning.[7]

Vancouver made the visit to the site of Cook's death the occasion for a ceremony designed to impress the natives. It was a Sunday, and the crews were in their best uniforms. A guard of marines was paraded on shore in honor of the king. Kamehameha was flattered by the compliment, and lower chiefs were duly impressed, as Vancouver had hoped. As a return compliment Kamehameha invited the English officers to witness a sham battle the next day. This proved to be a form of game in which the opposing sides approached and cast blunt spears at each other. Some of the more skillful warriors stepped out in front of the others, taunting the opposition and inviting special attention. They parried some of the spears cast at them with a spear held in the left hand while catching others flying past with the right hand. Kamehameha himself took part for a while, and on one occasion handled six spears cast at him almost simultaneously. Three he caught, two he parried with his own spear, and one flew past him harmlessly as he dodged it with a twist of the body. The game lasted most of the afternoon, and that night Vancouver added his own touch to the festivities with a fireworks display.

Vancouver also took advantage of the presence of a large number of the leading chiefs to urge that some means be found to restore peace to the islands and bring the civil war to an end. As a first step he suggested that a meeting be held of the leading kings or chiefs of the various islands, but he found too much distrust among the opposing kings for this to be considered at the time. Vancouver also urged Kamehameha to place the island of Hawaii under the dominion of the English king. That shrewd chieftain refused to consider the move unless one of the ships was left at the island to assist in its defense, adding that it would be imprudent for Vancouver to accept the island without providing the means for guarding it. He clinched his argument by asking, "Could it be expected that Owhyeaians would fight with firmness for their country if they imprudently had given it away to those who would not protect it?" [8] Vancouver would not go so far as to leave one of his ships at the island. In offering his proposal for cession of the island to England he had more than the welfare of the natives in mind; he was thinking in terms of empire and British dominion. Although agreement on this matter was not reached until his return the following year, he planted the seeds of the idea at this time and was wise enough not to press the point but to shift his interest in native politics into the channel of interisland peace.

Discussing with Kamehameha and his advisers various ways and means to restore peace, Vancouver offered to take one of the chiefs to Maui and there open negotiations with Kahekili and Kaeo. This was opposed on the ground that the chief would be safe only as long as he remained under Vancouver's immediate protection. A better idea, it was suggested, would be to take the chief to Maui to open the negotiations and then to bring Kaeo to Hawaii to complete the terms of peace, with Vancouver acting as referee on all disputed points. Vancouver saw the merit in the suggestion but was unwilling to devote the necessary time to it. It became clear to him, as the discussions continued, that what Kamehameha really wanted of him was open support for an invasion of his enemies' realm. Vancouver would not even consider actively taking part in the war. After further talk he drew out Kamehameha's terms for peace: Maui, Molokai, and the adjacent islands were to be ceded to Kamehameha while Kahekili and Kaeo retired to Oahu and Kauai in peace. Realizing that such terms would be completely unacceptable to the opposing kings, Vancouver offered his own suggestion, which was, in effect, a recognition of the *status quo*. He would sound out Kahekili and Kaeo for their ideas and promised to let Kamehameha know the results.

From a study of these conversations it becomes clear that Vancouver had a humanitarian as well as a material interest in restoring peace in the islands. Kamehameha, on the other hand, was bent on conquest and clearly wanted help in subduing his powerful neighbors. He supported his arguments by repeating that the murders of the officers and men of the *Daedalus,* on Oahu, had been committed by Kahekili's people. Revenge for that crime should be sufficient reason for Vancouver to help Kamehameha against Kahekili. While these differences of opinion arose between Vancouver and Kamehameha, the discussions were kept on a high plane and always within the limits of friendship and mutual respect.

Vancouver had spent about two weeks in Kealakekua Bay, and he was ready to move along the chain of islands. As a parting present Kamehameha gave him a cloak of red and yellow feathers, and as a special present for King George the king gave Vancouver the yellow-feathered royal cloak that he had worn on the occasion of his first formal visit to the ship. Vancouver, for his part, was lavish with his presents. Some were very practical, such as rigging one of Kamehameha's larger canoes as a schooner with canvas sails and fitting it out with a Union Jack and a suitable pennant. Kamehameha was highly pleased with that improvement in his fleet but suggested that it would look even better with some swivel guns mounted on it. Vancouver agreed that that might be so, but "Taboo King George" ended the talk about arming the canoe.

Vancouver's generous presents to Kamehameha had a much greater significance than mere flattery to the vanity of the king. In reality they amounted to a payment for the hogs and vegetables that were so abundantly supplied to his ships. An American visitor, Ebenezer Townsend, who was in the islands a few years after Vancouver had been there, found that Kamehameha had an exalted opinion of the English. This was due, he felt, to the fact that their ships were men-of-war, whose captains made their purchases through giving presents to the king on a lavish scale and securing supplies from him personally in return. By using that device Vancouver did not have to resort to the barter system of buying from lower chiefs or individual natives as the general run of trading-vessel captains did.[9] Vancouver himself noted that, after his ships were fully stocked and he permitted general trading among the crews, essential supplies disappeared from the canoes. Prices rose up to 500 per cent for the souvenirs for which the sailors outbid each other.

Towereroo, who had been brought to Hawaii from England the year before, was a daily visitor to the ships, but he received little attention from Vancouver. Other members of the expedition, not fully understanding his position, were critical of that neglect. The native fared better with Puget, from whom he received a number of presents. They were intended to enhance his prestige among his own people but only succeeded in arousing jealousies and even threats on his life.[10] Although Vancouver had formed a rather low opinion of the man on the voyage out to the island, on this occasion his failure to show him any special favor resulted less from that feeling than from a deep understanding of native customs and the delicate relationships existing among the various ranks of chieftains. Towereroo had no native rank, and to make him a relatively wealthy man among his people tended to flaunt those relationships, a condition apt to be more harmful than good for the man himself.

En route to his hoped for meeting with Kahekili and Kaeo on Maui, Vancouver's first objective was to survey the southern and western coasts of the island. While she was being worked along the western coast, the *Discovery* was boarded by a chief who proved to be an emissary from Kahekili. He wanted to know who the strangers were and if their intentions were friendly, being suspicious of their motives in view of the murder of Hergest and his men on Oahu. Vancouver assured him that he had no drastic action in mind but was anxious to meet the king in order to investigate those murders as well as to learn his views on restoring peace in the islands. This first visit was followed by one from Kamohomoho, a younger brother of Kahekili, who suggested that the best anchorage thereabouts was off the village of Lahaina, in the northwestern part of the island. On the subject of the murders on Oahu the year before Kamohomoho insisted that neither Kahekili nor Kaeo had any responsibility for that incident. Kahekili had already had three guilty men executed for their part in the crime. Vancouver was sure that there were more than three men implicated, and he intended to investigate the affair at Oahu to insure that full justice was done. Although he anchored off Lahaina he did not press the point with Kahekili until after Whidbey had completed a boat survey of the nearby coast and Menzies had returned from a botanical excursion in the interior of the island.[11]

Vancouver found Maui much impoverished, both as a direct result of the civil wars and because Kahekili maintained a large army on the island. This created added demands for the available food and took the men away from the cultivation of the soil. Nevertheless, Vancouver was able to obtain about one thousand muskmelons, grown from seed left on the island by an English captain six years before.

If a durable peace could be established, Vancouver reasoned, the soldiers would be released to return to their normal occupations, which

. . . would be immediately resumed with great energy; and the ability of procuring European commodities, for the purpose of imitating our manners and fashions, by the produce of their own labour and ingenuity, would stimulate them to an industry and exertion, that would be attended with so abundant an increase of productions, as would render the supplies of these islands almost inexhaustible; especially, as the breed of black cattle, sheep, and goats, already introduced, when established under such happy circumstances, would soon greatly increase.[12]

This was a truly desirable objective and shows again that the interest in re-establishing peace had a very material and realistic basis, as well as an altruistic one. On another occasion Manby was even more specific and realistic on the subject:

... should Great Britain ever attempt to Colonize any part of the Northwest Coast of America, these islands will give them a very ample store of provisions and provided industry is closely pursued a sufficiency of Rum and sugar might with ease be produced.[13]

The aged king of Maui and the other islands to the west was treated with the same consideration and honors that Vancouver had shown to Kamehameha. Among the first presents to the king was a cloth cloak similar to one given to the Hawaiian king. When the subject of peace was broached Kahekili listened intently and welcomed the idea, but he was distrustful of Kamehameha's ambition. Disbanding his army, he argued, would be an invitation for an invasion of Maui, but Vancouver countered that Kamehameha was sincere and would abide by any agreement reached. In that, as later Hawaiian history shows, Vancouver was overly optimistic. Kahekili died in 1794, and, taking advantage of the internal strife among his successors, Kamehameha struck suddenly and within a year conquered Oahu and the islands between Oahu and Hawaii, including Maui.

Kaeo, king of Kauai and, like Kamohomoho, a younger brother of Kahekili, joined the group from neighboring Molokai. As soon as they met he reminded Vancouver that he still had a lock of the latter's hair, given to him during Cook's third voyage. Vancouver had heard the tale at Kauai the year before but could remember neither the chief nor the incident. When, the next morning, Kaeo produced a lock of hair the same color as Vancouver's he had to conclude that the incident had taken place, and he was much impressed by the evidence of Kaeo's faithfulness to a memory.

With Kaeo at the council table the peace discussions were resumed. Kaeo believed that the only way peace could be restored was for Vancouver to return to Hawaii, but the Englishman had already rejected that idea. Kaeo then asked that when Vancouver returned to the islands the following year he should first stop at Maui, where Kaeo would embark with him and personally treat with Kamehameha on Hawaii. This was agreed to, and Vancouver sent off a letter explaining the agreement to Young on Hawaii. The bearer was to be a chief who was also to open preliminary negotiations with Kamehameha.

As he had found on Hawaii, the leaders on Maui were suspicious of Vancouver's motives in urging peace among the islands. Why did he advise peace when the captains of all of the trading vessels advised the opposite? He could only answer that those men were not true friends but were influenced by their own profitable trade in arms and ammunition. The most that Vancouver accomplished in his self-chosen role of peacemaker was to get agreement in principle. At least a start was made, and with that he had to be content while he turned his attention to more pressing problems of his voyage.

BRITISH JUSTICE

Native divers examined the bottom of the *Chatham* and found that much of her copper sheathing underwater had been torn away and lost. With another difficult season of surveying in prospect, it was desirable that this be replaced at once. The logical place for her to haul out on the beach was Nootka, for the range of the tides in the Hawaiian Islands was too small for the purpose. To gain time Vancouver sent her to Nootka in advance of his own sailing, while he went to Oahu to complete the investigation of the Hergest murders. In the middle of March the ships parted company at Maui, and the *Chatham* delayed only to survey the north coast of Molokai before proceeding to Nootka. She reached Vancouver Island after a fast passage of only three weeks.

In questioning Kahekili about the murder of Hergest and his men, Vancouver found that the Englishmen had given no offense to the natives and that the murders had been committed by a lawless group of men living on the western side of Oahu. No important chief was involved, and three or four of the guilty men escaped into the hills, but they were then living near an estate belonging to Kamohomoho at Waikiki. Vancouver demanded that the guilty men be apprehended and punished publicly by the natives themselves. All of the natives must be impressed with the fact that the punishment was for the murders, and that in the future anyone guilty of a similar offense could be sure of receiving the same punishment. Kahekili accepted the conditions and named Kamohomoho as his representative to carry out the necessary measures on Oahu.

The day before he left Maui, Vancouver landed to pay a formal visit to Kahekili, and in the evening he invited the king and his party on board the *Discovery* for a fireworks display. As a heavy surf was running at the beach he permitted the king's party to sleep on board in his cabin. He was kept awake most of the night by conversation among that group, consisting chiefly of speculation on the destructiveness of fireworks and the havoc they would cause among enemies if only a supply could be obtained and used in war. Then, as Vancouver described the event:

> The next morning *Titeree* [Kahekili] departed in a very sudden manner, and without my knowledge. I became apprehensive that some accidental offense had been given him, but Taio [Kaeo] assured me of the contrary, and that such was his common practice of retiring.[14]

There Vancouver suffered a lapse of memory or was covering up his own conduct, for Menzies recorded the reason for Kahekili's sudden departure in this manner:

> [One of the Niihau girls] missed a piece of ribbon which it was supposed some of those who had slept in the Cabin stole from her. Captain Vancouver in endeavouring to recover this trifle put himself in such a passion & threatnd the Chiefs with such menacing threats that he terrified some of them out of the ship with great precipitation; the King in particular came running into my Cabin before I knew any thing of the business, & instantly jumping into his canoe through the port hole, paddled to the shore & we saw no more of him.[15]

It was Kaeo, less easily frightened, who told Menzies what had happened. The old king, estimated by Vancouver to be more than sixty, was actually over eighty years old, and must have been very frightened indeed to create the scene that Menzies described. More significant in that incident was Vancouver's sudden burst of temper over what could have been only a trivial matter at best. This is one of the more clearly described incidents indicating that Vancouver was suffering from a hyperthyroid condition.

The *Discovery* sailed for Oahu, making a survey of the south

Mount Hualalai, Hawaii, from a plate in Vancouver's *Voyage of Discovery*

Mount St. Elias, Alaska, from a plate in Vancouver's *Voyage of Discovery*

shore of Molokai on the way. Vancouver planned to go around to the west-coast village on Oahu that was the scene of the murders, but Kamohomoho insisted that the guilty men were then living near Waikiki. On that basis the *Discovery* anchored in Waikiki Bay, and Vancouver began at once his investigation of Hergest's murderers.

When the *Daedalus* had called at Oahu in 1792, she had anchored near Waimea, on the northwestern side of the island. Her commander, with Mr. Gooch, the astronomer, landed with a small party to arrange with the natives for fresh water. After the work of watering was started, Hergest and Gooch walked to a native village some distance inland where they were well received. In their absence a fight broke out at the watering place between seamen and natives, and one of the seamen was killed. When word of that fight reached the village the friendliness disappeared and the unarmed Hergest and Gooch were killed by the villagers, presumably to prevent Hergest from returning to his ship and taking revenge.[16]

When the *Discovery* anchored in Waikiki Bay she was boarded by James Coleman, an American seaman who had been on Kauai the year before but was at this time in Kahekili's service. He brought with him an English-speaking native, who had been with Hergest in the *Daedalus,* to give his version of the murder incident. He claimed that he had warned Hergest not to land at that point as there was no chief present and the natives in that vicinity were known to be a troublesome group. The man who stabbed Gooch and wounded Hergest, together with two other principals in the affair, had been seized and executed by Kahekili's order. Coleman assured Vancouver that he had heard the man's story many times to the same effect and that it was confirmed by other natives.

The next morning Kamohomoho came off to the ship with Coleman and reported that he had in his canoe the man who had killed Hergest and two others implicated in the murders. They were brought on board, and Vancouver set about satisfying himself that the men were guilty of a part in the murders. A chief pointed out the principal offender, and Coleman confirmed that he was reported to be the one who killed Hergest, but he knew nothing about the other two men. Master's Mate Dobson, who had been in the *Daedalus* at the time of the murders, also identified one of the men as one who had been ejected from the ship by Hergest for his insolence. Kamohomoho said that there was a fourth man involved who could not then be found. Vancouver insisted that the English-speaking native, who feared reprisal from his fellows if he testified, come off to the ship to add his testimony to what had been given, but by then he also could not be found. Menzies reported that he had fled to the mountains, afraid to appear because of "some harsh reproofs received the preceeding evening from Captain Vancouver." [17] The leading chief of the island, who claimed to be ill, sent word assuring Vancouver that the men were guilty. The Englishman wished that he could gather more complete evidence than he had, but, since the men were accused by their neighbors and condemned by their own chief, he reluctantly consented to their execution. A full day was spent in the investigation, and he postponed the executions to the next day, much against the wishes of Kamohomoho and some other chiefs who wanted to get the business over with.

Before carrying out the executions Vancouver heard from the accused men themselves. They disclaimed any knowledge that any such incident as Hergest's murder had ever occurred on the island. Vancouver was justifiably skeptical of those claims for they must at least have known of the executions ordered by Kahekili. The sentences were executed in a solemn and public event in order to impress the natives with the seriousness of the crime. With several canoes lying off and with the crew of the ship drawn up at quarters, the condemned men were bound and taken into a double canoe alongside, and there executed by their own chief with a pistol.

Vancouver's account asserts that he was personally convinced that the three men were guilty of the crime and not just three hapless victims selected to appease him. Others were not so sure. Bell, whose journal reveals that he was greatly incensed over the crime, strongly supported Vancouver's action and defended him against possible future criticism in England for not having more evidence against two of the men. He even lamented that more men implicated in the murder could not be found and given the same treatment. The page and a half of his journal where he expressed those thoughts was later crossed out, and on the margin of one of them is this note: "1815 My opinion is altered now—I am 20 years older." [18] By 1794, when the *Daedalus* returned to Australia with a report of Vancouver's action, it was felt that the three men were not actually guilty but were simply an equal number of natives selected to compensate for the Englishmen killed in the first place. There is considerable later evidence to confirm that view.[19]

Whether or not the men executed were really guilty of a part in the crime, Vancouver had handled the situation with restraint and judgment. Rather than take some arbitrary punitive action as many would have done, he conducted an investigation and satisfied himself that the men were sufficiently implicated to warrant the punishment.[20] By having the executions performed by the natives themselves he placed the onus for any miscarriage of justice on their own chiefs. He succeeded in impressing them with the seriousness of the crime in English eyes and with the fact that future similar crimes would demand the same punishment. His fairness in the case could not fail to enhance his stature in the native minds. As a culmination of the grim and ceremonious visit to Waikiki, and to impress the natives still more with his power, Vancouver had one of his fireworks displays set off in the evening of his departure.

There remained but one task to keep the *Discovery* in the Hawaiian Islands—the return of the two girls embarked at Nootka to their native Niihau. But just before the ship left Oahu there was a native report that required investigation. Vancouver was told of a large bay in the southwestern part of the island, accessible by a narrow and winding channel, which was capable of sheltering large ships. Whidbey was sent to survey the reported bay and its channel. He found a shallow sandbar blocking the entrance, but some distance inside the channel he found "two bays, about a mile to the northward, forming a very snug and convenient little port. Unfortunately, the bar without renders it fit only for the reception of very small craft." [21] This was one of the earliest European appraisals of Pearl Harbor.

On the passage from Oahu to Kauai the *Discovery* met the largest canoe yet seen in the islands. It was over sixty-one feet long and was reported to be made from a single tree of the fir family. Vancouver had no doubt that the tree had been carried to Kauai from the northwest coast of America by ocean currents. He learned later that many other large trees had drifted ashore on Kauai.

At Kauai the acquaintances of the year before were renewed. The young prince of the island again visited the ship, as did many of the chiefs, and all expressed warm friendship. Reports of Vancouver's efforts to restore peace had already reached Kauai and were applauded there. By this time Vancouver's early suspicions and distrust of the Hawaiian islanders had almost completely disappeared. On hearing reports that a drought on Niihau had driven most of the natives from that island, he wanted to leave the two girls on Kauai. He realized that they had picked up many European customs and habits which would be disapproved of by their own kind after he left them. The chiefs assured him that the girls would not be mistreated if they were left on Kauai, and the chief of the Waimea district offered to give each of them an estate nearby. To make doubly sure that they would be well treated in the future Vancouver had the chief make the estates a gift to him, so that he could allow the girls to live on them as his tenants. After inspecting the estates and finding them large and well equipped, he was still suspicious of the sincerity of the chief. He was again reassured on that point, and the girls moved ashore, accompanied by many presents.

With that arranged, and after seven weeks in the islands, the *Discovery* set sail for Nootka and the continuation of the great survey at the end of March, 1793.

11

Inside Passage
(1793)

WHEN THE fresh meat and vegetables obtained in the islands were consumed, about ten days after the *Discovery* left Kauai, Vancouver ordered a double portion of sauerkraut and portable soup to be served regularly to the crew. He had used these antiscorbutic supplements to the normal ration sparingly the year before because of the uncertainty of a new supply. With his ships fully replenished from the *Daedalus,* and with arrangements made for her return to him with further supplies, he was anxious to preserve the excellent health of the men after their stay in California and the Hawaiian Islands.

The *Discovery*'s passage to the mainland was slow because of variable winds and overcast weather. A leak near the bow, as she neared the mainland coast, also caused anxiety. Upon sighting the land near Cape Mendocino on April 26, she beat her way northward against adverse winds and anchored in Trinidad Bay to repair the leak a week later. That bay was discovered by the Spaniards in 1775 and named by them Porto Trinidad. Vancouver had passed it by the year before, but this time he wanted to survey it and replenish his wood and water as well as repair the leak. He was not impressed by the port's potentialities, and after a three-day stay he sailed for Nootka. It required two more weeks of beating up the coast to reach Nootka, where it was learned that the

Chatham had completed her repairs and sailed for the north only two days before to resume the survey.

Puget made the run from Molokai to near Nootka in only three weeks, but a threatening storm caused him to put into Esperanza Inlet, a rocky cove about fifteen miles northwest of Nootka Sound. After unsuccessfully trying to work the *Chatham* through what was supposed to be an inner passage, he reached Friendly Cove in the middle of April. The governor, Señor Fidalgo, was very cordial and helpful and asked Puget and his officers to share his quarters and table ashore. His men helped the *Chatham*'s crew to career the ship and to repair her damaged underwater sheathing. The Spaniards were out of tobacco, and the *Princessa*, a Spanish war-ship in port, had many cases of scurvy on board. The *Chatham* had plenty of tobacco and also supplied some antiscorbutics for the sufferers, to reciprocate the Spanish hospitality. Puget took advantage of the repair period to change the rake of the *Chatham*'s foremast, hoping that it might improve her sailing qualities, for, as he wrote, "We had one consolation in that Alteration, in knowing the Impossibility that any change we made though it might not accelerate her usual way through the water, it was almost certain it would not diminish it." [1] The *Chatham* must have been a diffi-cult and cranky little ship to handle at sea to merit the recurring criticisms of her sailing qualities. Yet her record for speed, as shown once again by her fast passage from Molokai, certainly com-pared favorably with that of her larger consort, the *Discovery*.

When the work on his ship was completed, about the middle of May, Puget opened his sealed orders and found that he was to pro-ceed without delay to continue the continental survey from the point where it had been stopped the year before. Complying with that order, he sailed without waiting for the *Discovery* to arrive at Nootka.

The *San Carlos,* from San Blas, with Don Ramon Saavedra on board, arrived at Nootka the same day as the *Discovery*. Saavedra was to replace Fidalgo as the governor of the port. The *San Carlos* brought letters to Vancouver from Viceroy Revilla Gigedo and from Quadra at San Blas, but none from England. The letters were very friendly in tone, and in one of them the viceroy assured him of his continued support and assistance in his work. Vancouver was also told of the measures the two Spaniards had taken to speed Broughton on his way to England. A brief outline of Broughton's activities after his arrival in England is included here as a final mention, for he did not succeed in rejoining Vancouver in the Pacific.

After reaching England in June, 1793, Broughton was sent to Madrid to assist in reaching the final agreement on the Nootka Sound question. The French declarations of war on England and Spain in February and March, 1793, had brought the two countries closer together than they had been for many years. One sign of the new relationship was a quick agreement fixing the indemnity for the Nootka seizures at 210,000 Spanish dollars, although the disposition of Nootka itself was not agreed upon until February, 1794. The indemnity money was sent to England promptly, and only Meares seems to have been dissatisfied with the settlement. In June, 1793, he petitioned the government for further compensation, but he was cut off sharply by a reply which stated, "[The] Government has punctually and fully discharged its duty to you." [2] After participating in the discussions with the Spanish, Broughton, in 1796, returned to the Pacific on another surveying expedition. He arrived, however, after Vancouver had sailed for England.

Vancouver, at Nootka in the spring of 1793, found that during the winter the Spaniards had built a fort armed with nine guns on one of the islands dominating the cove. To some in his expedition this was an indication that the Spaniards did not intend to give up the port. It was even suspected that the negotiations of the year before had been prolonged in order to gain time for strengthening the place. It was also noticed that Americans were moving about and trading freely, in violation of the order Quadra had received that only Spaniards and Englishmen were to be permitted to trade on that coast. Fidalgo told Puget at first that he had no such orders but later confided to him that the orders were secret; they directed him only to warn the Americans to stay away from Nootka, and to report their movements to the viceroy.

Already well behind his planned schedule for the season, Vancouver stayed only two days at Nootka. He sailed to join Puget in Restoration Cove, Burke Channel, in British Columbia, which he reached late in May. Promptly Johnstone was sent with two boats to complete the survey of an arm that had been left unfinished the year before. Vancouver himself, with two of the *Discovery*'s boats, set out to extend the continental survey to the north. He was out for ten days on this boat expedition, carrying the survey of the continental shore to a point near Milbanke Sound. After he returned the ships were moved forward to that point, and Johnstone and Master's Mate Barrie, of the *Discovery*, were sent out with two boats to continue the survey.

This was the pattern of the work for the rest of the season. Tracing the continental shore line with the boats was a slow and tedious job because of the numerous deep fiords that cut back into the coastal mountain range. But it was necessary to explore each arm thoroughly if Vancouver was to prove or disprove the existence of a Northwest Passage.

Expecting from their experience of the season before that there would be heavy rains in that part of the world, Vancouver had had awnings and canopies made for all the boats while the ships were in southern latitudes. Each boat also had a tent with a painted floor cloth large enough to shelter the entire boat's crew. Provisions and spare clothing were packed in painted canvas bags.[3] Since it rained nearly every day during all the boat expeditions, this foresight paid rich dividends in added comfort for the boat crews.

But the health of the crew could not always be safeguarded. On Johnstone's second boat expedition several of the men roasted and ate some mussels that they found in a cove. Many of them became sick and one man died, the third man lost in the voyage up to this time. Carter Bay, across the channel from Sarah Island, commemorates this loss.

ALEXANDER MACKENZIE AND CHARLES VANCOUVER

By an interesting historical accident, just one month separated the visit to the same spot of two of the leading explorers whose names are associated with the northwest coast. Vancouver moved out of his first anchorage in Restoration Cove in the middle of June. On July 20 Alexander Mackenzie descended the Bella Coola

River and reached tidewater in North Bentinck Arm, not far from Vancouver's anchorage. He was an explorer for the Northwest Fur Company of Montreal, then a bitter rival of the Hudson's Bay Company, and he was in search of new sources of furs. A few years before, in 1789, Mackenzie descended the Mackenzie River to its mouth in the Arctic Ocean. In his 1793 expedition he was the first white man to cross the continent north of Mexico and the Californias; he was more than ten years ahead of Lewis and Clark.

Mackenzie spent several days exploring the vicinity of North Bentinck Arm and learned that other Europeans had been there shortly before his own arrival. Near Point Menzies, so named by Vancouver, he met several Indians who gave him an account of the earlier visitors:

> One of them, in particular, made me understand, with an air of insolence, that a large canoe had lately been in the bay, with people in her like me, and that one of them, whom he called Macubah, had fired on him and his friends, and that Bensins had struck him on the back with the flat of his sword. He also mentioned another name, the articulation of which I could not determine. . . . I do not doubt but that he well deserved the treatment which he described.[4]

"Macubah" is readily recognized, of course, as Vancouver, and "Bensins" as Menzies, the botanist. There is no indication in any of the accounts of the Vancouver expedition of any trouble with or firing on the Indians in that vicinity. On the contrary, they show that the natives thereabouts were inclined to be docile and shy. Mackenzie's informant was either boasting or referring to some incident with a trading vessel in that general region.

On a prominent rock Mackenzie painted a record of his visit, and he took possession of the country for England, duplicating a similar act by Vancouver. The spot is now marked by a monument that summer cruise ships sometimes pass in order that passengers may see the historic landmark. Had chance permitted them to meet at that remote spot, Mackenzie could have solved the problem of a Northwest Passage for Vancouver. But, even if the meeting had taken place, at that stage of his work it is unlikely that Vancouver would have modified his plans in any way or given up any part of his survey.

By still another interesting coincidence Charles Vancouver,

older brother of George, was at the same time trying to get government backing in London for an overland voyage similar to the one Mackenzie had just completed.[5] After the failure of several of his settlement projects in the eastern United States between 1785 and 1792, Charles proposed to the British government an exploring expedition to be conducted overland from Quebec to the headwaters of the Columbia River, and thence by boat to the Pacific. Although Charles was introduced to Sir Joseph Banks, nothing came of his proposal.

Captain George Vancouver knew nothing of the activities of Mackenzie and of his own brother Charles, as he pushed his survey northward in the summer of 1793.

CLOSE CALL

The heaviest load of the survey work fell on Whidbey of the *Discovery* and Johnstone of the *Chatham,* who were in charge of the numerous boat expeditions. As the continental shore line was slowly traced out by the boats, the ships moved forward in steps to keep abreast, in or near the present well-known Inside Passage to Alaska. The channels in which those movements were made are generally quite deep, and the ships often anchored so close to the shore that steadying lines were run out to trees on the steep mountainsides.

Puget was with Whidbey on his fourth boat trip early in July. In the course of that ten-day trip the boats entered the Skeena River, not far from present-day Prince Rupert, but they did not ascend it very far when it was found that the water was fresh at low tide. Puget recognized it as a river and passed off any possible criticism of its cursory examination by noting that "no breach appeared in the Mountains & the Difficult & Intricate Navigation of the Channel leaves no doubt in my mind that its Source is derived from the Snow." [6] Vancouver also recognized it as a river, although it does not appear as one on his chart.

In July, when the ships entered a cove near Chatham Sound, they fell in with the *Butterworth* of London, Captain Brown, with the schooners *Prince Lee Boo* and *Jackall* in company. Brown had been trading for furs in that region for several weeks, and his schooners had ranged extensively in the inland waters nearby. He offered to have one of them lead the *Discovery* and the *Chatham* into an arm of the sea where there was a secure anchorage. This was Observatory Inlet, near the present Alaska–British Columbia boundary. There the two ships prepared for an extended stay, and the observatory was set up for the first time that season. Johnstone went off to bring the survey forward to the anchorage. The *Discovery's* yawl and launch were fitted out with provisions for two weeks, and Vancouver himself, for the first time since May, with Puget, Menzies, Lieutenant Swaine, and Midshipmen Sykes and Pitt went in these boats to continue the survey northward. Vancouver considered this expedition to be very important, for he believed that he was in or near an opening that Caamano, in 1792, had indicated on his chart as the fabled River Los Reyes of de Fonté.

One day, after the boats had been out for more than three weeks, Vancouver was preparing to land at a point on Revilla Gigedo Island. He had already traced the continental shore around and to the north of that island, which he named for the Mexican viceroy. His boat was on the point of beaching when it was approached by several Indian canoes. While Vancouver landed to take compass angles from a prominent point nearby, Puget remained with the beached yawl. The launch waited a short distance offshore. The Indian canoes closed in and crowded around the yawl, and Puget noticed that while they were apparently friendly they were also inclined to be thievish. Vancouver returned to the boat, and it was almost clear of the beach when an old woman, apparently a leader, seized a line and made her canoe fast to the boat. At about the same time an Indian snatched a musket from the boat as the others began to hold their spears in a threatening manner. The situation was suddenly critical, and Vancouver took a musket to the forward part of the boat in an effort to parley with a chief who had climbed aboard and to gain time for the launch to come to their assistance. The chief left the boat and indicated by gestures that the Indians would lay down their spears if he would lay down his musket. For a moment the tension was eased, but the old woman's screams egged the Indians on, and the boat was again surrounded.

By then the launch was within pistol shot range. Suddenly the Indians started seizing everything loose in the yawl, and several spears were thrown at the officers and men. In that desperate situation Vancouver gave the order for both boats to open fire on the Indians. The succeeding volley caused them to flee to the shore and into the woods on higher ground. They managed to take with them three guns and a pair of pistols from the boat, but the arms chest was still intact. After getting the boat well clear and offshore, Vancouver considered landing again to destroy the Indians' canoes. Considering the fact that they were a long distance from the ship and that provisions were low, and finding two of the men already wounded by spears, he gave up the plan to land again. Menzies estimated that six or eight Indians were killed by the volley, and Puget's estimate was eight or ten. The site of the skirmish received the name Escape Point, and it is still so called on the chart of the northwestern shore of Revilla Gigedo Island.

This was the second serious skirmish with natives during the voyage, although harmless warning shots had been fired on several occasions. Vancouver was genuinely disturbed that it had occurred and at first thought some provocation had been given while he was away from the boat taking the compass angles. When he was satisfied that there had been none, he sought some other explanation. Puget freely admitted that he was completely surprised and was disarmed by the early friendly manner of the Indians. The arms chest in the boat, he noted, was "terribly lumbered up with Bags of Provisions." [7] The weapons that were stolen were in the rods of the canopy. The lack of early caution, brought about in part by generally friendly relations with other Indians encountered in that region, was probably responsible for the actual attack, in Vancouver's opinion. The real motive was much deeper than that, he thought.

The Indians had obviously had contact with traders, for some of them had muskets. One of them made it clear to him that one or more of their muskets had burst when fired. He had heard similar complaints of faulty weapons received in trade from the chiefs on Hawaii. He was convinced that the Indians in this fracas had a grievance against white men that stemmed from earlier brushes with traders. Captain Brown, of the *Butterworth,* told him of firing on and killing some Indians in Observatory Inlet earlier in the year. Vancouver concluded:

I am extremely concerned to be compelled to state here, that many of the traders from the civilized world have not only pursued a line of conduct, diametrically opposed to the true principles of justice in their commercial dealings, but have fomented discords, and stirred up contentions, between the different tribes, in order to increase the demand for these destructive engines. They have been likewise eager to instruct the natives in the use of European arms of all descriptions; and have shewn by their own example, that they consider gain as the only object of pursuit; and whether this be acquired by fair and honorable means, or otherwise, the manner how it is obtained seems to have been, with too many of them, but a secondary consideration.[8]

The boats returned to the ships without incident. They had been away for twenty-three days, covered about seven hundred miles of travel, yet advanced the map of the continental shore only about sixty miles in a direct line from the ships' anchorage. Such a record is still another vivid illustration of the laborious and tedious work that went into the survey. The myth of the de Fonté legend was disposed of by finding the shore line solid, although marked with many deep fiords.

The ships were moved up to a cove not far from the scene of the Indian skirmish, and Whidbey, this time with Lieutenant Baker, first lieutenant of the *Discovery,* and Johnstone, set out again to continue the survey. On this trip Johnstone discovered the mouth of the Stikine River, in Alaska, but he found no more than nine feet of water in it. Once again the ships moved forward, following a channel that today is one of the main inner steamship routes in southeastern Alaska. They anchored in a small cove that Vancouver called Port Protection, as it proved to be a secure harbor in a heavy storm that struck soon after they anchored. A final pair of boat expeditions sent Whidbey and Johnstone out for the seventh time that season. On their return, after an especially disagreeable time in stormy weather, Vancouver discontinued the survey for the season, ending it at Cape Decision. It was then nearing the end of September, and the stormy season was at hand. He was disappointed at the relatively short lateral distance of coast that had

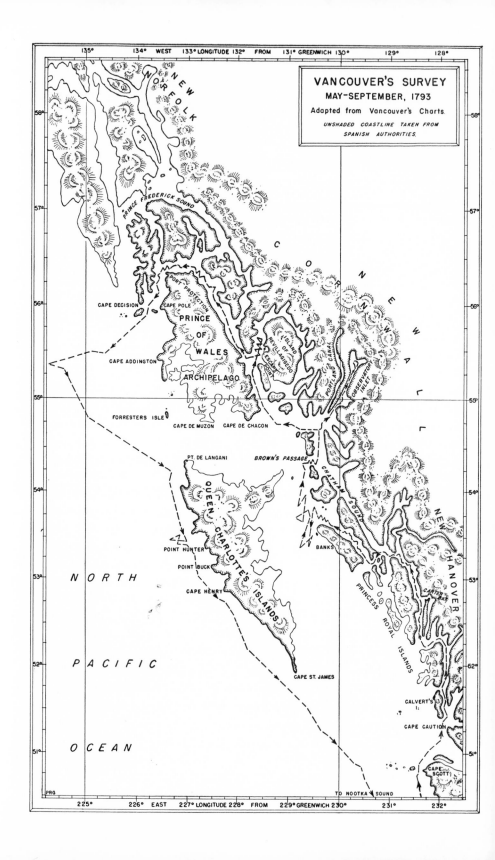

VANCOUVER'S SURVEY
MAY–SEPTEMBER, 1793
Adapted from Vancouver's Charts.
UNSHADED COASTLINE TAKEN FROM
SPANISH AUTHORITIES.

been covered, but he believed that the worst was over. He was well pleased that he had definitely proved the fallacy of the pretended discoveries of both de Fuca and de Fonté.

Puget pays another tribute to the officers and men who made the numerous boat trips, praising the

> . . . indefatigable exertion and Attention that has on all Occasions been paid by the Officers under whose direction they were conducted and also the Seamen who performed the Labourious task [of pulling at the oars and who] always performed their duty with Alacrity, not even a Murmur was heard. Necessity obliged us frequently to pull till Eleven at Night, which still made no difference in the hour of Departure.[9]

The entire season had been spent in the inner channels and fiords of British Columbia and southeastern Alaska, an area that even today is a wilderness whose few small towns seem from off-shore to be fighting off a forest trying to reclaim its own.

ARRILLAGA

As the ships sailed southward, a survey was made of the western coasts of the Queen Charlotte Islands. At Nootka Vancouver found there was still no word for him from Europe, nor was there any report of the *Daedalus* or any other ship with supplies for him. Remaining but three days and leaving word for the *Daedalus* to join him, he sailed for California. He hoped to meet Quadra with recent instructions for settling the Nootka affair, either at San Francisco or at Monterey. The expedition again followed the coast on the way south and this time sighted the Coos River, in Oregon, which had been missed in the earlier passages. The *Chatham* was sent to examine Port Bodega, a few miles north of San Francisco Bay. Fog prevented Puget from making a thorough examination of that bay, and he soon joined the *Discovery* at San Francisco.

At San Francisco the Englishmen received news of affairs in Europe. Louis XVI of France had been beheaded, and all Europe was in arms. Señor Sal, the commandant of the San Francisco presidio, came on board the *Discovery* to renew old friendships and to offer his services. But the atmosphere at San Francisco, at first friendly, quickly changed, for the next morning Vancouver received two letters from Sal. In one he was asked to report his arrival and to state what he wanted in the port and how long he intended to remain. In the other he was notified that no one other than Vancouver himself would be permitted ashore except to secure wood and water; Vancouver, with an officer or midshipman, could visit the presidio.

These restrictions had been ordered by Captain José Joaquin de Arrillaga, the acting governor at Monterey. Arrillaga was lieutenant governor of the Californias at Loreto, on the Gulf of California, and became acting governor in April, 1792. In September the viceroy ordered him to Monterey, where he arrived in July, 1793. He was not pleased when he learned of the liberties that had been allowed Vancouver the year before, especially the trip to Santa Clara. He had instructions from the viceroy to give minimum assistance to foreigners and to keep Spanish military weakness from becoming known to them. This prompted him to issue orders to Sal, in October, to furnish Vancouver only with his urgent needs and to direct him to sail at once without stopping at any other Spanish port.

Vancouver accepted the conditions imposed by Sal, intending to go to Monterery after about three days to learn the reason for them, for he believed that Sal was acting as an unwilling agent. Several of his officers were displeased with Vancouver's acceptance of Sal's restrictions. Puget resented seeing an armed guard supervising the taking on of wood and water on shore, but he withheld final judgment until they reached Monterey. He thought that one reason for the restrictions might have been the arrival of the *Butterworth* off the port some time before. Menzies was unhappy because Vancouver would not permit him to go on shore to collect botanical specimens. Bell, of the *Chatham*, was the most critical. He believed that Vancouver acted beneath his dignity as the captain of a British man-of-war, and that he "treated the matter too lightly, he even permitted the limits of the ground he was to walk over to be pointed out to him, and a guard accompanied him to prevent their being encroached upon." [10]

Soon after the *Discovery* and the *Chatham* left San Francisco Bay they were joined by the *Daedalus*. She had arrived at Nootka the evening of the day the two ships sailed from there, having left

Australia four months earlier. In Australia she was considered to be a colonial ship, and her commander had strict orders to return to Port Jackson immediately after supplying Vancouver's ships. The acting governor of New South Wales complained of Vancouver's request for her return to him, stating that "the *Daedalus* is sent here more for the purpose of asking than giving assistance." [11] Nevertheless he wanted Vancouver to secure and send him more cattle in spite of the poor results of the first attempt to send them from California to Australia.

At Monterey, after an exchange of formal gun salutes, Vancouver and Lieutenant Hanson, of the *Daedalus,* called formally on Arrillaga. Puget, in the *Chatham,* had become separated from the other ships in a fog and had arrived at Monterey a day ahead of the other two. He had already called on the governor and was with him again when Vancouver and Hanson arrived. According to Vancouver's version of the meeting, he first inquired about the deserters of the year before and then started to give his reasons for being in the port. Arrillaga stopped him and said the matter could best be handled by an exchange of correspondence. Puget's journal confirms that the meeting was very formal and brief. Menzies, however, quoted Puget as saying that Vancouver expressed his intentions to go to San Diego for dispatches from home, to repair his vessels, to take supplies from the *Daedalus,* and to rest and refresh his crews after their arduous season's work. The governor told him not to go to San Diego for Monterey would serve just as well for his needs. All accounts agree that the meeting was strained. Arrillaga was suspicious of Vancouver's return after all that he had seen the year before, and Vancouver was both surprised and annoyed at his cold reception, which was in sharp contrast to his earlier one.

Later in the afternoon two short letters were delivered on board the *Discovery.* In one of them Arrillaga asked the purpose of Vancouver's visit to the port and stated that he had no orders to receive foreign vessels. The other informed him of the orders to the commanders of the various ports that only the commanders of vessels and one or two others would be permitted on shore. Although Arrillaga offered assistance in securing wood and water, notice must be given before these supplies could be obtained.

The next day Vancouver sent a long reply outlining in detail the purpose of his voyage as one of exploration. He had been directed to visit that region and had understood before he left England that he would be hospitably received. He also understood that Spanish officers would forward his dispatches and charts to Europe. He expected that the British Court would publish the results of his voyage, thus benefiting Spain, and he was authorized to give Spanish officers copies of his surveys. He had given them to Quadra the year before and intended to do so again. In view of the viceroy's assurance that the attentions of the year before only complied with his sovereign's desires, he expected the same treatment this year from one he considered a friend and ally. Vancouver went on to explain his desires, which were to repair the ships' rigging, to transfer stores, to set up the observatory ashore, to pursue botanical studies, and to provide exercise and recreation to his men on shore.

Arrillaga's rather sharp reply two days later was, so Vancouver reported, in "a sneering, forbidding and ungracious stile." [12] He expressed himself as satisfied with Vancouver's "polite ingenuity and solicitude" in advising him of the objects of the visit, which were well known to him. Arrillaga said he was thoroughly familiar with Vancouver's treatment the year before but did not believe that the viceroy intended him to make a second visit. There was no royal sanction for Vancouver's visit to the California ports such as had been issued to La Pérouse. He offered the use of a warehouse for the temporary storage of the supplies from the *Daedalus*, the key of which he would lend to Vancouver. If that was unsatisfactory some other place could be chosen, but only two men could care for the cargo at night under Spanish supervision. The observatory could be set up near the cargo, but it could be operated only in the daytime within sight of the presidio. Officers could exercise on foot within sight of the presidio, but all the personnel, except the warehouse guards, must be on board at night. Vancouver should promise to get his work done in the shortest time and be on his way.[13]

These terms, restrictive and lacking in hospitality, were not ones to which a man of Vancouver's temperament could accede. No English captain of that era would have been likely to accept them.

According to Puget, "To accept the terms Mr. Arrillaga wanted, would never be compatible with the Character of a British Officer." [14] Vancouver declined to enter into further correspondence with Arrillaga and decided to secure his necessary services in Hawaii, where he felt he would be assured of a more cordial welcome. On leaving Monterey he wrote to Arrillaga regretting his inability to pay for supplies that he had received at San Francisco. Arrillaga replied that he should ease his mind on that point and returned a draft that Vancouver had made in favor of Sal. He also asked Vancouver to accept some cattle as a present.

Arrillaga was the only Spanish official with whom Vancouver and his officers were not on the best of terms. The basis of the friction was Arrillaga's caution in his temporary position and his belief that Vancouver had already learned too much about California and its defenses. Bancroft, in his *History of California,* discusses this incident at length as a highlight of an otherwise uneventful regime for Arrillaga. He concludes that Vancouver was unfair to Arrillaga in his version of the affair, citing a number of Spanish documents to support that view.[15] The key letter of the disagreement, containing Arrillaga's conditions for Vancouver's stay at Monterey, is capable of different interpretations, but it is unfriendly in tone, offering assistance without hospitality. The following year Vancouver received a letter from the viceroy, dated October, 1793, and addressed to him at Monterey, indicating that his return was expected. The other English officers were as critical of Arrillaga as Vancouver was. Puget looked forward to an asylum with the Hawaiian Islanders, though it had been refused by "Officers of a civilized nation with whom England is now joined as a Friend and Ally." [16] Arrillaga was "callous to every feeling of humanity," according to Menzies.[17] What was resented most was the denial of the chance to get ashore and exercise after the long and hard season's work. The viceroy later approved Arrillaga's position, but at the same time he desired that good relations be maintained with Vancouver.

Vancouver was not beyond criticism in his stand at Monterey. His instructions required him to survey the coast to latitude 30° north (in Lower California) , but they also implied close cooperation with the Spaniards by requiring that he maintain good relations with them. In spite of Arrillaga's admonition against visiting other ports in California he continued his survey after leaving Monterey; he stopped at three missions, while checking and adding to the Spanish charts in his possession.

His first stop after Monterey was at Santa Barbara, "Queen of the Missions." Señor Don Felipe Goycochea, the commandant, received the ships cordially and offered them wood, water, and provisions, and recreation on shore. He had orders similar to Sal's but chose to disregard them so long as the conduct of the Englishmen was good. In a few days Father Vincente Sta. Maria, from the mission of San Buenaventura, several miles down the coast, arrived with ten sheep and twenty mule loads of vegetables for the ships. He had made a number of ocean voyages and knew what fresh provisions meant on board ship. Extremely grateful for that gesture, Vancouver invited him to ride in the *Discovery* back to his mission. When the ships anchored off San Buenaventura a surf was running, too heavy for the ship's boats to risk landing. The priest did not want to try landing in an Indian canoe, many of which were ferrying provisions through the surf. He became nervous and distressed when he learned that one of his servants had taken his Bible and Prayer Book ashore. In the evening his fears were eased and his good humor restored when his precious books were returned to him undamaged. The next morning he went ashore happy and to an enthusiastic welcome from his Indian charges.[18]

Following the coast to the southeast the ships searched for some sign of the pueblo of Los Angeles, the "country town of the Angels," Vancouver called it. Nothing was seen of the forerunner of that great modern city that took its name from the pueblo. Vancouver added to the predominantly Spanish names along the California coast wherever he found gaps in the Spanish charts, using the names of military and mission figures whom he had met. Point Sal, for the commandant at San Francisco; Point Arguello, for the garrison commander at Monterey; Point Dume and Point Vincente, for the priests of San Buenaventura; and Point Fermin, for the president of the Franciscan order in California, are examples.

Headed for San Diego the ships passed the mission of San Juan

Capistrano, and from close offshore the men noted its beautiful and lush setting. At San Diego, reached at the end of November, the commandant, Don Antonio Grajero, was expecting them; but he also had orders from Arrillaga to restrict their visit. Without openly violating his orders, which included a ban on allowing any cattle to be taken from the country, Grajero and his officers made the ships' stay as pleasant as possible.[19] The Spanish officers openly expressed their dislike for the orders they were under, and they promised to bring Arrillaga's treatment of Vancouver to the attention of the viceroy. No word had reached San Diego from England, and a week was spent preparing dispatches and copies of charts to be sent to England and to Quadra at San Blas. As a parting present Vancouver gave Father Fermin, whose headquarters were at San Diego, an organ that was in his cabin.

After leaving San Diego the ships followed the coast southward, without special incident, to the prescribed limit of the survey near Rosario, about one-fourth of the way down the peninsula of Lower California. In just two seasons Vancouver had mapped the continental shore line from latitude 56° north, in southeastern Alaska, to his assigned southern limit. The air-line distance between the two points is about seventeen hundred miles, but in actual shore-line distance it is many times that figure. It was a remarkable accomplishment, a tribute to Vancouver's tenacity, drive, and energy.

With that part of the survey completed he headed for Hawaii and a needed rest for himself and his officers and crews. There, as he expressed it, he could

. . . firmly rely on the sincerity of *Tamaahmaah* [Kamehameha], and the professions of the rest of our rude uncivilized friends in those islands, for a hearty welcome, a kind reception, and every service and accommodation in their humble power to afford; without any of the unhospitable restrictions we must have been under from the then *civilized* governor at Monterrey.[20]

12

Cession of Hawaii
(1794)

On the run from Lower California to Hawaii the three ships passed close to the island of Guadalupe, about 175 miles off the coast, in order to check its geographical position. From that island the track was laid to run a few miles south of the route of the year before; the possibility of sighting the island group of Los Majos still existed. Nothing was seen, or really expected, and early in January, 1794, the east coast of Hawaii was sighted, only twenty-four days after the ships left the California coast. The fast passage was due partly to the steady ocean current which carried the ships along; as they approached Hawaii the current set them westward as much as twenty-five miles each day.

In their conversations of the year before, Kamehameha had told Vancouver of a good harbor on the northeast coast of Hawaii. On this occasion, off present-day Hilo, Vancouver sent Whidbey with a boat to examine the harbor before risking taking the ships in. While Whidbey was away on that service, Kamehameha made his appearance on board the *Discovery*. He was anxious for Vancouver to stay at Hilo for a while, but Whidbey reported that the bay was too much exposed to the prevailing wind for their purposes. Vancouver then decided to return to Kealakekua Bay on the protected western coast of the island.

Kamehameha was invited to go to Kealakekua Bay in the ship,

but he demurred, giving as his excuse a local ceremony that required his presence. This had been more than a mere social invitation, for Vancouver believed that Kamehameha's presence while the *Daedalus* was being unloaded would prevent possible trouble with the natives. Resorting to a ruse, he pretended to be offended by Kamehameha's refusal and threatened to go instead to Maui and seek out Kahekili, Kamehameha's archenemy.[1] This worked, and the king soon found a way to be excused from his local religious duties. While the details were being worked out, Vancouver learned that the king and his favorite young wife, Kaahumanu, were separated; she was suspected of having had an affair with Kaiana. His offer of mediation in that domestic affair was refused curtly and abruptly.

By mid-January the ships were securely moored in Kealakekua Bay. Kamehameha offered to provide a guard for the *Daedalus'* stores on shore, and to have his own people assist with the ship's work and fill all the water casks. To avoid contact between the Englishmen and several local chiefs, Kamehameha asked Vancouver to inform him of his desires. He himself would supply all their needs. This arrangement proved to be a great convenience and help to the ships, but it was not entirely free of a selfish motive, as Puget suggested:

> I certainly join with others in Admiration of the King's conduct in this respect, but I differ in Opinion of the Motives from which it Springs, he sees with the utmost jealousy any Attention paid to the other chiefs & appears extremely anxious to prevent their Receiving any Benefit from our Visit—Every present made them he regards as an Acquisition of Power for by distributing these things with Liberality among their Adherents, it fixes more firmly their Attachment. Therefore if His Majesty can under the Cloak of Princely Liberality monopolize the Articles of Traffic (for he is to have on our Departure as much as he wishes for) it will not only serve himself in that particular, but be the means of giving him additional Consequence. . . .[2]

Puget's observation is certainly in keeping with the character of that ambitious native king.

Vancouver welcomed Kamehameha's offer, and provisions began flowing into the three ships in large quantities. Kamehameha also issued strict orders for the conduct of his people toward the visitors, and he warned Vancouver that he had several enemies among the chiefs of the island who might want to cause trouble. Vancouver, for his part, reissued his orders of the year before, restricting the officers from going ashore armed and limiting the midshipmen to going ashore only with officers. Those orders were no more popular at this time than they were when first issued.

One of Vancouver's first acts was to send ashore from the *Discovery* the bull and two cows and two pairs of sheep that Arrillaga had given him at Monterey. The animals left on Hawaii the year before were thriving, and he had high hopes of creating a substantial herd for the future. At a later meeting with Kamehameha and the chiefs of the island he had a ten-year taboo placed on killing any of the animals he brought to the island. Because of this wise precaution he can be considered the founder of the cattle industry in the Hawaiian Islands.

The work of overhauling the ships' rigging and taking on of stores from the *Daedalus* got under way and continued throughout the stay without a hitch. Whidbey was again placed in charge of the observatory on shore. Menzies and some of the officers set out under the guidance of a minor chief to climb Mount Hualalai, about fifteen miles north of the bay, and they returned from a successful trip nine days later. Puget and another party went off to visit a nearby village, where they met the man who was supposed to have first stabbed Captain Cook.

While the work and recreation were going on around him, Vancouver was deeply involved with his favorite projects of trying to reach a peaceful settlement of the civil war and persuading Kamehameha to cede the island of Hawaii to Great Britain. His well-intentioned effort of the year before to arrange a meeting between Kaeo and Kamehameha had come to an unfortunate end. One of his first questions was whether his letter to Young from Maui had been received. It had not been, and all Vancouver could learn was a vague story about a party from Maui that had tried to land on the western side of Hawaii some months before. Kamehameha was reluctant to discuss the matter but finally seemed to agree that the party probably was an embassy from Kahekili bearing the letter. That it actually was, and it was driven off from Hawaii without being allowed to land.[3] Vancouver regretfully concluded that the only way in which he could bring the warring factions together was to shuttle his ship between Maui and Hawaii, directing the negotiations himself. This he would not do, both because of the time required and because of the inevitable wear and tear on the aging rigging of his ship.

The serious meetings on the cession of Hawaii had to wait for an assembly of the leading chiefs of the island. During the wait an incident occurred that marred somewhat the existing happy relations. Since boarding the ship at Hilo all of Kamehameha's personal retinue had lived on board the *Discovery*, a circumstance that shows how much Vancouver's suspicions of native treachery had waned. One morning five of his table knives were missing. He sent all the party but Kamehameha himself out of the ship and insisted that the knives be returned. Kamehameha went ashore and personally recovered three of them. Another was recovered some time later, but the fifth was not returned. Vancouver learned that it had been given to a powerful chief from whom Kamehameha did not want to force its return. The ivory handles were the attraction; they were wanted for neck ornaments. Kamehameha was never suspected in the theft in any way, and he remained in good standing throughout.

When Vancouver learned that one of Kamehameha's white retainers, a former mate of the *Lady Washington* named Boid, wanted to build a European-style schooner for the king, he offered to have his ships' carpenters build the keel and frame. He sailed from Kealakekua Bay before the new vessel was completed, but she was far enough along to be easily finished. He left behind all the necessary ironwork, masts, sails, canvas, and twine to outfit completely the thirty-six-foot schooner, which received the imposing name *Britannia*.

By the end of the first week in February all the essential work was completed, but Vancouver stayed on at Hawaii for two more weeks. He did not want to resume the survey of the northwest coast until April because of the severe weather to be expected in Alaska any earlier in the year. At Hawaii he could obtain an abundance of fresh provisions without trading in firearms, the one thing he refused to consider in all his relations with natives. Besides, his business with Kamehameha and the chiefs of the islands was not yet completed.

After discharging all the supplies and provisions that the two other ships could stow, the *Daedalus* sailed for Australia. In her went two midshipmen from the *Discovery,* the Honorable Thomas Pitt and Thomas Clarke, and one from the *Chatham,* Augustus Grant. Pitt and Grant were discharged from their ships for disciplinary reasons and were sent to Australia on the first leg of their return to England. Vancouver's later relations with Pitt and the subsequent troubles he had over his treatment of the young man form such an important part of his career and life that a full discussion of them is better postponed until a later chapter.

With two more weeks of relative leisure in prospect, Menzies, with Lieutenant Baker and Midshipmen Heddington and Mackenzie, set off to try to climb the peak of Moana Loa. This mountain and its sister volcano, Moana Kea, are the two highest mountains on Hawaii. Menzies arranged to have special barometer readings taken on the ship every two hours during his absence. He planned to take similar readings at the same times on a portable mercurial barometer that he carried with him. He obviously understood the principle of using differences in barometric pressure for measuring altitudes. By that knowledge the able botanist of the expedition showed that he was a well-informed general scientist as well as proficient in his own specialty. On the first day of the ascent the party could only reach the snow line by dark. The next day Menzies, Baker, Mackenzie, and a servant reached the peak and took the necessary barometer reading. Menzies computed the altitude of the peak of Moana Loa to be 13,634 feet,[4] a remarkably accurate measurement, considering that it was made in 1794, since the present official altitude is 13,680 feet. Unfortunately, Menzies' journal ends with the return from the peak to his camp at snow line, and there is no record of his opinions and observations for the rest of the voyage.

Vancouver had neither time nor inclination for such diversions, but he was always actively promoting his political projects. Since relations with the natives had been uniformly excellent, he relaxed his restrictions on the shore excursions of the midshipmen. Altogether he was very pleased at having selected Hawaii as the place for doing the ships' work:

Our reception and entertainment by these unlettered people, who in general have been distinguished by the appellation of savages, was such as, I believe, is seldom equalled by the most civilized nations of Europe, and made me no longer regret the inhospitality we had met at St. Francisco and Monterrey.[5]

Through Kamehameha he obtained permission from the high priests to be present at one of the solemn native religious rites, something normally forbidden. He also renewed his efforts to bring about a reconciliation between the king and his young wife Kaahumanu. She was rarely seen in the vicinity of Kealakekua Bay and the ships, but her father, Keeaumoku, was a constant visitor. He assured Vancouver that she desired the reconciliation. Kamehameha had refused all offers of assistance in the affair from his chiefs, but he, too, seemed anxious for a reconciliation and finally consented to allow Vancouver to bring about a meeting. Together they worked out a scheme that would appear to make the meeting one of pure chance. Vancouver was to invite the queen on board his ship with members of her family and distribute presents among them. During the conversation he would find out if she desired a reconciliation. Then, as a seeming joke on Kamehameha, he would have a scrap of paper carefully wrapped in native cloth and sent ashore as a present to the king. By prearranged marks on the paper Kamehameha would be told of her sentiments. If they were favorable, he was to rush on board with profuse thanks for remembering him, and thus come face to face with Kaahumanu. The scheme worked perfectly; Kamehameha played his part like a veteran actor, feigning great surprise when he saw his queen in the cabin. There the two were happily reunited, and Vancouver was understandably proud of his part in the little plot. The only cloud on the affair was her final request that he exact a solemn promise from Kamehameha not to beat her after she returned to her home.

Aside from his political ambitions for the island, Vancouver continued to show a genuine interest in the welfare of the Hawaiian people. For Young, Davis, and Boid, Kamehameha's own foreign retainers and advisers, he had high praise as wise and good counselors. He offered to take Young and Davis home with him, but they were perfectly content where they were and chose to remain. But there were seven former sailors, who had attached themselves to lower chiefs on Hawaii, whom he considered renegades and potentially dangerous. The men called themselves Americans, but they seemed to Vancouver to be British subjects.[6] While he was at Hawaii he was given a letter from Captain Brown, of the *Butterworth,* telling of similar small bands of former sailors on Oahu and Kauai. These men had joined with a chief in a rebellion and had schemed with the natives to capture an American brig. Vancouver recognized a real danger in having such men in the islands, and he tried to have those on Hawaii delivered to him. Neither Kamehameha nor the other chiefs would listen to his plea to give the men up, because of the exiles' knowledge of European firearms. Vancouver, in turn, was unwilling to seize them by force, thereby risking a breach in the excellent relations that existed between himself and the chiefs.

THE CESSION OF HAWAII TO ENGLAND

Kamehameha, with his domestic affairs in order, next turned to the question of cession. Vancouver's goal was quite clear, for he saw very well the growing threat from traders of several countries who called at the islands and trafficked in arms. This practice could easily lead some day to seizure of the group by some other nation. To forestall such a possibility he wanted to establish an indisputable first claim, over Hawaii at least, by a formal and voluntary act of cession. In this he was also guided by his recent experience at Nootka. He summed up his position in this way:

The long continued practice of all civilized nations, of claiming the sovereignty and territorial right of newly discovered countries, had heretofore been assumed in consequence only of priority of seeing, or of visiting such parts of the earth as were unknown before; but in the case of Nootka a material alteration had taken place, and great stress had been laid on the cession that *Maquinna* was stated to have made of the village and friendly cove to Senr Martinez. Notwithstanding that on the principles of the priority of claim that England had to the Sandwich Islands; yet I considered, that the voluntary resignation of these territories, by the formal surrender of the king and the people to the power and authority of Great Britain, might probably be the means of establishing an incontrovertible right, and of preventing any altercation with other states hereafter.[7]

Kamehameha, having been convinced of the desirability of the move, called a meeting of all of the principal chiefs of the island. Until then Vancouver had refused to see Kemeeiamoku, chief of the Kohala district, in the northern part of the island. It was he and his people who had captured the *Fair American* in 1790. But in order to make the forthcoming formalities as complete and unanimous as possible he relented and agreed to receive the chief. The latter's trip to Kealakekua Bay was made with great hesitation and fear of retaliation, and he stopped at every *morai* on the way for spiritual reassurance. He apologized profusely for his treatment of the Americans and claimed to have been beaten by Mr. Metcalf. After some discussion Vancouver shook his hand as a token of forgiveness, thus easing the chief's tension. Bell, who believed in maintaining British authority with strong punitive action, felt that in receiving rather than punishing Kemeeaimoku Vancouver's "comity has in this instance been carried to too great a length." [8]

An even greater concession was made when Vancouver received, as a member of the king's party, the man who had reputedly stabbed Cook. According to Puget, this chief, whom he called Papeah, still bore scars from wounds received in that fight, and he was honored among his fellows for the deed.

The preliminary meetings brought to Kealakekua Bay a large gathering of important people from all over the island, and there was much entertainment. Vancouver watched and described at length two or three theatrical performances and dances on shore. He also contributed to the festivities with the ever popular fireworks display.

When the fateful day arrived the king and queen and their personal entourage, with the chiefs of the districts of Kona, Kau, Puna, and Kohala, assembled on board the *Discovery* in the presence of Vancouver, Puget, and the officers of the ship.[9] Kamehameha opened the formalities with a speech in which he gave his reasons for offering to place the island of Hawaii under the protection of Great Britain. He named the various nations whose ships had called at the island in recent years and stressed that the island was not strong enough to resist these nations in case of attack. For that reason it would be desirable to be under the protection of one of them whose people were favorably known to the native islanders. He was followed by Keeaumoku, who gave a more local and material reason why the step should be taken. He argued that Maui should be brought under the control of Hawaii, and that when the expected force arrived from England that should be its first task. Kavaheero, of Kau, was more moderate in his views but saw in the arrangement greater security for the people of the island. Kaiana agreed that a garrison and ships should be sent out from England for protection of the islanders. Some of the officers then present should return with those forces, he argued, to assure them that they were actually King George's men. Vancouver's account of the deliberations stressed that in every one of the speeches

> . . . their religion, government, and domestic oeconomy was noticed; and it was clearly understood, that no interference was to take place in either; that *Tamaahmaah*, the chiefs and priests, were to continue as usual to officiate with the same authority as before in their respective stations, and that no alteration in those particulars was in any degree thought or intended.[10]

Such matters being fully discussed and understood by all parties, the king and his entire group stated that "they were no longer *Tanata no Owhyhee,* the people of Owhyhee; but *Tanata no Britannee,* the people of Britain." [11] Puget then landed, displayed the English colors, and took formal possession of the island for Great Britain. The ceremonies were completed with a gun salute from both vessels, and a copper plate with the following inscription was placed in Kamehameha's house:

> On the 25th of February, 1794, Tamaahmaah, king of Owhyhee, in council with the principal chiefs of the island assembled on board His Britannic Majesty's sloop Discovery in Karakakooa bay, and in the presence of George Vancouver, commander of the said sloop; Lieutenant Peter Puget, commander of his said Majesty's armed tender the Chatham; and the other officers of the Discovery; after due consideration, unanimously ceded the said island of Owhyhee to His Britannic Majesty, and acknowledged themselves to be subjects of Great Britain.[12]

Immediately after these formalities the *Discovery* and the *Chatham* sailed from Kealakekua Bay. Some parts of the other islands in the chain remained to be surveyed, and after calling at two or three villages on the northwest coast of Hawaii and taking

178

leave of Kamehameha and his queen, Vancouver turned to the job of surveying the east coast of Maui. He had not given up entirely his role of peacemaker and still had two pairs of sheep that he intended to give to Kahekili and Kaeo as presents. At Maui he learned that Kahekili was on Oahu and Kaeo was on Molokai. Vancouver stopped at a village on the southeast coast of Molokai, where he understood that Kaeo lived. A strict taboo was in force, and he was told that Kaeo could not come to see him. It is possible that this chief's ill-starred attempt, at Vancouver's urging, to enter into negotiations with Kamehameha on Hawaii may have influenced the strictness of the taboo.

Vancouver's next move was to the west coast of Oahu, which he included in his survey. There he stopped near the village where Hergest had been killed only to learn that Kahekili was at Waikiki, on the opposite side of the island. Without taking the time to go to Waikiki to see the king, he completed his survey and moved on to Kauai. It is very noticeable that after he received the cession of Hawaii from Kamehameha Vancouver's interest in Kahekili and Kaeo declined.

At Waimea Vancouver found the two girls he had left there the year before well cared for, but they were apprehensive that their treatment might change upon his final departure from the islands. Vancouver drew promises from the local chiefs that such would not be the case. He left his remaining sheep with the regent of Kauai, asking for the same ten-year taboo that the cattle on Hawaii were under. A final call at Niihau completed Vancouver's visits to the Hawaiian Islands, and in mid-March, 1794, the *Discovery* and the *Chatham* sailed for the final leg of the continental survey. During the coming season Vancouver planned to begin at the western limit of the survey, in Cook Inlet, and trace the continental shore line eastward to join with the past season's work.

VANCOUVER'S INFLUENCE ON THE FUTURE OF THE ISLANDS

It is interesting to examine something of Vancouver's lasting influence and work in the Hawaiian Islands, and the ultimate significance of the cession of Hawaii to England.

Native Hawaiian historical accounts contend that Kamehameha

did not intend to give away the land but only wanted to get assistance against his enemies. Ralph S. Kuykendall, the Hawaiian historian, points out that these accounts were written down, with the influence of American missionaries, many years after the events, and they may be biased.[13] But he concluded that there can be no doubt that one thing the Hawaiian chiefs wanted was protection against their enemies. It is quite clear from Vancouver's own account that they expected warships, and possibly troops, to be sent out from England for their protection. Early in the negotiations Vancouver refused to leave the *Chatham* at Hawaii, but he promised faithfully that the desire of the chiefs to have warships stationed there would be presented to his government. Kuykendall also points out that Kamehameha adhered to the spirit of the agreement and was openly partial to the English, although he treated the ships of all nations in a friendly manner. Within a year of the cession, he conquered the whole island chain except Kauai and Niihau, and became king of the Hawaiian Islands as Kamehameha I. In 1810, in a letter to King George of England, he referred to himself as a subject of that sovereign. Foreign naval officers visiting the islands recognized that they had a special relationship with England, either as a protectorate or in an alliance. Only the island of Hawaii itself was involved in the cession, but Kamehameha and the others seem to have interpreted the agreement to include his expanded domain.

From Vancouver's careful explanation that native economy and rule would not be disturbed, it is apparent that the agreement actually established a protectorate, rather than making an outright cession. This is supported by the fact that there was no mention of a specific compensation to Kamehameha and his chiefs for yielding sovereignty of the island to England. Vancouver's account does mention the distribution of "useful presents or ornamental articles," which he and Kamehameha disbursed after the ceremony on the basis of the ranks of the several chiefs. Vancouver's general lavishness with presents to Kamehameha and the other chiefs, and his promise to urge that armed assistance be sent to the island, could be considered as a form of compensation. But as he described the ceremony the cession was a unilateral action on the part of the Hawaiians.

For the islanders themselves the protectorate probably had definite benefits. One notable example of this was the case of George A. Scheffer, a German doctor in the service of the Russian American Company in 1816. He made an agreement with Kaumualii, king of Kauai, placing that island under the protection of Russia. Baranof, the governor of the Russian American Company at Sitka, Alaska, repudiated the action of his agent because of the English protectorate. Scheffer's domineering manner caused Kaumualii to have a change of heart, and some time later, at Kamehameha's instigation, he expelled the Russian agent. Scheffer went to Russia for support in 1819, but he was unsuccessful in his efforts to have the Russian government exploit the islands.

What Vancouver expected from his unwritten treaty is clear from the record. He recognized the great commercial value of the islands, and he wanted them under the British flag. He also knew of his country's plans to found a convict colony on the northwest coast of North America, and the great strategic value that the Hawaiian Islands would have as a link between that coast and Australia is obvious. Reared as he was in an atmosphere of British imperial expansion, he did his best to bring about an arrangement so desirable from his country's point of view.

When he brought his report of the cession back to England that country had been at war with France and her allies for two and one half years. Except for one short breathing spell it would continue to be locked in the tremendous struggle of the Napoleonic era until 1815. Under such circumstances the fate and status of a remote and little-known island in the far-off Pacific was unlikely to receive much consideration.

Furthermore, the experience of the American Revolution led many in England to believe that colonies were certain to break away from the mother country when they were economically sufficiently developed. The British islands in the West Indies had been immensely valuable economically, but they had always required strong protection in the numerous wars of the past. Some people even considered island possessions as a liability. In the 1790's British governments, with such past experience to guide them, were growing wary of making new annexations, especially of islands.

In this general change of attitude toward imperial expansion can be seen early manifestations of the "Little Englander" movement that became so prominent in nineteenth-century British history. With that feeling nascent, and with a great war in progress, Vancouver's timing was not right for affirmative action on the cession of Hawaii.

His agreement with Kamehameha was not entirely forgotten in England, however. In 1822 an armed schooner, built in Australia for the purpose of fulfilling Vancouver's promise, was delivered to the Hawaiian king at Honolulu. In acknowledging the gift Kamehameha II, ruler since 1819, wrote to the British king reporting the death of his father and renewing the recognition of a British protectorate.[14] Kamehameha II and his queen sailed to England in 1823, and they were received and entertained by the British government. The Admiralty's attitude toward the islands at that time was made clear in a letter to the Foreign Office, for the attention of Mr. Canning, then Foreign Minister:

> . . . these islands, first discovered by Captain Cook in his last voyage, were afterwards distinctly ceded to His Majesty and placed under the protection of Great Britain by Tamaahmaah, son of Terreoboo. The latter appeared in Captain Cook's time to be the supreme chief of these islands, and the former equally appeared to Captain Vancouver, to whom the cession was made in 1794, to have succeeded to the supreme authority. The details of this transaction and Captain Vancouver's reason for accepting the cession are to be found in the third volume of his voyage.[15]

Both the king and the queen died in England, and their bodies were returned to Honolulu in 1825 in the frigate *Blonde,* Lord Byron commanding. Byron's secret orders instructed him to be prepared to assert England's rights in the islands, but he was to avoid discussion of them as much as possible. He was to treat subjects of other powers with moderation, and, should any dispute arise between himself and one of them, he was to suggest that the matter be referred to their respective governments. Soon after Byron's arrival Karaimoku, the regent, announced that he considered that the islands belonged to Great Britain. He hoped that Byron had brought laws and regulations for them. Byron replied that he was willing to give his advice whenever he could but that they must make their own laws, "as they best know how to govern their own people, but as far as protecting them from foreign interference, I thought they might rely on the friendship of Great Britain." [16]

Byron's orders and guarded attitude reflect the policy of the British government at that time. It was unwilling actually to annex the islands but stood ready to assert its claims if any other nation seemed ready to move into them. This was not what Vancouver had wanted or had in mind, for he certainly visualized an outright annexation when he observed that, "whether this addition to the empire will ever be of any importance to Great Britain, or whether the surrender of the island will ever be attended with any additional happiness for its people, time alone must determine." [17]

Not the least of Vancouver's accomplishments in the Hawaiian Islands was his survey of the entire chain. His chart was the first complete and accurate map of the group. Its errors are minor ones and not easy to detect; the most noticeable is a small displacement in the longitude of the eastern islands of the chain.

Native historical tradition relates that Vancouver also talked with Kamehameha about Christianity and promised to have missionaries sent out from England. There is nothing in his own work or in the various journals of the expedition to confirm that tradition. His great admiration for the good work of the Franciscan missionaries in California may have suggested the idea to him. There was no chaplain in his expedition, and the idea, if he did have it, would have been his own. There is one nearly contemporary account that tends to confirm that he did discuss with Kamehameha the idea of introducing Christianity into the islands. The American traveler Ebenezer Townsend, in a letter written from Niihau in August, 1798, related the following anecdote:

Captain Vancouver was very anxious to Christianize these people, but that can never be done until they are more civilized. The king Amma-amma-hah told Capt. Vancouver that he would go with him on to the high mountain Mona Roah and they would both jump off together, each calling on their separate gods for protection, and if Captain Vancouver's god saved him but himself not saved by his god, then his people should believe as Capt. Vancouver did. Capt. Vancouver had management enough to get all the islands ceded to the King of England; this will be sufficient excuse to the world-monopolizing disposition of that government to take possession whenever they think it for their interest to do so.[18]

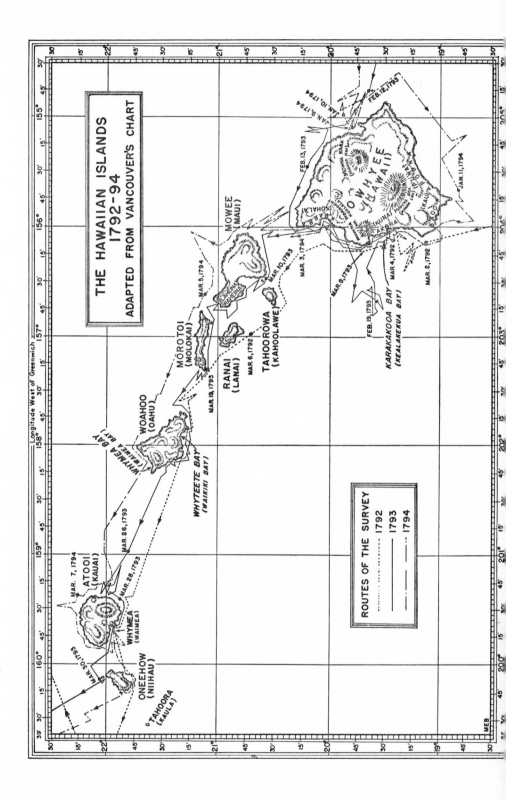

THE HAWAIIAN ISLANDS
1792-94
ADAPTED FROM VANCOUVER'S CHART

Longitude West of Greenwich

MOWEE
(MAUI)

MÔROTOI
(MOLOKAI)

LAHAINA
(RHEINA)

MAR.5,1794

MAR.10,1793

MAR.3,1794

TAHOOROWA
(KAHOOLAWE)

RANAI
(LANAI)

MAR.6,1792

MAR.19,1793

FEB.13,1793

MONNA KOAH

OWHYEE
(HAWAII)

MONNA ROA

(KAUN)

(KAUAI)

(KOHALA)

(KAILUA)

MAR.8,1793

MAR.4,1792

MAR.2,1792

FEB.19,1793

KARAKAKOOA BAY
(KEALAKEKUA BAY)

JAN.5,1794

JAN.10,1794

FEB.12,1793

JAN.11,1794

WOAHOO
(OAHU)

WHYMEA
BAY
(WAIMEA
BAY)

WHYTEETE BAY
(WAIKIKI BAY)

MAR. 7, 1794

ATOOI
(KAUAI)

MAR.26,1793

MAR.28,1793

WHYMEA
(WAIMEA)

MAR.30,1793

ONEEHOW
(NIIHAU)

TAHOORA
(KAULA)

ROUTES OF THE SURVEY
.... 1792
_____ 1793
— · — · — 1794

MEB

This was written only four years after Vancouver's final visit to the islands, and Townsend could have heard the tale only from local sources at a time when the memory of Vancouver was still fresh in the minds of the people. It would be interesting to know Vancouver's answer to Kamehameha's challenge, but unfortunately Townsend did not record it, and Vancouver's own account has no mention of the incident.

When Broughton came back to Kealakekua Bay in January, 1796, he found that the cattle Vancouver left there were in excellent condition and observed that "the people in general spoke very highly of Captain Vancouver." [19] Dr. Herbert H. Gowen, in his study of Kamehameha, noted that Vancouver's memory was "universally respected" among the natives.[20] Well it might be, for he left them enriched with a generous supply of European products, and with his cattle he brought a new industry and source of wealth to the islands. His visits among them were marked by a total absence of violence except for his insistence on the execution of the murderers of Lieutenant Hergest. The fact that parties from his ships could travel safely into the interior of the island of Hawaii reveals the depth of the natives' respect for him.

Vancouver's one-man peaceful "conquest" of Hawaii was a great monument to his diplomatic skill, tact, and judgment. At least until about the 1820's, when American missionary influence began to be important, the islands lay ready and seemingly anxious to become a part of the British Empire. The fact that the British government did not choose to accept them in no way detracts from Vancouver's accomplishment.

In sum, it can perhaps be said that, thanks to Vancouver's initiative, the Hawaiian Islands were the only important inhabited group in the Pacific that retained its independence through the nineteenth century. And it is significant that the jack of the Hawaiian flag is the Union Jack of England. What greater monument can a man have than the enduring respect of a people whose civilization differed so markedly from his own?

13

The Great Survey
(1794-95)

WHEN THE *Discovery* and the *Chatham* cleared the island of Niihau in the middle of March, 1794, Vancouver veered off to the northwest for 150 miles to check the position of Nihoa, or Bird Island as Captain Colnett called it in 1788. Satisfied with a short sight of that sheer and barren rock, which rises to over nine hundred feet, he then laid a course for Cook Inlet in Alaska. The *Chatham* soon dropped far astern and by the next morning she was out of sight. The two ships rejoined in Cook Inlet, where the *Chatham* was first to arrive.

When Puget opened his sealed orders after losing touch with the *Discovery*, he found that he was to proceed to Cape Douglas, a prominent point at the northern end of the Alaska peninsula, and there resume the survey northeastward. Anticipating that raw and cold weather would be common that season Puget had obtained from the *Daedalus* some damaged blankets which he issued to the crew for making cold weather clothing. His foresight was richly rewarded for shortly after sighting Kodiak Island on April 10 the *Chatham* was driven into a small harbor on the Kenai Peninsula to ride out a storm with heavy snow squalls. During the next few days the temperature in Puget's cabin dropped below freezing. It was not a propitious start for a surveying season, but Puget still felt that Vancouver's plan for reaching Cape Decision that season and completing the survey was a good one: ". . . The Principle on which Captain Vancouver formed his plans for the ensuing Summer was certainly excellent & if an early Spring had set in it would have greatly contributed towards a speedy Conclusion." [1]

The *Chatham* was kept in port for nearly two weeks by recurring storms, after which Puget went to Cape Douglas and traced the western shore of Cook Inlet northward through the first week in May. Some visiting Indians then indicated to him that the *Discovery* was anchored further up the inlet, and there he rejoined his commander later in the day.

After losing touch with the *Chatham*, the *Discovery* had had an uneventful passage until she approached the Alaskan coast, where she too experienced freezing weather and heavy snow storms. On one occasion the temperature in her cabin dropped to 7° Fahrenheit. Vancouver's first landfall was an island southwest of Kodiak which he identified with Bering's voyage of 1740-42, and which he named appropriately for Bering's lieutenant, Chirikof. After coasting along the eastern shore of Kodiak Island the *Discovery* entered Cook Inlet two days later than the *Chatham*. She passed not far off the harbor where the *Chatham* was then lying, but neither vessel had any indication of the presence of the other. Leaving the lower part of the inlet for Puget to survey, Vancouver worked the *Discovery* up to an anchorage near the present city of Anchorage. This was tedious and dangerous work for the inlet was filled with ice chunks carried back and forth by the strong tidal currents, which run at five knots and at times may reach eight knots. The maximum range of the tides in Cook Inlet, one of the highest ranges in the world, is up to thirty-three feet; the *Discovery* could therefore move up only on the inrushing flood tide. The bottom of the inlet is covered with boulders which are dangerous for the navigation of ships in shoal waters.

From the anchorage Whidbey set out with the boats to examine the Turnagain Arm of Cook's third voyage, a channel reaching eastward from the main part of the inlet. During his absence Vancouver received a visit from some Russians from Port Etches, on Hinchinbrook Island in Prince William Sound. They came overland from an inlet in that sound to Turnagain Arm, through a low pass only about fifteen miles long. It was a regular trade route for them, and with the knowledge of that route Vancouver recognized that the Kenai Peninsula was a peninsula whose shore line would not require the same detailed examination that was devoted to other parts of the coast.

Whidbey needed but a few days to confirm that Turnagain Arm was a closed inlet. After his return to the ship Vancouver led a boat expedition to trace the northern upper part of the inlet. He found its head much encumbered with shoals and backed by high mountains all around, thus exploding a theory, popular in some circles at home, that Cook Inlet was actually the western outlet of the Northwest Passage. It was one of the few times that season that Vancouver went out in the boats, for his health was failing fast and he was sick most of the time.[2] He had just returned from that excursion when the *Chatham* joined him. In commenting on having proved that the inlet was not a large river, as Cook had described it, he noted that, had its discoverer

... dedicated one more day to its further examination, he would have spared the theoretical navigators . . . the task of ingeniously ascribing to this arm of the ocean a channel, through which a north-west passage existing according to their doctrines, might ultimately be discovered.[3]

Vancouver changed the name of the arm to Cook's Inlet (now Cook Inlet), in preference to the earlier Cook's River.

While working the ships southward out of Cook Inlet, Vancouver visited a Russian outpost on the eastern side of the inlet. Its large central log house appeared to him to be warm and relatively comfortable, but there was a complete lack of sanitation. As he approached the house over a poor path he was greeted by "a most intolerable stench, the worst, excepting the skunk, I had ever the inconvenience of experiencing." [4] On the whole, however, he found that the Russians had a well-organized fur collecting system; the Indians seemed well treated, faithful, and apparently very friendly to the Russians.

This was not an accurate impression of actual conditions, for at that time there were two competing Russian trading companies in that region. Only the year before Alexander Baranof, chief factor of the Shelikof company at Kodiak and later to achieve fame as governor of the Russian American Company, had stopped an internecine war between Russians and Indians. Before then the Indians were troublesome, but by 1794 Baranof had asserted his leadership, and fairly good order was restored and enforced.[5] The lack of an interpreter prevented Vancouver from getting a truer idea of conditions in the Russian zone of trading operations. He did learn correctly that the easternmost Russian settlement at that time was in Prince William Sound.

Near the entrance to Cook Inlet he waited for a few days for a promised meeting with Baranof, who was reported several times to be arriving very shortly but never appeared. The next anchorage was in a bay on the western end of Montague Island, lying across the outer side of and protecting Prince William Sound. Knowing that there was a narrow land communication between upper Cook Inlet and that sound, Vancouver was little concerned with the outer coast of the Kenai Peninsula. He knew of a harbor there called by Portlock Port Andrews and by the Russians Blying Sound, where, with the help of two Englishmen, the Russians were building a ship the size of the *Discovery*. He was tempted to stop in the harbor to work on his own ship, but it was not well placed for continuing the survey and he passed it by. Residents of the modern town of Seward, on Resurrection Bay, as the harbor is now called, proudly claim that their town is the site of the first shipyard in that part of the world.

From the new anchorage boat expeditions under Whidbey and Johnstone were sent to trace the shores of the sound. By then it was mid-May and the weather had improved, but the boats still had a difficult time in occasional storms and heavy rains. Nearly a month was required to complete that part of the survey. In June the *Chatham* was sent ahead to examine the coast of the mainland from Prince William Sound to Port Mulgrave, in Yakutat Bay, well to the east. The *Discovery* was to follow her in a few days.

The *Chatham* carried out her mission without special incident and reached Yakutat Bay at the end of June. She spent several days there surveying that large bay. Dixon had named it Admiralty Bay in 1787, but Vancouver named it for Bering, in the mistaken belief that it was the one described by that earlier explorer in the Russian service. Puget found there a large party of more than a thousand Kodiak Indians taking sea otters under a Russian agent. The mainland Indians, though less numerous, were more warlike than those from Kodiak, and they resented the Russian-led intruders. The Russian agent appealed to Puget for help should the local Indians attack his party, and Puget agreed to help if necessary. A large-scale Indian battle was thus probably averted by the *Chatham*'s presence and by the later arrival of Captain Brown, the English trader, in his tender *Jackall*.

The *Discovery* arrived off Yakutat Bay early in July. She fired a gun in answer to one heard from the inner bay, and early the next morning Manby was sent out to help pilot the larger ship into the bay. He failed to return to the *Chatham*, and lacking any word from Vancouver Puget sailed three days later to join the *Discovery* in Cross Sound, the outer end of the Inside Passage.

Vancouver left Prince William Sound four days after the *Chatham* sailed from there. The *Discovery* was slowed by adverse winds for several days off Kayak Island, but near the end of June she reached the vicinity of Mount St. Elias, an imposing 18,008-foot peak that dominates the region. Vancouver paid tribute to its beauty in these words:

> . . . The coast is again composed of a spacious margin of low land, rising with a gradual and uniform ascent to the foot of the still connected chain of lofty mountains, whose summits are but the base from whence mount St. Elias towers, majestically conspicuous in regions of perpetual frost.[6]

When Manby came out to the *Discovery* off Yakutat Bay the Indian canoe that brought him made its own way back into the harbor and left him stranded on board. By then the ship had drifted to leeward past the bay, and Vancouver, anxious to keep the survey moving and unwilling to make a long beat upwind, continued along the coast fully expecting that Puget would join him later in Cross Sound. The next day a strange sail was sighted which proved to be the *Jackall*, tender to the *Butterworth*, with Captain Brown on board. She was on a trading cruise and was headed for Yakutat Bay. Brown had left Canton the previous February, and he gave Vancouver the latest news of the war in Europe. It included disturbing reports of discontent in England, influenced by social ideas springing from the French Revolution. It is well to recall that this "latest" news was then about a year old, having traveled to China around the Cape of Good Hope.

One natural phenomenon that puzzled Vancouver was the nature and origin of glaciers, which are numerous in the vicinity of Mount Fairweather and discharge directly into the open sea. He speculated that they were rivers of ice but assured his readers that he was doing so only to describe them better. Written by one who was not familiar with glaciers, his description and guess as to their nature is vivid and stands up well with reality when read today.

After he arrived in Cross Sound and was joined by the *Chatham,* Vancouver found a snug anchorage in Port Althorp, a protected arm off the southeastern corner of the sound. Because of floating ice chunks in the sound, Vancouver sent Whidbey with three boats, instead of the usual two, to continue the survey, working from north to south toward the last season's terminal point.[7]

A few days later, while temporarily feeling well, Vancouver became restless and decided to survey the islands marking the inner side of Cross Sound himself. He set out in a boat early in the morning but was forced to return to the ship by noon, being "seized with a most violent indisposition, which terminated in a bilious colic, that confined me for several days to my apartments." [8] He was obviously a very sick man by then, and this was his final attempt to do boat survey work. Johnstone and Whidbey were in charge of the final boat expeditions. As Whidbey's allotted two weeks passed without his return, Vancouver began to worry for his safety, and he was noticeably relieved when the boats did return after having been away for sixteen days.

Whidbey started his boat work at Cape Spencer, the northern entrance to Cross Sound, and followed the continental shore through Icy Strait and Lynn Canal and along the western side of Admiralty Island to a point from which he could see the Cape Decision of the year before. He did not discover that Admiralty Island was an island until his next boat expedition.

In Lynn Canal Whidbey's alertness averted what might have been a tragic incident with the Indians. His boat was approached one afternoon by a large canoe in which was an ornately dressed chief. The chief appeared to be friendly and courteous, giving Whidbey a sea otter for which he received a present in return. The canoe remained in company with the boats until dark when, as a precaution, Whidbey had the men sleep in the boats at anchor in a small cove, and a watch was kept. At daylight it was seen that several more canoes had slipped into the cove undetected. All were filled with well-armed Indians, some with muskets. Whidbey tried to ease his boats out of the cove to avoid possible trouble, but the chief who had kept him company the day before closed his boat and tried to jump into it. The awning rigging of the boat slowed him, and before others could follow he was forced out of the boat. By then the boats were surrounded with more than two hundred Indians in canoes. The boats' crews were armed and alert for an attack, and this caused the Indians to hold back and resort to taunts and threats. Whidbey withheld fire until it should be necessary to save his men, and, after following the boats about three miles along the shore, the threatening Indians withdrew.

Late in the evening of the same day, while moving through a narrow channel toward the point where present-day Juneau is located, the boats were again followed by a large canoe which was joined by another. Whidbey tried to drive the Indians away by having a shot fired over their heads, but this only made them bolder. When he tried to land to camp for the night, the canoes rushed in and beached and the Indians formed to oppose the landing. Rather than risk a fight with them Whidbey kept the crews at their oars all night and retired into Lynn Canal.

With the end of the survey close at hand, Vancouver showed a pronounced nostalgia as he named Lynn Canal for his birthplace. A bay on the eastern side of that Channel was named Berners Bay, and the two points at its mouth were named St. Mary's and Bridget. Bridget Berners was the maiden name of Vancouver's mother, and Wiggenhall St. Mary's, a few miles upriver from King's Lynn, was his mother's family seat. Other feminine names he gave to landmarks in this area were Lavinia, Augusta, Sophia, Amelia, and Mary. The subjects of the names have not been identified, but they may have honored relatives or friends. His three sisters were Bridget, Sarah, and Mary, but Sarah's name was not used in that region.

Vancouver's map of the northwest coast was nearly complete with the results of Whidbey's boat expedition. There remained only about one degree of latitude to be covered, and one more boat expedition should finish that part. To work his ships through the ice-filled inland waterway and follow Whidbey's return route

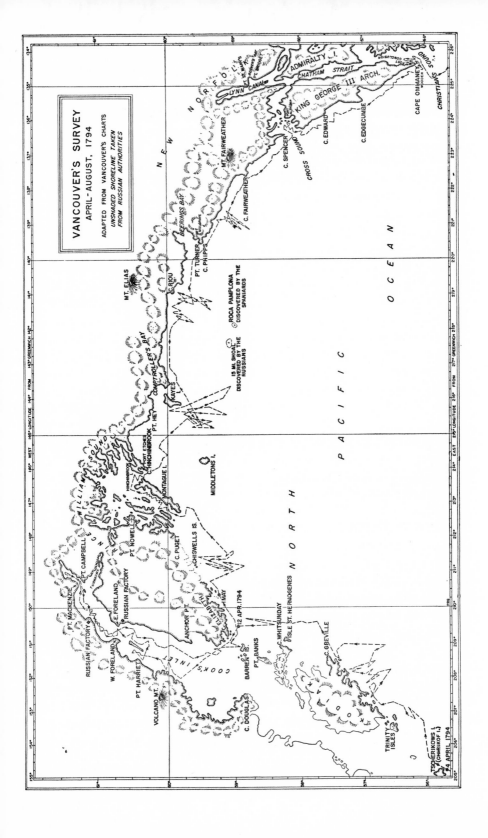

VANCOUVER'S SURVEY
APRIL-AUGUST, 1794

ADAPTED FROM VANCOUVER'S CHARTS
UNSHADED SHORELINE TAKEN
FROM RUSSIAN AUTHORITIES

would have been dangerous and time consuming. It was much easier to do as Vancouver did—sail down along the outer coast to some cove not far from Cape Decision. The port selected was on the inner coast near the southern end of Baranof Island, and it was named Port Conclusion. From there two boat expeditions were sent out under Whidbey and Johnstone. The latter went to Cape Decision to start where the previous year's survey had ended, and Whidbey started at the point he had reached in his earlier expedition. Each party was to trace the continental shore until the two met. When the two weeks estimated as required to accomplish this had passed by, Vancouver again fretted and worried over the safety of the boats and their crews. This time they returned after being out for eighteen days and reported the successful completion of the survey. It was a joyful occasion for it meant that at long last the tedious and laborious boat work was ended and the ships could be headed for home. By coincidence Vancouver was promoted to post captain just ten days after the end of the survey, on August 28, a timely and fitting climax to his great accomplishment.[9]

Whidbey had another close call with the Indians near the end of his boat trip. On a rare clear day he landed on a beach in a small cove to dry wet clothes and clean the boats. A large canoe filled with Indians came into the cove and assumed a hostile attitude after first seeming to be friendly. Whidbey pulled off the beach and continued his survey, stopping to land for dinner some distance away. The canoe reappeared around a point and paddled rapidly toward the Englishmen. Whidbey ordered a shot fired over the canoe to warn the Indians away, but they only closed faster. He then had a shot fired at the canoe, upon which it turned away and disappeared behind the point. Not wanting to be surprised on shore in an ambush, he re-embarked his party and pulled clear of the beach. It was just in time, for suddenly the canoe again came in sight and a group of Indians burst out of the woods behind the spot where the men had been eating. Vancouver reasoned that such treacherous acts by the Indians were outgrowths of earlier unpleasant contacts with traders. In addition, the fact that in each case Whidbey would not trade with them might have made the Indians angry. It was probably the only time that they had seen Europeans who were unwilling to trade and they must have been puzzled by the attitude of the members of the survey parties, who were so different from the other white men. Johnstone also reported meeting Indians so persistent in their efforts to trade that he had trouble in chasing them away.

Soon after Whidbey's brush with the Indians, Johnstone's boats approached, signaling the end of the survey. The boats met at a spot on Kupreanof Island, nearly opposite Point Vandeput on the mainland, and not far from the location of the present town of Petersburg, Alaska. Heading back to the ships, the united party moved to a cove a few miles to the west to camp for the night. Vancouver noted that during the evening

> . . . no small portion of facetious mirth passed amongst the seamen, in consequence of our having sailed from old England on the *first of April,* for the purpose of discovering a north-west passage, by following up the discoveries of De Fuca, De Fonte, and a numerous train of hypothetical navigators.[10]

At Vancouver's direction Whidbey took formal possession of the country before returning to the ships. Vancouver was justifiably proud of the work that had then been completed. In apologizing for the minute detail in which he described the boat expeditions and the ships' tracks, he explained his purpose to make "the history of our transactions on the north west coast of America, *as conclusive as possible,* against all speculative opinions respecting the existence of a *hyperborean* or *mediterranean ocean* within the limits of our survey." [11]

HOMEWARD BOUND

The day following the return of the boat parties to the ships was set aside as a holiday for the crews to celebrate. For that purpose, "they were served such an additional allowance of grog as was fully sufficient to answer every purpose of festivity on the occasion." [12] One cannot help wondering if this festivity had any connection with Vancouver's report that a southeast gale with heavy rain and fog held up their departure for the south for four days.

With the return of moderate weather the ships sailed from Port Conclusion on August 22, but they were two more days getting into the open sea. In light winds and fog the *Discovery* drifted close to a rock off Cape Ommaney, the southern point of Baranof Island, on which heavy surf was breaking. The boats were launched, and, after the ship had been towed to safety, one of the boat's crew fell overboard while his boat was being hoisted in. Another boat was sent to his rescue, but the man could not swim; he had bumped his head on the gunwale in the fall, and he disappeared almost at once. It was the fourth fatality of the voyage. Wooden Island, off Cape Ommaney, preserves the memory of the man.

The *Discovery* arrived at Nootka early in September, for once a few hours ahead of the *Chatham*. The new governor, Brigadier General Don José Alava, had arrived there only the day before. He was appointed to replace Quadra, whose death the preceding March was mourned deeply by all the Englishmen. Alava expected to be the Spanish commissioner for the final settlement of the Nootka Sound incident, but as yet he had no specific instructions. He had no word for Vancouver, but he was expecting his own documents to reach Nootka by the middle of October at the latest. Disappointed at receiving no word for himself, Vancouver decided to wait at Nootka with Alava. There was much work to be done on the ships to prepare them for the voyage home, and Alava offered every assistance within his power.

By a Spanish ship sailing south Vancouver sent a letter to the Admiralty reporting the completion of his survey. The delay in receiving instructions from home was irksome, and in a letter written at the same time to his London agent, James Sykes, he expressed his hope of getting back soon to take an active part in the war. He still had no reply to his dispatches sent home by Mudge and Broughton. "Thus you see my good friend I am once more entrap'd in this infernal Ocean, and am totally at a loss to say when I shall be able to quit it. . . ." [13]

Another letter sent at the same time is of special significance to us for it is the only known personal letter from Vancouver to a member of his family. Addressed to his older brother John, it is surprisingly lacking in real news and was obviously dashed off hurriedly, in sharp contrast to his normally carefully composed letters:

Nootka Discovery
Sept ye 8th 1794

My Dearest Van

I have the pleasure of informing if you are as *I trust in God you are* in the midst of all the horrid riot and confusion in which Europe has been thrown since our departure, by a banditry of vagabonds in quest of disorder plunder and thirst for human blood, a true and loyal subject to our King & constitution   I have the pleasure I say of informing you, that in good health in the land of the living *or rather existing* after having finally executed the investigation of coast of NW America we arrived a few days ago in this port, whence I expected to find sufficient documents for the the purpose of negotiating the business of these territories but that not being the case it is at present out of my power to form any judgement of the time when we are likely to return to England   I am however in hourly expectation of receiving some dispatches to that effect and shall when such period may arrive in all probability have it in my power to give you more positive information of my future expectations; our situation in these remote and uncouth regions afford me no opportunity of executing epistolary correspondence excepting on subjects of our transactions which is in my power to communicate only in an official capacity to the Ministers of our Court. You must therefore my dearest Van be content in being informed of my wellfare thus far: being at the same time assured that I trust divine providence will bestow its benediction on the whole of our family friends & connections to whom you will do me the particular kindness to remember me in such terms as I may be deemed to merit in their good opinions and be assured

I am My Dearest Van
Unalterably your ever affectionate
& Sincere friend and Brother

Geo Vancouver[14]

Spirits were raised early in October when it was reported that the expected packet from San Blas was in sight, but the newcomer proved to be the *Jackall* instead, coming in from her season of trading in the north. Captain Brown's arrival was welcomed for he was helpful in clearing up some minor points of the survey in southeastern Alaska.

When October 16 came and there was still no ship from Mexico, the *Discovery* and the *Chatham* sailed for Monterey in company with Governor Alava in the *Princessa*. Soon after leaving Nootka the ships were separated in a dense fog. The *Discovery* then ran south near the coast, and below Cape Mendocino she was caught in one of the worst storms of the voyage. She arrived at Monterey on November 6, to find the *Chatham* snugly moored after her arrival four days before. The smaller ship had run south farther offshore and had missed the worst of the storm.

Arrillaga was no longer at Monterey, and Arguello, the commandant of the presidio, was in charge. He offered the facilities of the port to Vancouver and handed him a letter from Viceroy Revilla Gigedo, dated the preceding October. Vancouver derived much satisfaction from the fact that the viceroy had sent the letter to Monterey to be held for him, thus disproving Arrillaga's claim that his second visit to the port was not expected. Alava's instructions were not at Monterey, nor was there any word from England for Vancouver. Arguello sent a special courier to San Diego in the hope that some letter might be waiting there. It required ten or twelve days to make the round trip, meaning still further delay for the expedition. But as compensation there was an abundance of fresh beef for the crew, and game birds were brought in by the sportsmen of the expedition, a welcome relief from the salted meat diet for all hands. The officers and men were allowed to exercise ashore, and Vancouver himself, his health temporarily restored, joined one excursion into the nearby interior.

During the wait for the courier's return from San Diego, the newly appointed governor of California, Don Diego Borica, arrived at Monterey from Mexico City with his family, having been eight months en route on horseback. The same day an express arrived with Alava's instructions, but it brought nothing for Vancouver. Alava told him that the Nootka affair had been settled amicably nearly on the terms Vancouver had offered Quadra. He also said that London was issuing a new commission, and after his return to England Vancouver learned that originally this commission had been addressed to him.

The Nootka incident had an almost comic opera ending. In January, 1794, there was signed at Madrid a "Convention for the Mutual Abandonment of Nootka." It provided that new instructions would be issued to the commissioners to proceed to Nootka. There the land occupied by Meares's men in 1789 was to be formally delivered to the English commissioner. Thereupon the English flag was to be unfurled as a sign of possession. After that ceremony the two officials would withdraw their respective people from the port, which henceforth would be open to the free use of the nationals of both parties. Both agreed not to reoccupy the place permanently and not to assert a claim to the territory in the future.

This agreement was much closer to Quadra's offer than to Vancouver's, but it went much further than either in the mutual abandonment of the port. It was well that Vancouver did not carry out the ceremony, for surely it would have hurt his pride to do so. In March, 1795, Lieutenant Thomas Pierce, of the Marines, and Alava carried out the prescribed ceremony, and thereafter, except for casual visits by traders, the place was deserted by Europeans. Before long all signs of civilization disappeared, and Nootka reverted to the possession of the Indians. Today it is only a small fishing and lumbering village with but few marks of the prominence it once had in world affairs. In 1903 the Washington University Historical Society erected a granite monument there commemorating the meeting between Vancouver and Quadra, and in 1924 the Canadian Historical Sites and Monuments Board unveiled a commemorative tablet. It is no longer an important place, but for a few years Nootka was a name known in every court in Europe, and a minor dispute there came close to causing a major war.

At Monterey the Spaniards held six deserters for Vancouver's arrival. He found that only three of them were his own men: the armorer and a marine from the *Chatham,* and a former convict stowaway from the *Daedalus.* The other three were not Englishmen, and he refused to accept them. He was presented with a bill for 425 Spanish dollars for the expenses of the men while they were in Spanish custody. Without instructions on how to deal with the matter and having no Spanish money, he did not pay the bill but promised to lay the matter before the Admiralty upon his return to England, and this arrangement seemed quite agreeable to the governor.

By the end of November the watering, provisioning, and other business on shore were completed, and early in December the *Discovery* and the *Chatham* sailed from Monterey toward home. Thomas Manby, master of the *Chatham,* returned to the *Discovery* as third lieutenant; and Harry Humphreys, master's mate, moved to the *Chatham* as master.

With his survey still in mind, instead of proceeding by the direct route to Cape Horn Vancouver headed for Cape San Lucas, the southernmost point of Lower California, arriving there two weeks later. He had Spanish charts for that part of California, and he knew that the correct longitude of Cape San Lucas was known. It had been determined in 1769 from observation of the transit of Venus by a French scientific expedition organized for the same purpose as Cook's first voyage. Vancouver found that his own calculation of the longitude of Cape San Lucas varied from the known one by only one minute of arc, a remarkably close agreement with a discrepancy of less than one mile. So rewarding a confirmation of his mapping was ample justification for all the laborious work with the observatory and the constant taking of astronomical sights throughout the survey. In a notable understatement Vancouver concluded that his recorded positions and charts would be found to be "tolerably correct."

A detailed comparison of Vancouver's chart of the Pacific coast of North America, the first complete one to be produced, with modern charts of the same region shows only one error of any consequence. Some features of islands such as the Queen Charlotte Islands and Kodiak were taken from Spanish and Russian charts, and these are shown on his charts in lighter lines than those for his own work. Since the continental shore line was his primary interest it is there that the comparison is most revealing. The longitude error at Cape San Lucas was practically zero, but in the vicinity of Puget Sound his longitudes of land features average about one-third of a degree to the east of the true values. Near Cook Inlet, in the extreme northern part of his charts, the error increases to about one degree to the east, roughly about thirty miles. The latitudes of the land features are extremely accurate throughout, rarely varying more than a mile or two from the correct values. The longitude error is as if a correct map, pivoted at Cape San Lucas, were rotated about one-half a degree of arc toward the true north-south axis. Vancouver frequently noted a discrepancy between his longitudes and Cook's, but he believed that since his were based on many observations they were more accurate. In southeastern Alaska, where overcast weather prevented him from taking a large number of astronomical observations, the discrepancies in his chart are more numerous, yet many of the positions are very close to the true positions as known today. Off Point Arena, California, in 1793, Puget found that his computation of the longitude of that point was about one-third of a degree west of Vancouver's figure, and Puget's result was close to the correct value.[15]

The error in Vancouver's longitudes was one in celestial navigation, and it is impossible to establish without having his actual observations and mathematical formulas and tables to check. It was a function of latitude, as the error increases uniformly with the latitude. The fact that the error is consistent is mute testimony to the care and thoroughness with which his computations were made. Even today the navigational charts of the coastal waters of upper British Columbia have a small error in orientation of some of the channels, and traces of Vancouver's original survey can be found on them. Pilots running the narrow channels of the Inside Passage depend upon compass courses and distances known from long experience rather than on the charts.

After confirming the accuracy of his longitude at Cape San Lucas, Vancouver had every reason to be confident of the accuracy of all of his work. Not content with that geographical accomplishment, he next took his ships to check the Marias Islands, off the Mexican coast not far from San Blas. Once again too sick to go himself, he sent Whidbey and Manby in the boats in search of fresh water, but none was found. Beyond the Marias Islands the coast of the mainland was sighted, and from Cape Corrientes Vancouver headed for Cocos Island, about five hundred miles west and slightly south of Panama.

On the fourth Christmas away from home extra rations of grog were served according to custom, and Vancouver noted that the crew spontaneously toasted the memory of Quadra and the health of Kamehameha, showing that the admiration and affection for those men, who had done so much for the comfort and health of the expedition, was not confined to the officers.

At the beginning of the year 1795 both ships faced a critical shortage of fresh water due to old and leaky water casks, especially in the *Chatham*. Light winds meant slow progress, and in a few days the *Discovery* began distilling sea water, getting from fifteen to eighteen gallons per day from her distilling apparatus. Puget already had his officers on a strict water ration, and his distilling machine was producing from three quarts to one gallon per day. Cocos Island, which had first been reported by the buccaneers with its exact position doubtful, became an urgent target. Several days were spent searching for it before it was sighted in the latter part of January. There the ships spent several days and found an abundance of fresh water, firewood, and coconuts. Vegetable seeds were planted for the benefit of future visitors.

The next planned stop after Cocos Island was Juan Fernandez Island, in the South Pacific off the coast of Chile. It was the island from which Alexander Selkirk, whose experiences inspired Defoe's *Robinson Crusoe,* was rescued. While passing close to the Galapagos Islands en route to Juan Fernandez, the ships spent three days checking their geographical positions and searching for wood and water. The impatience to get home and the petulance that existed in the expedition by this time is clearly revealed by Puget's reaction to this delay:

> I believe we never quitted a Place with such general heart-felt joy as we did this Barren group—Had our examination been *likely* productive of any addition to geography or beneficial to future visitors in pointing out Situations where refreshment could have been found then cheerfully the task would have been performed but in neither of those points have we succeeded.[16]

A few days after the departure from the Galapagos the sailing qualities of the *Chatham* again came under fire, and Vancouver told Puget that he was proceeding ahead to Juan Fernandez; the *Chatham* should join him there. Added to the order was a criticism of the *Chatham*'s station-keeping that aroused Puget's resentment. His journal reports that the *Discovery* frequently changed course without making a signal, and that she could sail closer to the wind than the *Chatham*. "Where the blame lies is obvious & any impartial person could see" that the better sailing qualities of the *Discovery* gave her a wide choice of courses with respect to the wind that the *Chatham* could not match.[17]

The *Discovery* sailed southward until during a squall the mainmast was found to be badly sprung. The upper masts were taken down and temporary sails were rigged while the carpenters worked on the mast. The new rigging reduced the *Discovery* to the equivalent of a two-masted ship. Then another trouble developed when Menzies reported that scurvy was appearing in the crew. This worried Vancouver for he had been careful to enforce his antiscorbutic measures after the mild outbreak off California. The source of the malady was revealed unexpectedly when the cook reported that he had disobeyed orders and given members of the crew grease skimmings from the boiled salted meat to mix with their "pulse" (peas).

Vancouver was so pleased to find the probable source of the scurvy that he did not punish the cook for his disobedience but accepted instead a promise to stop the practice. Also, he could not resist a thrust at Sir Joseph Banks at that point, for he felt there might be some on board who "seemed to be acquainted with the opinions of the president of the Royal Society, and who stated, that *he* conceived that pulse with any kind of grease was not only a wholesome food, but also very antiscorbutic." [18] Active treatment of the scurvy with lemon juice was started, but the recovery was slow and the number of cases increased. From this Vancouver was convinced that the practice of using fat skimmings was of long standing and was fairly general among the crew.

VALPARAISO AND CAPE HORN

Two weeks after the accident to the mainmast a sail was sighted far astern. On its closing it proved to be the *Chatham,* now a match for her crippled consort in sailing qualities. Puget reported that the captain of a Spanish merchantman, to whom he had spoken several days before, told him that Juan Fernandez was a poor place to repair the ships and to get wood and water. He recommended Valparaiso, Chile, as the best place for such purposes in that part of the world. The *Discovery*'s mast proved to be in worse condition than had been thought, and Vancouver was in a quandary, for his instructions forbade him to stop at any part of Spanish America between latitude 30° North and Chiloe Island, in latitude 44° South. Valparaiso was in latitude 33° South, and about 650 miles north of Chiloe Island, well inside the forbidden zone. Normally he made all his decisions with little or no consultation with his juniors, but in this case he asked for the advice of Puget and the officers of the *Discovery*. Such a consultation could help to answer any censure he might receive later for disobeying his orders. Puget, Baker, Swaine, Manby, and Whidbey signed a letter addressed to Vancouver and strongly urging him to proceed to the nearest port to secure a new mainmast.

Near the end of March, almost four months out of Monterey, the ships anchored in Valparaiso harbor. A real European settlement, the first since Capetown nearly four years before, was a welcome sight. The local governor, Don Louis Alava, a brother of the governor at Nootka, welcomed them heartily but told Vancouver that he would have to get permission from the president and captain general of Chile at Santiago for them to do their desired work. That official was Don Ambrosio O'Higgins de Vallenar, father of Bernardo O'Higgins, the Chilean national hero. The courier would require about four days to return from Santiago, but meanwhile there would be no restraint on the officers in visiting the town, and the ships could take on wood, water, and provisions. That was welcome news, for the *Discovery* still had seventeen cases of scurvy, and there were also some cases in the *Chatham*, arising from the same forbidden practice of using fat skimmings in the food.

The president's answer, giving full permission for the ships' work to be done and inviting Vancouver to visit Santiago, came through promptly. Before accepting the invitation he felt it was his duty to see that all the essential work was started. Since there was no mast timber available in Valparaiso to replace the *Discovery*'s mainmast, it was necessary to take the old one ashore to be spliced and patched as well as possible with the material available. When he was satisfied with the progress of the work, Vancouver, with Puget, Menzies, and the senior officers of the two vessels, set out on horseback for Santiago, escorted by two dragoons.

There they were warmly welcomed by the president general, who gave the group rooms in the palace. That official was much interested in Vancouver's work, and he in turn was pleased by

O'Higgins' compliments. They were entertained in a series of levies and parties at which the Englishmen were ill at ease, in the presence of the brilliantly dressed Spaniards, because of their threadbare uniforms. The president general noticed their embarrassment and explained to everyone the hardships they had endured and the great work they had done. In the course of the rounds of sightseeing and parties Vancouver's observant eye missed little. For Don Ambrosio and his work he had great respect and admiration. He had built a series of dams to control floods in the river that supplied water to the city, and he had been very successful in quieting the feuds of the natives and in curbing factional fighting. Vancouver rated his soldiers the equal of any in Europe and learned that eight thousand men could be assembled in twenty-four hours for the defense of Valparaiso, in case that seaport should be attacked. So pleasant were Santiago and its people that Vancouver's party did not return to Valparaiso for two weeks.

There was still much work remaining to be done at Valparaiso, and because of his poor health Vancouver obtained quarters for himself ashore from Governor Alava. Even with all the work being done on them the ships were still in poor condition, with worn and rotting sails and ropes that were repaired and replaced as much as possible.

Vancouver's instructions told him to survey the coast of Chile south of Chiloe Island if this seemed practicable to him. In view of the condition of his ships, and with the winter season approaching, he reluctantly gave up the idea of attempting that survey. It was a fortunate decision, for that part of the Chilean coast is mountainous and deeply indented with channels and inlets for 750 miles, very similar to the coast of British Columbia and southeastern Alaska. At that stage of the voyage Vancouver's ships and men would not have been equal to the task.

He was fortunate in being able to get supplies at Valparaiso; otherwise he might have had to make the long run directly to the Cape of Good Hope with meager supplies. Well stocked with provisions, and with his ships repaired as well as possible, he decided to go next to St. Helena, in the south Atlantic, and there join a convoy for home. He consulted Puget on this point, and the decision to go from St. Helena to England in convoy arose from a question as to whether or not the French had issued them a safe-conduct, as Louis XVI had done for Cook's ships in 1788. If not it would be safer to be in a convoy.

Early in May, with the ships as ready as they could be made, and with the health of all hands except Vancouver excellent, the two ships sailed from Valparaiso. As they approached Cape Horn wintry gales and snow storms battered them about, especially the little *Chatham*. On the day the ships rounded the Horn she had only five men in a watch able to keep to the deck; the rest were sick from exposure and cold. Once the ships were well past that stormy cape and working northward in the Atlantic, the weather gradually moderated. The *Chatham* once more fell astern, and the *Discovery* went on alone. On that leg of the voyage a seaman, Richard Jones, fell overboard and was lost, the fifth man lost on the voyage. A grating was thrown over for him and the ship hove to in an effort to rescue him, but he was seen no more. Early in July, as the *Discovery* was approaching St. Helena, the *Chatham* caught up with her for the last time and both ships entered the harbor together.

With their arrival at St. Helena in July, 1795, the scientific and geographical part of Vancouver's voyage ended. From the time he had first heard of the war with France he had been anxious to get back to European waters where he could have an active part in it. The first opportunity for this came at St. Helena, changing the character of his expedition from a scientific one eligible for safe-conduct from the French to one composed of men-of-war, actively engaged in the war.

14

Half Pay
(1795-96)

DURING Vancouver's first call on Governor Brooke at St. Helena he learned that the war then in progress had expanded to include Holland among England's enemies. The French overran that country in the winter of 1794-95 and captured the Dutch fleet while it was frozen in the ice in the Texel. England then declared war on Holland.

On seeing a Dutch East Indiaman, the *Macassar,* approaching the harbor at St. Helena, Vancouver sent an officer and a party of men to board and take possession of her as a prize, probably the first inkling the Dutch captain had of the new state of affairs. This action on Vancouver's part, a direct participation in the war, was enough to void any safe-conduct passport the French might have issued in his favor. A week after he took the ship he was told by another captain, in from the Cape of Good Hope, that such a decree in his favor had been issued. That the French National Assembly did issue a safe-conduct decree for Vancouver has not been confirmed, but one probably was issued. Early in 1801, when the Englishman Flinders was setting out to survey the Australian coast, the French government granted him such a passport.

While the ever necessary repairs to the ships were being made for the final leg of the voyage home, Vancouver became more deeply involved in military affairs. A few days after his arrival the

Sphinx came into port with dispatches from Vice Admiral Sir George Keith Elphinstone (Lord Keith), at the Cape of Good Hope. Elphinstone was then in command of an expedition sent out to capture Capetown from the Dutch. The *Sphinx* carried orders to Major General Clarke, then waiting with his troops embarked at Bahia St. Salvadore, Brazil, for instructions to join the admiral. After consulting with Governor Brooke about disturbing reports on the military situation at the Cape, Vancouver offered to proceed there in the *Discovery* with troops and supplies. A few days after he made his offer the *Arniston,* an East Indiaman in naval service, arrived from the Cape with duplicate dispatches. With the *Arniston* available for a return trip, and in view of the generally poor condition of the *Discovery,* Brooke declined Vancouver's offer of assistance. Among other things it was reported that the British troops at the Cape were short of camp equipment and light artillery. The four three-pounder field guns, tents, axes, and shovels used by the expedition during the survey were no longer needed, and Vancouver placed them in the *Arniston* for the use of Elphinstone's troops.

It was the captain of the *Arniston* who told him of the French decree of safe-conduct for his expedition. But Vancouver had already committed himself too deeply in the hostilities to reverse his actions. In a letter to Elphinstone he reported that since his arrival at St. Helena he had

... been honoured with the confidence and consultation of the Honourable Governor Brooke, and have thence been induced to take probably a more active part in the military operations going forward in this island than the spirit of my commission and the orders I am under may contain.[1]

There is in that passage a suggestion of a guilty conscience, yet we can certainly sympathize with him, for, as he pointed out in the same letter, "The measures I thus pursue (on this *uninstructed occasion* since I have not received a single line from either the *Admiralty or Secretary of State Office since August* 1791) will I hope meet your approbation."

This letter reminds us again how far Vancouver was from our own age of almost instantaneous radio communication services. For four years he was without a single official word, even in acknowledgment of his long progress reports, which were sent home at every opportunity. There was, of course, no direct channel to him except through Spanish hands, and relations with that country were no longer as cordial as they had been when France first declared war on the two countries. Vancouver's letter from Nootka of September 8, 1794, reporting the completion of the survey, was received in the Admiralty late in April, 1795. Lieutenant Pierce, carrying his new instructions for the final settlement of the Nootka affair, may have had some directions for Vancouver's future conduct; but the fact that Pierce went ahead with the ceremony indicates that it was expected that Vancouver might be on his way home. The Admiralty sent no word even about the French safe-conduct to likely stopping places on the way home, and Vancouver was still acting entirely on his own resources and judgment.

In addition to the duplicate dispatches for General Walker at Bahia, the *Arniston* brought dispatches for London that Elphinstone wanted Governor Brooke to forward immediately. Vancouver next offered to send the *Chatham* to Bahia with the duplicate dispatches, and Brooke did accept that offer. As soon as the *Chatham* was ready for sea, within two weeks of her arrival at St. Helena, Puget sailed for Bahia. Still considering the possibility that a French safe-conduct existed for his ships, Vancouver changed his mind about waiting until the *Discovery* could join a convoy. A large convoy had left St. Helena the morning his ships arrived there, and with luck he might overtake it and join it at sea. Taking Elphinstone's urgent dispatches for the Admiralty, he sailed on July 16 after placing Lieutenant Johnstone with a prize crew on board the *Macassar* to await a convoy for home.[2] Brooke was very appreciative of Vancouver's help at St. Helena. He wrote to Elphinstone:

> It appears fortunate for the service that Captain Vancouver arrived here with his two vessels at such a time. In the first place he has been able to afford unexpected assistance; in the next place all your wishes respecting dispatches to the place of rendezvous, as well as to Europe, have been complied with, and I have been enabled to return the Orpheus to you without a moment's delay.[3]

A month after leaving St. Helena the *Discovery* overtook the convoy under escort of the *Sceptre*, Captain Essington. During the run her guns were rigged for action and the men were exercised at them daily. This made her a welcome addition to the convoy, which included a number of valuable Dutch prizes. Possibly to ease his conscience, Vancouver recorded that Captain Essington believed that the existence of a French safe-conduct in favor of his ships was very doubtful. Whether it existed or not, it was comforting to be under the protection of a convoy.

Just before the *Discovery* joined the convoy there was an unpleasant incident between Vancouver and Menzies, the botanist and surgeon. Short-handed in the *Discovery* after putting the prize crew in the *Macassar,* Vancouver placed one of Menzies' servants on regular watches working the ship. During a downpour of rain some of Menzies plant frames on deck were left uncovered and many of the plants he was taking back to England were damaged or destroyed. Menzies wanted Vancouver to punish the man, whose normal duty it was to look after the frames, but, when the captain found that he was carrying out the orders of the officer of the watch at the time, he took no action. Menzies complained, apparently rather vigorously, that he was being treated unfairly in the matter, and Vancouver placed him under arrest for insolence and contempt, a charge that Menzies later denied.[4] At the end of the voyage Vancouver recommended to the Admiralty that Menzies be court-martialed, and orders were prepared for trying him; but a month later, while winding up the *Discovery*'s affairs, Vancouver withdrew his charges after receiving an apology from Menzies, and the order was canceled.

Vancouver, like most sailors, apparently felt an intense affection for his ship and her boats. When a Dutch prize in the convoy made a distress signal the *Discovery* sent her cutter to investigate. The prize was sinking and was so far gone that she was abandoned and set on fire. As the *Discovery* was hoisting in her cutter afterward it was stove in and broken to pieces. This inspired one of the most moving passages in Vancouver's account of the voyage:

I do not recollect that my feelings ever suffered so much on any occasion of a similar nature, as at this moment. The cutter was the boat I had constantly used; in her I had travelled very many miles; in her I had repeatedly escaped from danger; she had always brought me safely home; and although she was but an inanimate conveniency, to which, it may possibly be thought, no affection could be attached, yet I felt myself under such an obligation for her services, that when she was dashed to pieces before my eyes an involuntary emotion suddenly seized my breast, and I was compelled to turn away to hide a weakness (for which though my own gratitude might find an apology) I should have thought improper to have publicly manifested.[5]

As the convoy approached the English Channel, the danger of meeting strong French raiders increased daily. For that reason, and because it was a valuable East India convoy, Captain Essington took it well clear of French waters and into the River Shannon on the western coast of Ireland. There it was to wait until stronger protection could be obtained for the final run to England. And there the *Discovery* anchored with the rest of the convoy on September 13, 1795.

Another misunderstanding with Menzies occurred just before the *Discovery* reached port. On the day before she reached St. Helena, Vancouver had called for all the journals of the officers and midshipmen as his instructions from the Admiralty required him to do. At that time Menzies evaded the demand by asking for more time in which to finish writing his journal. His own instructions for the voyage, prepared by Sir Joseph Banks, required that his journals and drawings be delivered to the secretary of state for home affairs. With the coast of Ireland in sight Vancouver issued a written order to Menzies to deliver his journals. The Scot, then under arrest and facing a court-martial, showed a stubborn streak. He noted that Vancouver's order was addressed to him as surgeon of the *Discovery*. In that capacity his only journal was the sick book, which he was ready to deliver at any time. As for his journals, drawings, and sketches as the botanist of the expedition, his original orders required him to deliver them to the secretary of state, and he felt that he was not authorized to deliver them to anyone else. All Vancouver could do was report to the Admiralty Menzies' refusal to give up the journals.

As soon as the ships were anchored, Captain Essington ordered Vancouver to proceed to London with his important Elphinstone dispatches. Leaving Lieutenant Baker, the first lieutenant, to sail the *Discovery* on the last leg of the voyage to England, Vancouver reached London a few days later. This did not end the voyage for him, as there was the task of settling the ship's affairs and disposing of her crew. The *Discovery* reached Deal, on the Strait of Dover, in mid-October, and Deptford, on the Thames, on October 20. There Vancouver rejoined her for the final work of closing out his voyage.

The *Chatham* reached Bahia late in July, where she found the *Sphinx* and twelve East Indiamen with General Clarke's troops embarked, preparing to sail for the Cape of Good Hope. Elphinstone's orders had already been received, making the *Chatham*'s own mission with the duplicates superfluous. Puget wanted to make a complete survey of the bay, but his short stay in the port permitted only a reconnaissance. Some of his men were showing early symptoms of scurvy, but he was able to purchase an abundance of salad greens, yams, pineapples, and citrus fruit to relieve the symptoms. Each man in the crew was served four oranges a day.

After a three-week stay in the port, the *Chatham* sailed alone for England and had an uneventful passage. She almost caught the *Discovery* again, for on October 16 she anchored at Plymouth, just one day after the *Discovery* reached Deal.[6]

CLOSE OF THE VOYAGE

Except to mapmakers who were already reproducing parts of Vancouver's map of the northwest coast of America[7] the return of the ships attracted very little public attention, for war news was being eagerly sought. *The London Chronicle,* on September 17, quoted the purser of a ship as reporting that Vancouver had joined the *Sceptre* convoy, but most of the news item dealt with Vancouver's report of military events at the Cape of Good Hope. The same newspaper noted the *Discovery*'s arrival at Deal on October 15 and the *Chatham*'s arrival at Plymouth the following day. In the latter case two short paragraphs gave a summary of the voyage; but the newswriters were much more interested in letters Puget brought from Bahia than in the ship's travels. The *Annual Register* reported the conclusion of the voyage in the following notice, dated September 24:

> The Discovery sloop of war, captain Vancouver, arrived at Limerick on the 13th inst. in company with the homeward bound East India Fleet, having

completely effected the object of her expedition, and made some important discoveries on the northwest coast of America. She sailed from England with 150 [*sic*] men on board, and such was the attention of the officers to their health, that only one died in the course of a very fatiguing voyage of four years. They speak in the highest terms of the inhabitants of the Sandwich Islands, from whom they experienced every possible courtesy and attention.[8]

And thus, after four years, six and one-half months, ended one of the most notable voyages in the annals of navigation. From the standpoint of distance traveled it was one of the longest, if not actually the longest, of the voyages on record to that time. The tracks of the ships have been plotted from positions given in Vancouver's *Voyage of Discovery* and from tables and positions given in journals of the expedition. On the basis of this plot it is estimated that the *Discovery* covered about sixty-five thousand miles during the voyage, some ten thousand miles more than the *Resolution* sailed in Cook's second voyage. Added to that should be the phenomenal performance of the small boats during the survey. From the various accounts of the boat expeditions and from a trace of the boats' tracks, it is estimated that they covered about ten thousand miles, with most of that distance under oars!

The ships were almost entirely upon their own resources, having been supplied just twice from the *Daedalus,* and this fact alone is ample proof of the resourcefulness, ingenuity, and seamanship of Vancouver and his officers. At Nootka, in California, and at Valparaiso they had some help from the Spaniards, but there was at these places no dockyard service, such as was needed for major repairs. Sails and ropes could be replaced only from their own stock of supplies, and careful conservation of those resources and constant repairs to the hulls of the ships were the only way in which they could be kept seaworthy enough to continue. There was much improvising; for example, toward the end of the voyage spare anchor cables were raveled out and converted to smaller ropes to replace rotten ropes in the rigging.

In the preservation of the health of the men, Vancouver's record compares very favorably with that of any navigator of the time. The only serious outbreak of scurvy that took place resulted from disobedience of his orders. The *Discovery* lost six men during the course of the entire voyage: one man died from disease, one was poisoned, one was an apparent suicide, and three were lost through accident. Vancouver's losses by death were about one-third the normal mortality rate in England at that time. The *Chatham* did not lose a man during the entire voyage.

When the *Discovery* reached Deptford, Vancouver rejoined her and spent about two weeks closing out her records, turning in her stores to the dockyard, and paying off and transferring her crew. One of his first concerns was for the future of his officers and midshipmen. Spelman Swaine and Thomas Manby began the voyage as master's mates, but both had passed their examinations for lieutenant, and during the voyage Vancouver had promoted them to be second and third lieutenants of the *Discovery* to fill vacancies. As they were to be transferred from the *Discovery*, he recommended to the Admiralty that their appointments be confirmed and that their commissions be dated as of the dates he had appointed them, an important advantage in fixing their seniority. The Lords of the Admiralty could find no precedent for such a concession and would only commission them as of the present date.

Understanding that an Admiralty order to transfer the *Discovery*'s men to another ship included his midshipmen and mates, Vancouver interceded for them in order that they might have the opportunity to take their examinations for lieutenant. This intercession was successful, for only two weeks later, in a letter concerning witnesses for the court-martial of the *Discovery*'s former carpenter, he mentioned "Lieutenant" Robert Barrie and "Lieutenant" Volant V. Ballard; one had been a master's mate and the other a midshipman on an earlier list. Vancouver also pleaded clemency for a seaman who had deserted from the *Alfred* and had voluntarily surrendered to him at Nootka in September, 1794. The man was entered on the *Discovery*'s rolls and proved to be a very good and sober seaman.

At the end of October the *Discovery* was ready to be decommissioned and delivered to the dockyard authorities. By November 3 all the formalities were completed and Vancouver went on half pay the next day, ending his active service in the navy. The next two months he spent in London. The final adjustment and clearance of his accounts required him to ask the Admiralty to approve such details as his issue of clothing to Kamehameha's white retainers and extra issues of grog for the boats' crews when on surveying trips.

In January, 1796, Vancouver was taking a well-earned rest at Bristol Hot Wells, a fashionable resort at the west coast seaport of Bristol. His chronic illness, so pronounced in the final year of the voyage, had continued to grow worse at home. His brother John, who helped in the preparation of his journal for publication, wrote in his own preface to that work:

> Ever since Captain Vancouver's return to England, his health has been in a very debilitated state, and his constitution was evidently so much impaired by the arduous services in which, from his earliest youth, he had been constantly engaged, that his friends dared to indulge but little hope that he would continue many years amongst them.[9]

The vacation was interrupted by a letter from the Admiralty asking for Vancouver's answer to a Spanish complaint that he had refused to reimburse the viceroy of Mexico for the expenses of the deserters at Monterey in 1794. Vancouver was annoyed at this interruption to his rest and pointed out testily to the Lords, "The whole of the said transactions have been transmitted by me at three different periods for their Lordships' information."[10] Once more he reviewed his actions at Monterey in detail. His explanation was apparently satisfactory, for the Admiralty agreed to pay the charges, and no further complaints were received from the Spaniards.

By the end of March, 1796, Vancouver was back in London ready to begin the last large project in connection with his voyage, the preparation of his journal for publication. He asked the Admiralty to authorize the return of his journals and drawings and to pay the expenses of engravers for the charts and plates required. The Admiralty approved the request, but for some unexplained reason Vancouver was not notified of that action for several months. Meanwhile he looked about for a place to settle himself where he could concentrate on his work. He selected the little

215

village of Petersham, in the borough of Richmond, Surrey, a few miles up the Thames from London. At that time it was an aristocratic village and the home of many prominent families in England. The old "Star and Garter," on the side of Richmond Hill overlooking Petersham, was then the most famous hotel in England, and Vancouver stopped there before he moved into Petersham. According to local tradition and a story handed down by word of mouth, it was at that hotel that he was supposed to have said, "In all my travels I never clept eyes on a more beautiful spot than this. Here would I live and here I would die." [11]

The reader has already seen enough of Vancouver's written words to judge whether he might have spoken those words, for they are certainly unlike anything that he wrote. On the other hand, the view from Richmond Hill up the valley of the Thames and of the village of Petersham lying below is a charming one, and it appears today much as it must have looked in 1796. Little is known of Vancouver's life there, but that he lived in the village is certain, for most of his letters after July, 1796, are dated from Petersham.

He was already at work on his journal in July when he again asked the Admiralty to approve the expense of engraving the charts and plates to be included in his account of the voyage. He pointed out that in his expedition there had been no extra expense for civilian draftsmen or an astronomer, such as had accompanied Cook. He understood that three thousand pounds had been granted for the publication of the account of Cook's third voyage and hinted that he should have the same. As for his personal finances he had received no pay since December, 1790, and he had been put to considerable personal expense for entertaining Spanish officials during the voyage. He had applied to the Home Office for reimbursement for those expenses, but there was little prospect of its being granted. He therefore requested a sufficient grant-in-aid to enable him to do a more finished work than his private means would permit. The Lords advised him that they would authorize the employment of engravers for the plates but that they would decide which views and plates would actually be engraved. With this assurance Vancouver settled down in earnest at his work.

15

The Camelford Affair
and Vancouver as a Disciplinarian
(1796-97)

BARON CAMELFORD

The next outstanding episode in Vancouver's life was a scandal which further damaged his health and affected his career. Among the three midshipmen discharged for disciplinary reasons from Vancouver's ships in the Pacific and sent home in the *Daedalus* from Hawaii in 1794 was a young nobleman, the Honorable Thomas Pitt. Pitt was the son of Baron Camelford, a prominent member of the great Pitt family who was a first cousin of the prime minister, William Pitt; of the Earl of Chatham, then First Lord of the Admiralty; and of the wife of the foreign minister, Lord Grenville. It would have been hard to find a youth in England with more influential or powerful family connections than the Honorable Thomas Pitt.

The *Daedalus* arrived in Australia in April, 1794, where Pitt learned that he had succeeded to the title of Baron Camelford. He sailed to India and at Malacca joined the *Resistance,* Captain Edward Pakenham; he was appointed a lieutenant and for a time paid strict attention to his duties, but he was summarily dismissed from that ship in November, 1795. He returned to England by September, 1796, and challenged Vancouver to a duel for alleged mistreatment received while serving in the *Discovery*.[1] Although

Vancouver was accused of flogging Pitt, there is no surviving record in any of the journals of a specific incident in which this occurred, and the nature of Pitt's offense and of the punishment administered has never been entirely clarified. Vancouver's reply to the challenge in 1796 was that his actions were necessary for the preservation of discipline and that Camelford had brought the punishment upon himself by his own misconduct.

Vancouver offered to submit the affair to the judgment of any flag officer in the navy, and if it was decided that he should give satisfaction he would then take part in the duel. To the volatile young Camelford, Vancouver's offer was unacceptable. ". . . As fighting was more agreeable to his lordship than expostulation, this mode of settling the dispute was declined, and [he] threatened personally to insult the Captain." [2]

With his offer thus rejected, and threatened with personal injury and insult, Vancouver decided to seek the protection of the law. He was on his way to the Lord Chancellor's office in London with his brother Charles when he met Camelford on Conduit Street. The young nobleman created a scene and attacked Vancouver with his cane, aiming several blows at him which were deflected by Charles. After that scene Lord Loughborough, the Lord Chancellor, sent for Camelford. The young man appeared at his house in a rage but was slowly calmed down and was bound by surety to keep the peace.

The incident was made the subject of a bitter caricature dedicated to the flag officers of the navy by James Gillray and entitled, "The Caneing in Conduit Street." Gillray was the most eminent English caricaturist of that day, and his products were bought eagerly throughout Europe. In the caricature Vancouver is pictured as rather short and very fat. Over his shoulder is a feather cloak with the caption, "The Present from the king of Owyhee to George III, forgot to be delivered." Gillray's source for this jibe is not known; Kamehameha's feather cloak, given to Vancouver as a present for King George in 1793, was presented to the king by the Duke of Portland in 1797. Why Vancouver delayed so long in delivering it and why he was not present at the ceremony of presentation was not explained; his illness or this unpleasant incident may have been the reason.

Dangling from Vancouver's sword in the caricature is a paper inscribed, "List of those disgraced during the voyage—Put under arrest—all the ship's Crew—Put in irons, every Gentleman on Board—Broke, every man of honor and Spirit—Promoted, Spies, etc." Under Vancouver's foot is a paper with the motto, "Every officer is the Guardian of his own Honor." In Charles's coat pocket is a paper labeled "Chas Rearcover, Letter to be published after the parties are bound to keep Peace." Vancouver is pictured as a coward, and the effect of the caricature is a violent indictment of him as an individual and as a representative of naval authority.

This incident, and the resulting inquiry into Vancouver's conduct, further weakened his health and ended his career in the navy. As for Camelford, he developed from a hot-tempered and quarrelsome youth into an overbearing and insulting officer whose appearance bore "evident marks of insanity." [3] After many escapades as a naval officer, including the killing of a fellow lieutenant in an alleged mutiny,[4] his name was stricken from the commander's list of the navy, and the last five years of his life were marked by adventures, disputes, and duels that made him notorious. His career was brought to a violent end in March, 1804, when he was killed in a duel.

Vancouver's judgment must be criticized, for in flogging a gentleman, if that is indeed what he did, he violated the social code of the time. Nevertheless it can be seen that Camelford's character was without doubt one to arouse anger in a superior officer, and he was probably guilty of insubordination more than once.

INVESTIGATION

In view of Camelford's position, some sort of action against Vancouver was inevitable. Another reason for investigation was the seriousness of the charge against Vancouver, for flogging a midshipman was almost without precedent. The regulations for the navy forbade a captain to strike an officer, and although midshipmen were not formally officers they were candidates for commissions and were, socially, members of the officer class.

There was neither a court of inquiry nor a court-martial in Vancouver's case, and a full record of the investigation that took place is not available. That some official action was taken, however, is evident. A contemporary biographer of Camelford wrote, "[The] affair was . . . left to legal jurisdiction to settle." [5] At Petersham, in March, 1797, when Vancouver was so sick that his brother had to write for him, he wrote in a letter to his agent in London, ". . . Ascertaining and refuting the *falsehood* in Question is an indispensable duty, which I owe to all those, whom at the time I had the honor to command. . . ." [6] In the same letter he referred to an investigation apparently then under way: "If the investigation is to stand over until I can personally attend to it, most likely the whole business will be settled long ere that period arrive, as . . . it will be some months before I shall be able to venture a visit to London."

Another indication that an investigation was made into Vancouver's relationship with Pitt is the mystifying absence of any mention of Pitt in most of the surviving journals and correspondence relating to the voyage to the Northwest. Still intact are Puget's and Bell's reports that Pitt was transferred to the *Daedalus* in February, 1794, but these reports give no further details. Many of the journals end in February, 1794, when Camelford was discharged from the *Discovery,* and Menzies' record, up to that time a detailed and important report, is missing after that date. Two journals delivered to the Admiralty at the end of the voyage are not now in the archives. One is that of Joseph Whidbey, master of the *Discovery;* it was one of the official complete records of the ship. The other is the journal of Robert Barrie, one of Camelford's closest friends. In the journal of H. M. Orchard, clerk of the *Discovery,* were recorded all punishments meted out. The pages of this journal are missing for the periods from May 27 to June 10 and from August 16 to September 6, 1793. Menzies wrote on August 28, 1793, of "punishments [that] were inflicted on the Discovery of a very unpleasant nature." [7] This was soon after Vancouver returned from the boat expedition on which there was a skirmish with the Indians, and Camelford had been a member of that expedition. In a letter to Evan Nepean at Whitehall in January, 1793, Vancouver wrote that the conduct of "Mr. T. Pit has been too bad for me to represent in any one respect." [8] Aside from these meager clues there is no record left of what offenses

Camelford committed that resulted in the alleged floggings, or when they occurred. The absence of any detailed report of Pitt's actions suggests that each journal has been carefully searched for any item that might have a bearing on his case and that such items have been removed to be used in some way. On the cover sheet of the personal journals now in the Public Record Office is a penciled note, "Rec'd 25th Oct 1802—W"; this indicates that they were returned to the central office after several years' absence.

Vancouver's conduct during the voyage, therefore, came under a most searching investigation, which included the examination of all the journals kept on the voyage; and he was in spite of this never formally charged with undue severity. The Camelford incident, however, has been the basis for describing him as a harsh and brutal officer, and a modern reader of the journals kept on the voyage might readily concur in this description. A more realistic judgment requires a review of disciplinary measures in the naval service of the time.

PUNISHMENTS IN THE NAVY

One of England's leading historians of naval life holds that the first criticism of the eighteenth-century naval captain is that he was a bully, and that his conduct was marked by tyranny and brutality.[9] A dozen lashes with the cat-o'-nine-tails was the punishment prescribed in the King's Regulations for most offenses, and the slightest offense was likely to draw the lash from a capricious captain. Punishment for especially serious crimes was, according to the Regulations, to be decided upon by the Admiralty in formal court-martial; but many captains, far from home and the naval courts, administered severe punishments, which often consisted of unlimited flogging or running the gantlet through a double line of the crew armed with tarred ropes.

Although officers and men seemed to accept flogging as a matter of course, rarely discussing the practice in their journals, mutinies are occasionally reported. Death was the penalty for mutiny, yet during the 1790's seamen frequently became desperate enough to rebel for better food and better pay. Complaints in connection with cruel treatment were usually directed at brutal excesses on the part of officers, rather than at the legal regulations concerning punishment. In some cases exceptionally tyrannical captains were forced from their ships after formal inquiry by the Admiralty, but the naval courts as a rule defended severity of discipline on the part of officers.

Vancouver, with an independent command in the Pacific and unable to apply to the Admiralty for court-martial without long delay, frequently awarded more than the dozen lashes specified in the Regulations for common offenses. For drunkenness, especially when combined with neglect of duty or insolence and contempt, he delivered as much as five dozen lashes; and theft, always a serious offense at sea, was met with heavy punishment. One seaman received a total of 72 lashes for theft, administered on two occasions, and one of the marines received a total of 144 lashes on four occasions. For striking his superior officer, an offense that would have earned an extremely severe penalty in the courts, one of the carpenter's mates received 72 lashes. One of the most severe punishments was that of the seaman who deserted at Monterey in 1792. His was an offense that would have called for a court-martial and heavy penalty from the Admiralty; from Vancouver he received a total of 144 lashes.

In the *Discovery* in 1795 there were fifteen instances of flogging; in 1792 the number was thirty-five; in 1793 there were thirty-three instances; and in 1794 there were twelve. This record is not unlike those of Vancouver's former commanders; it shows him to have been a strict and taut captain but not a capricious or brutal one. Several incidents reveal that he was at times lenient and more than customarily concerned for the welfare of his men. He excused his cook for disobedience in connection with the outbreak of scurvy near Valparaiso; he interceded with the Admiralty on behalf of the deserter who gave himself up at Nootka; and at the end of the voyage he went out of his way to secure proper recognition of the services of his officers and men.

In none of the journals of the expedition has there been found any suggestion of a tendency to mutiny, and friction between Vancouver and his officers was settled in most cases without serious consequences. Only one man, the carpenter of the *Discovery*, was brought to trial by court-martial. Thomas Manby incurred Vancouver's wrath early in the voyage, but he was later promoted to master of the *Chatham* and third lieutenant of the *Discovery*. Vancouver's relations with Menzies were seriously strained at times, but they were cleared up without the need for formal action. Vancouver was inclined to be reticent and aloof. Puget reported, "[Since] Captain Vancouver's Intentions, however trifling in themselves are always under a seal we can form no judgment of the present plan." [10] Bell was critical of Vancouver's orders regulating conduct on shore at Tahiti and Hawaii, but had he been informed of the captain's reasons for issuing such orders he might have proved more understanding. Yet such reticence on the part of a captain was not unusual in the eighteenth-century navy; indeed, it was the exception for a commander to take his subordinates into his confidence.

The charges of tyranny and brutality that were lodged against Vancouver in 1796 grew entirely out of his relations with Camelford, and his subsequent reputation was affected by the criticism of Sir Joseph Banks, who had formed an early dislike for him. The record of the voyage shows Vancouver to have been an able and conscientious officer, whose ill health and occasional outbursts of temper did not prevent him from working as hard as his men or from taking a personal interest in their health and welfare.

16

Conclusion

VANCOUVER'S DEATH

WHILE THE furor over the Camelford affair was at its height, Vancouver was working for his share of the prize money for the *Macassar,* the Dutch prize taken at St. Helena in 1795. The problem was, according to his letter to the Admiralty, that she had been taken before the actual declaration of hostilities and had been condemned to the crown, and only a portion of the prize money was to be awarded to the *Discovery* and the *Chatham.*[1] Admiral Elphinstone also claimed an admiral's share as commander in chief at the time of the capture. He was not actually Vancouver's commander in chief, but few admirals passed by any chance for a share of prize money. Vancouver appealed to the Admiralty for a ruling on the point to be given to the Treasury, and the matter was eventually settled in his favor.

The rest of the year 1797 Vancouver spent at Petersham working on his journal and supervising the engraving of the plates for the publication of his account. In this work he was assisted by his brother John, but his correspondence at the time shows that he was most meticulous in seeing to every detail himself. With the Admiralty's approval Vancouver engaged some of the finest engravers in England to prepare the plates for the work, and the results are among the best illustrations in any eighteenth-century

224

account of a voyage. Among the engravers were John Landseer, father of the painter Edwin Landseer, James Fittler, James Heath, and Benjamin T. Pouncy, all well known. Other equally expert cartographic engravers made the plates for the navigational charts and views. The scenic engravings were made from sketches done on the voyage by members of the expedition. Most of the sketches were by John Sykes, master's mate in the *Discovery;* others were by Harry Humphreys, also a master's mate in the *Discovery,* and by Thomas Heddington, midshipman in the *Chatham* and the youngest member of the expedition, only fifteen years old at the start of the voyage.

The Lords of the Admiralty kept a watchful eye on the progress of the project. One of Vancouver's letters in September, 1797, reveals how carefully he prepared every detail. Commenting on some proofs of plates submitted for the inspection of the Lords he noted:

These proofs you will observe are not titled, and it is therefore necessary you should be made acquainted that the lettering, or writing, of copper plates is a distinct business of itself; which as I consider will be better done by one person I wait until I have received all the plates, in order for it to be executed at home under my own inspection.[2]

By February, 1798, all the prospective plates were finished and Vancouver submitted an itemized list of the cost of the various engravings. He was not sure that the Lords had approved the view of Nootka which he included, but he considered it to be essential. He was proud of the fact that the charge for six plates of views of headlands useful in navigation was only £371, "considered fair for Mr. Carey's estimate was £520." [3] The total charge to the government for all the engravings was £1038 15s. 0d.

Still another activity in which Vancouver was engaged late in 1797 was negotiating with the Admiralty for payment for the nearly five years of arduous service on the voyage to the Northwest. He had received no pay from the time he took command of the *Discovery* until October, 1797. He was then paid for the time spent on the voyage at the rate of six shillings, sixpence, per day, but he asked that this be increased to eight shillings since he had acted as purser of the ship. The Admiralty, finding a precedent in the case of Captain Bligh, finally ordered that he be paid at the higher rate, but the long delay in paying him was not explained. This episode is an excellent example of why an English naval officer of that day had to have independent means in order to serve his country.

During the last few months of his life, Vancouver was preparing to settle in Berkshire and was negotiating for the purchase of a house there. His last letter of report to the Admiralty was dated March 29, 1798; in it was enclosed Landseer's bill for engraving. By then he must have realized that he had not long to live, for a month later he drew up a new will. He died at Petersham on May 12, 1798,[4] and was buried in the churchyard of St. Peter's Church, Petersham, on May 18. There is no record of the cause of his death. It has been suggested that he suffered from tuberculosis,[5] but to this author the pattern of his energetic activity and recurring relapses and the tendency to sudden outbursts of temper seem more nearly to conform to an improperly treated hyperthyroid condition.

Vancouver had never married. In his will he left a small sum to his agent, small annuities to two of his sisters and his brother Charles, and the bulk of his estate to his brother John.

THE VOYAGE OF DISCOVERY

At the time of George Vancouver's death five books of the six projected for the account of his voyage had been completed by him and were ready for publication, and more than half of the sixth book was also ready. John, with the help of Puget, finished the part that covered the passage around Cape Horn and home, faithfully following Vancouver's journal. The Admiralty had underwritten the cost of the work, but its preparation was not without personal expense to George Vancouver. As late as January, 1798, he had applied to his agent for an additional credit of £200 to meet incidental expenses connected with the books.

The *Voyage of Discovery to the North Pacific Ocean and round the World* was published in 1798 in three quarto volumes of six books, with a separate atlas. That it was received with keen interest is indicated by the long reviews that greeted its publication. The *Annual Register* devoted twenty pages to it, summarizing the events of the voyage and challenging Vancouver's claim to have proved conclusively that a Northwest Passage did not exist within the limits of his survey. Stressing the fact that Vancouver had at first missed the Columbia River, the reviewer concluded that it was by no means yet proved that a navigable Northwest Passage did not exist.

Another reviewer, writing in the *Navy Chronicle,* was much more enthusiastic about the work. He felt that it should be ranked with the very best accounts of voyages, and praised the quality, arrangement, and substance of Vancouver's work.[6]

The *Voyage of Discovery* is a fitting monument to the officers and men who accomplished the voyage itself. There are 1,440 pages in the original edition. Much of the text consists of long descriptions of the natives of the Pacific, their customs and way of life, and of the countryside seen in the course of the survey. The more than three hundred names assigned to headlands, mountains, waterways, and other features of the Pacific coast of North America honor the leading figures in English public life as well as Vancouver's own officers and midshipmen.[7]

In writing the final draft Vancouver followed his daily rough journal very closely, and summaries of letters were inserted at the time they were written or came to his attention. Comparison of these summaries with the original letters shows that he omitted nothing of importance in abridging them. Unlike the accounts of Cook's voyages, which were edited by others, this was written by the captain himself, with assistance from his brother. The original manuscript of the *Voyage of Discovery,* which confirms this, was located by George Godwin among the unindexed manuscripts in the British Museum.[8]

A six-volume second edition of the *Voyage of Discovery* was published in 1801. The plates and illustrations in that edition are inferior to those in the first edition, for the copper plates from the first edition were stolen, according to the publisher's foreword. A German edition of the work appeared in two volumes in 1799-1800, a two-volume Swedish edition in 1800, a French edition in 1802, and a Russian edition in 1827-28. Copies of all these editions are now in the Pacific Northwest Collection of the University of Washington Library at Seattle.[9]

VANCOUVER'S PLACE IN HISTORY

Vancouver died obscurely, probably bitter over his treatment and the notoriety of the Camelford affair. The *Annual Register* made no note of his death, and his obituary in the *Gentleman's Magazine* was hardly flattering: "At Petersham, Surrey, Capt. Geo. Vancouver, of the royal navy, lately returned from a voyage round the world; an account of which, printed at the expense of the Board of Admiralty, is now ready for publication." [10]

At the time of his death England was deep in the war with France, with a growing coalition on the continent against her. The great Napoleonic Wars were to absorb England's attention for the next seventeen years, and an explorer and his account of a voyage in the Pacific could not attract the attention that they might in quieter times. An indication of this lack of interest is given in the following letter, published in the *Navy Chronicle* in 1805:

Mr. Editor:

During a walk through the beautiful meadows that extend from Richmond, I lately visited the churchyard of Petersham, that I might mark the spot where one of our latest Circumnavigators, Vancouver, was buried; and I must acknowledge my surprise when, after some time spent in the search, I found only a plain common Grave, with this singular inscription: CAPTAIN GEORGE VANCOUVER DIED IN THE YEAR 1798. Neither the day of his death, nor his having been an Officer in His Majesty's Navy, are mentioned. This singular Tombstone appears on the south side of the Churchyard.

S. [11]

The same simple headstone marks his grave today, although it is now well tended and is remembered annually by the people of British Columbia, who helped rebuild St. Peter's Church after the Second World War. Vancouver's family was well-to-do and could have afforded a more elaborate stone, and it may be presumed that the simple headstone was his own request.

Vancouver's contributions to history can be divided into two aspects, political and geographical. At Nootka he conscientiously carried out his government's directions as he understood them, aware of plans for colonizing the Northwest and unwilling to compromise with Quadra without further orders from the Admiralty. Although some of his superiors criticized him for not accepting Quadra's terms, it was recognized that he did not do so because of the nature of his instructions.[12]

At Hawaii, Vancouver's negotiations with Kamehameha were based on his own vision of an England someday strongly established in the Pacific, and he did a thorough job in laying the groundwork for that imperial position. While England never acted upon the cession of Hawaii, skillfully arranged by Vancouver, the right was reserved to assert England's claim in case any other country showed an acquisitive interest in the islands. This position may have kept Russia or France from trying to seize them.

Vancouver's survey exerted a direct influence on the settlement of the Oregon Boundary Dispute in 1846. A treaty between the United States and Spain in 1819 provided for the cession of Florida, fixed the western boundary of the Louisiana Purchase, and transferred to the United States any Spanish claims to territory in the Pacific north of latitude 42° North (the present boundary between Oregon and California). Thus the United States acquired, or claimed to acquire, Spain's rights under the Nootka Sound Convention. In 1818 England and the United States fixed the boundary between Canada and the United States, west of the Lake of the Woods as far as the Rocky Mountains, along the forty-ninth parallel of latitude. They were unable to agree upon a line west of the Rockies. The United States claimed the Columbia River watershed by virtue of Gray's discovery in 1792. England claimed the same region, basing her claim on Vancouver's discoveries and Broughton's exploration of the Columbia River. The United States advocated a boundary along the forty-ninth parallel all the way to the Pacific, but England was willing to allow the boundary to follow that parallel only to the headwaters of the Columbia; it was then to follow the river to the sea.

From 1820 to 1846 there developed, with rising heat on the American side at least, the Oregon Boundary Dispute. In 1824 the United States, because of its claim to former Spanish territory, negotiated a treaty with Russia, fixing latitude 54° 40′ North as the dividing line of their respective interests in the coastal region. A year later England concluded a similar treaty with Russia. "54-40 or Fight" became a campaign slogan in the American presidential campaign of 1844, and a great deal of propaganda was published about the issue. The prolonged and bitter dispute was settled by a treaty in 1846 which stipulated that the boundary was to follow the forty-ninth parallel to tidewater, then run in a winding line through the San Juan Islands and out to sea through the Strait of Juan de Fuca, avoiding a division of Vancouver Island.

Vancouver's name is linked with the Oregon Boundary Dispute because of his survey and because his *Voyage of Discovery* and charts were practically the only accurate source of information about the region. In 1844 Robert Greenhow, librarian of the State Department, published a history of Oregon and California which was in reality a defense of the American position in the great dispute.[13] It was written at the time of the greatest political furor over the issue. Legal arguments over the meaning of the Nootka Sound Convention had an important place in the dispute, and Vancouver's position in the local negotiations at Nootka received a searching analysis. Greenhow charged that Vancouver deliberately misrepresented the statements of the American captains Gray and Ingraham concerning the Martinez-Colnett incident in 1789. The book was highly critical of Vancouver, as might be expected in a brief of the American position in the midst of the dispute, and was an effort to discredit Vancouver's work.

In 1846 Travers Twiss, a noted English international jurist, published a defense of the British side of the dispute.[14] More moderate and legalistic than Greenhow's book, it was naturally favorable to Vancouver's work. Twiss wrote:

> The important services rendered to navigation and science by Vancouver and Lieutenant Broughton, were fully acknowledged by Mr. Gallatin in the negotiations of 1846; yet all these, it is contended by the Commissioners of the United States, are entirely superseded by Captain Gray having first entered the mouth of the chief river of the country.[15]

In this passage Twiss neatly summed up the substance of twenty years of negotiations as far as maritime discovery and exploration were concerned. The ultimate settlement was based upon so many involved issues that it is doubtful that the issue of the first discovery of the Columbia River was nearly as important as is indicated by the space it occupied in the negotiations. Without the solid foundation of Vancouver's monumental work as a base for the British position, however, it is conceivable that the northern boundary of Oregon might have been fixed at latitude 54° 40′ North, and Canada today would have no Pacific shores.

Vancouver's geographical accomplishments have received very little criticism. Most of the criticism expressed has been to the effect that he missed noting the larger rivers of the Pacific slope. This was not the case, and the fact that he did not emphasize them is readily explained when it is recalled that he was searching for a navigable passage, not for ordinary rivers. His failure to notice the Columbia River the first time he passed it was seized upon by his American critics, who had political motives, as a weakness in his work; but most modern historians and geographers have recognized and marveled at the magnitude and accuracy of the survey, considering the somewhat primitive equipment used.

Early British historians of exploration to some extent neglected Vancouver in their extreme admiration for Cook, his predecessor. Robert Kerr, who from 1811 to 1824 compiled an eighteen-volume history of voyages and travels purporting to be a complete history of navigation, discovery, and commerce, did not mention Vancouver or his voyage.[16] Kerr obtained some of his material from Sir Joseph Banks, and ignoring Vancouver's voyage must have been deliberate, a reflection of the antipathy of some toward Vancouver. Alexander Findlay, a compiler of sailing directions in the mid-nineteenth century, found that Vancouver lacked the varied talents and enterprise of Cook. Findlay conceded, however, that Vancouver "may be said to be the discoverer of much of the coast." [17]

Modern British historians and geographers have been more generous in their praise of Vancouver. Edward Heawood, the standard authority on eighteenth-century exploration, considered his survey the most arduous that any navigator had undertaken.[18] J. N. L. Baker, another modern British historian of geography, recognized the magnitude of Vancouver's work and thought that he had all but been forgotten because he did nothing to gain notoriety.[19]

The fullest recognition and praise have come from those who have had occasion to check his work in detail. Lieutenant Charles Wilkes, who headed a United States naval exploring expedition in the Pacific from 1838 to 1842, resurveyed Puget Sound in 1841. He marveled at the accuracy of Vancouver's work and found his descriptions of the bays and the countryside so realistic that it was hard to believe they had been written half a century before.[20] George Davidson, who spent many years with the United States Coast and Geodetic Survey and compiled sailing directions for Alaska in 1869, once told Professor Edmond S. Meany that he had been over all Vancouver's work on the Pacific Coast and considered him to be "a great big man." [21] William H. Dall, an early Alaskan explorer, stated in 1870 that Vancouver's explorations "have not been excelled by any other navigator," [22] and found in the 1880's that Vancouver was still the most trustworthy authority on Alaskan waters.

To compare Vancouver with Cook, as nineteenth-century British historians were so apt to do, means comparing two men with different purposes and methods. Cook was primarily interested in making discoveries rather than in carefully mapping or describing them; he combed the South Pacific in great sweeps, discovering many new lands in a wide unknown area. Vancouver, on the other hand, searched tenaciously for an entrance into a great land mass, of which the general location was already known. His idea of starting at a point known to be on the continent and following the continental shore line until he found the Northwest Passage, or proved it to be nonexistent, was praiseworthy in its simplicity. It is likely that he was prouder of proving the absence of a Northwest Passage within the limits of his survey than he was of the map that resulted from the search. This thorough investigation of a single area distinguishes him from Cook, the wide-ranging explorer.

The cloud on Vancouver's character, stemming from his treatment of the troublemaker Camelford, deprived him of the recogni-

232

tion he deserved and banished him to near oblivion until modern times. His most pronounced trait was an outstanding industry and capacity for work which enabled him to carry out the great survey with tenacity in spite of failing health. His energy, tight discipline, and meticulous attention to detail, all characteristics of a conscientious officer, were rewarded with respect by most of his officers and men, as well as by modern students of naval exploration.

Appendix

THE INSTRUCTIONS FOR THE VOYAGE.[1]

By the Commissioners for executing the office of Lord High Admiral of Great-Britain and Ireland, &c.

The King having judged it expedient, that an expedition should be immediately undertaken for acquiring a more complete knowledge, than has yet been obtained, of the northwest coast of America; and, the sloop you command, together with the Chatham armed tender, (the Lieutenant commanding which, has been directed to follow your orders) having been equipped for that service; you are, in pursuance of His Majesty's pleasure, signified to us by Lord Grenville, one of His principal Secretaries of State, hereby required and directed, to proceed, without loss of time, with the said sloop and tender, to the Sandwich islands in the north pacific ocean, where you are to remain during the next winter; employing yourself very diligently in the examination and further survey of the said islands; and, as soon as the weather shall be favorable, (which may be expected to be in february, or at latest in march, 1792) you are to repair to the north-west coast of America, for the purpose of acquiring a more complete knowledge of it, as above mentioned.

It having been agreed, by the late convention between His Majesty and the Catholic King, (a printed copy of which you will receive herewith) that the buildings and tracts of land, situated on the north-west coast above mentioned, or on islands adjacent thereto, of which the subjects of His Britannic Majesty were dispossessed about the month of april, 1789, by a Spanish officer, shall be restored to the said British subjects, the court of Spain has agreed to send orders, for that purpose to its officers in that part of the world; but, as the particular specification of the parts to be restored may still require some further time, it is intended that the King's orders, for this purpose, shall be sent out to the Sandwich Islands, by a vessel to be employed to carry thither a further store of provisions for the sloop and armed tender above mentioned, which it is meant shall sail from this country in time to reach those islands in the course of next winter.

234

If, therefore, in consequence of the arrangement to be made with the court of Spain, it should hereafter be determined that you should proceed, in the first instance, to Nootka, or elsewhere, in order to receive, from the Spanish officers, such lands or buildings as are to be restored to the British subjects; orders, to that effect, will be sent out by the vessel above mentioned. But, if no such orders should be received by you previous to the end of january, 1792, you are not to wait for them at the Sandwich islands, but to proceed, in such course as you may judge most expedient for the examination of the coast above mentioned, comprized between latitude 60° north and 30° north.

In which examination the principal objects which you are to keep in view, are,

1st, The acquiring accurate information with respect to the nature and extent of any water-communication which may tend, in any considerable degree, to facilitate an intercourse, for the purpose of commerce, between the north-west coast, and the country upon the opposite side of the continent, which are inhabited or occupied by His Majesty's subjects.

2dly, The ascertaining, with as much precision as possible, the number, extent, and situation of any settlements which have been made within the limits above mentioned, by any European nation, and the time when such settlement was first made.

With respect to the first object, it would be of great importance if it should be found that, by means of any considerable inlets of the sea, or even of large rivers, communicating with the lakes in the interior of the continent, such an intercourse, as hath already been mentioned, could be established; it will therefore be necessary, for the purpose of ascertaining this point, that the survey should be so conducted, as not only to ascertain the general line of the seacoast, but also the direction and extent of all such considerable inlets, whether made by arms of the sea, or by the mouths of large rivers, as may be likely to lead to, or facilitate, such communication as is above described.

This being the principal object of the examination, so far as relates to that part of the subject, it necessarily follows, that a considerable degree of discretion must be left, and is therefore left to you, as to the means of executing the service which His Majesty has in view; but, as far as any general instructions can here be given on the subject, it seems desirable that, in order to avoid any unnecessary loss of time, you should not, and are therefore hereby required and directed not to pursue any inlet or river further than it shall appear to be navigable by vessels of such burthen as might safely navigate the pacific ocean: but, as the navigation of such inlets or rivers, to the extent here stated, may possibly require that you should proceed further than it might be safe for the sloop you command to go, you are, in such case, to take command of the armed tender in person, at all such times, and in such situations as you shall judge it necessary and expedient.

The particular course of the survey must depend on the different circumstances which may arise in the execution of a service of this nature; it is, however, proper that you should, and you are therefore hereby required and directed to pay a particular attention to the examination of the supposed straits of Juan de Fuca, said to be situated between 48° and 49° north latitude, and to lead to an opening through which the sloop Washington is reported to have passed in 1789, and to have come out again to the northward of Nootka. The discovery of a near communication between any such sea or strait, and any river running into, or from the lake of the woods, would be particularly useful.

If you should fail of discovering any such inlet, as is above mentioned, to the southward of Cook's river, there is the greatest probability that it will be found that the said river rises in some of the lakes already known to the Canadian traders, and to the servants of the Hudson's bay company; which point it would, in that case, be material to ascertain; and you are, therefore, to endeavour to ascertain accordingly, with as much precision as the circumstances existing at the time may allow: but the discovery of any similar communication more to the southward (should any such exist) would be more advantageous for the purposes of commerce, and should, therefore, be preferably attended to, and you are, therefore, to give it a preferable attention accordingly.

With respect to the second object above mentioned, it is probable that more particular instructions will be given you by the vessel to be sent to the Sandwich islands as aforesaid; but, if not, you are to be particularly careful in the execution of that, and every other part of the service with which you are entrusted, to avoid, with the utmost caution, the giving any ground of jealousy or complaint to the subjects of His Catholic Majesty; and, if you should fall in with any Spanish ships employed on any service similar to that which is hereby committed to you, you are to afford to the officer commanding such ships every possible degree of assistance and information, and to offer to him, that you, and he, should make to each other, reciprocally, a free and unreserved communication of all plans and charts of discoveries made by you and him in your respective voyages.

If, in the course of any part of this service, you, or the people under your command, should meet with the subjects or vessels of any other power or state, you and they are to treat them in the most friendly manner, and to be careful not to do any thing which may give occasion to any interruption of that peace which now happily subsists between His Majesty and all other powers.

The whole of the survey above mentioned (if carried out with a view to the objects before stated, without too minute and particular an examination of the detail of the different parts of the coast laid down by it) may, as it is understood, probably be completed in the summers of 1792 and 1793; and you are hereby required and directed to repair accordingly, to the Sandwich islands; and, during your stay there, you are to endeavour to complete any part which may be unfinished of your examination of those islands.

After the conclusion of your survey in the summer of 1793, you are, if the state and circumstances of the sloop and tender under your command will admit of it, to return to England by Cape Horn, (for which the season will then probably be favorable); repairing to Spithead, where you are to remain until you receive further order; and sending to our secretary an account of your arrival and proceedings.

It seems doubtful, at present, how far the time may admit of your making any particular examination of the western coast of South America; but, if it should be practicable, you are to begin such examination from the south point of the island of Chiloe, which is in about 44° south latitude; and you are, in that case, to direct your attention to ascertaining what is the most southern Spanish settlement on that coast, and what harbours there are south of that settlement.

In the execution of every part of this service, it is very material that you should use, and you are therefore hereby strictly charged to use every possible care to avoid disputes with the natives of any of the parts where you may touch, and to be particularly attentive to endeavour, by a judicious distribution of the presents, (which have been put on board the sloop and tender under your command, by order of Lord Grenville) and by all other means, to conciliate their friendship and confidence. Given under our hands the 8th of March, 1791.

To	Chatham.
George Vancouver, Esq.	Rd. Hopkins.
commander of his Majesty's	Hood.
sloop the Discovery,	J.T. Townshend.
At Falmouth.	
By command of their Lordships.	
Ph. Stephens.	

ADDITIONAL INSTRUCTIONS.

By the Commissioners for executing the office of Lord High Admiral of Great-Britain and Ireland, &c.

Lieutenant Hergest, commanding the Daedalus transport, (by whom you will receive this) being instructed to put himself under your command, and to follow your orders for his further proceedings; you are hereby required and directed, to take him, and the said transport, under your command accordingly; receiving from her the provisions and stores intended for the use of the sloop you command, and the Chatham armed tender, or such parts thereof as the said ship and tender shall be able to stow.

And whereas you will receive herewith a duplicate of a letter from Count Florida Blanca, to the Spanish officer commanding at Nootka, (together with a translation thereof) signifying His Catholic Majesty's orders to cause such officer as may be appointed on the part of His Britannic Majesty, to be put in possession of the buildings, and districts, or parcels of lands therein described, which were occupied by His Majesty's subjects in the month of april, 1789, agreeable to the first article of the late convention, (a copy of which has been sent you) and to deliver up any persons in the service of British subjects who may have been detained in those parts; in case, therefore, you shall receive this at Nootka, you are to deliver to the Spanish officer, commanding at that port, the above-mentioned letter from Count Florida Blanca, and to receive from him, conformably thereto, on the part of His Britannic Majesty, possession of the buildings and districts, and parcels of land, of which His Majesty's subjects were possessed at the above-mentioned period.

In case, however, this shall not find you at Nootka, when Lieutenant Hergest arrives there, but be delivered to you at the Sandwich islands, or elsewhere, and the said lieutenant shall not have then carried into execution the service above mentioned, (which in the event of his not falling in with you he is directed to do) you are immediately to proceed to Nootka, and to carry that service into execution as above directed, taking the said lieutenant and transport with you if you shall judge it necessary. But as they are intended afterwards to proceed to New South Wales, to be employed there, under the orders of Commodore Phillip, you are not to detain them at Nootka, the Sandwich islands, or elsewhere, longer than may be absolutely necessary, but to direct Lieutenant Hergest to repair with the said transport to port Jackson, with such live stock, and other refreshments, as may be likely to be of use in the settlements there; and to touch at New Zealand in his way, from whence he is to use his best endeavours to take with him one or two flax-dressers, in order that the new settlers at port Jackson may, if possible, be properly instructed in the management of that valuable plant.

Previous, however, to your dispatching him to port Jackson, you are to consider whether, in case of your not being able to take on board the whole of the transport's cargo, any future supply of the articles of which it is composed, will be necessary to enable you to continue your intended survey; and, if so, you are to be careful to send notice thereof to Commodore Phillip, who will have directions, on the receipt of your application, to re-dispatch the transport, or to send such other vessel to you with the remainder of those supplies (as well as any others he may be able to furnish) to such rendezvous as you appoint.

And whereas Mr. Dundas has transmitted to us a sketch of the coast of North America, extending from Nootka down to the latitude of 47° 30″, including the inlet or gulph of Juan de Fuca; and as from the declarations which have lately been made, there appears to be the strongest disposition, on the part of the Spanish court, that every assistance and information should be given to His Britannic Majesty's officers employed on that coast, with a view to the enabling them to carry their orders into execution; we send you the said sketch herewith, for your information and use, and do hereby require and direct you, to do everything in your power to cultivate a good understanding with the officers and subjects of His Catholic Majesty who may fall in your way, in order that you may reap the good effects of this disposition of the Spanish court.

You are to take the utmost care in your power, on no account whatever, to touch at any port on the continent of America, to the southward of the latitude of 30° north, nor to the north of that part of South America, where, on your return home, you are directed to commence your intended survey; unless, from any accident, you shall find it absolutely necessary, for your immediate safety, to take shelter there: and, in case of such an event, to continue there no longer than your necessities require, in order that any complaint on the part of Spain on this point may, if possible, be prevented.

If, during your continuance on the American coast, you should meet with any of the Chinese who were employed by Mr. Meares and his associates, or any of His Majesty's subjects, who may have been in captivity, you are to receive them on board the sloop you command, and to accommodate them in the best manner you may be able, until such time as opportunities may be found of sending them to the different places to which they may be desirous of being conveyed; victualling them during their continuance on board, in the same manner as the other persons on board the said sloop are victualled.

Given under our hand the 20th of august, 1791.

To   Chatham.
     George Vancouver, Esq.   J.T. Townshend.
commander of His Majesty's sloop   A. Gardner.
the Discovery.
By command of their Lordships.
                 Ph. Stephens.

LETTER FROM COUNT FLORIDA BLANCA.
(Translated from the Spanish)

In conformity to the first article of the convention of 28th october, 1790, between our court and that of London, (printed copies of which you will have already received, and of which another copy is here enclosed, in case the first have not come to hand) you will give directions that His Britannic Majesty's officer, who will deliver this letter, shall immediately be put into possession of the buildings and districts, or parcels of land, which were occupied by the subjects of that sovereign in april, 1789, as well in the port of Nootka, or of Saint Lawrence, as in the other, said to be called port Cox, and to be situated about fifteen leagues distant from the former to the southward; and that such parcels or districts of land, of which the English subjects were dispossessed, be restored to said officer, in case the Spaniards should not have given them up.

239

You will also give orders, that if any individual in the service of British subjects, whether a Chinese, or of any other nation, should have been carried away and detained in those parts, such person shall be immediately delivered up to the above-mentioned officer.

I also communicate all this to the viceroy of New Spain by His Majesty's command, and by the same royal command I charge you with the most punctual and precise execution of this order.

May God preserve you many years.

        (Signed)   The Count Florida Blanca.

Aranjuez, 12th may, 1791.

To the governor or commander of the port at Saint Lawrence.

By the Commissioners for executing the office of Lord High Admiral of Great-Britain and Ireland, &c.

In addition to former orders, you are hereby required and directed, by all proper conveyances, to send to our secretary, for our information, accounts of your proceedings, and copies of the surveys and drawings you shall have made; and, upon your arrival in England, you are immediately to repair to this office, in order to lay before us a full account of your proceedings in the whole course of your voyage; taking care, before you leave the sloop, to demand from the officers, and petty-officers, the log-books, journals, drawings, &c. they may have kept, and to seal them up for our inspection; and en- joining them, and the whole crew, not to divulge where they have been until they shall have permission so to do: and you are to direct the lieutenant commanding the Chatham armed tender to do the same, with respect to the officers, petty-officers, and crew of that tender.

Given under our hands the 10th of August, 1791.

To	Chatham.
George Vancouver, Esq.	J.T. Townshend.
commander of His Majesty's sloop	A. Gardner.
the Discovery.	

    By command of their Lordships.

        Ph. Stephens.

Notes

Chapter 1

1. W. G. Perrin (ed.), *The Naval Miscellany* (Publications of the Navy Records Society, LXIII [London, 1928]), III, 362.

2. The word "tons," used to express the size of sailing ships of this period, can be confusing. It was not a measure of the weight of the ships but an arbitrary figure derived from formulas that differed from one shipbuilder to another. The usual formula was length in feet times width or beam times depth of hold, divided by one hundred. Thus a ship of three hundred tons might have a length of keel of about eighty-eight feet, or about one hundred feet on the main deck, a beam of about twenty-five feet, and a depth of hold of about thirteen feet. "Tons" was therefore a crude expression of volume rather than weight, and a rough approximation of the modern term "gross tonnage." Cook's *Resolution* was about 110 feet long on the main deck, with a 30-foot beam; the *Adventure* was about 100 feet long.

3. George Vancouver, *A Voyage of Discovery to the North Pacific Ocean and round the World* (London: C. J. and J. Robinson; J. Edwards, 1798), II, 379.

4. James Cook, *A Voyage towards the South Pole and round the World* (London: W. Strahan, 1777), I, 9.

5. *The Navy Chronicle*, I (1799), 125. Under "Naval Anecdotes": "Captain Vancouver used to say, that he had been nearer the south pole than any other man for when the immortal Cook in latitude 72, was stopped in his progress by impenetrable mountains of ice, and was prepared to tack about, he went to the very end of the bowsprit, and waving his hat, exclaimed *Ne Plus Ultra!*"

6. George Forster, *A Voyage round the World* (London: B. White, 1777), I, 542.

7. James Cook and James King, *A Voyage to the Pacific* (London: G. Nicol and T. Cadell, 1784), I, 9.

8. Vancouver, *Voyage of Discovery*, III, 91. This entry indicates a reason for the absence of Vancouver's journal from the collection in the Public Record Office in London of journals for Cook's third voyage. When preparing

his book Vancouver could scarcely have recalled this detail without reference to his earlier journal. He may have withdrawn the journal for use on his own voyage, but he surely made use of it in preparing his account of the voyage. In another reference, to the latitude of Point Breakers at Nootka, he also recollects his own observations on Cook's third voyage.

9. For a good account of the incident see Ralph S. Kuykendall, *The Hawaiian Kingdom, 1778-1854* (Honolulu: University of Hawaii Press, 1938), pp. 18-20.

10. Thomas Edgar, Journal, quoted in part in George Godwin, *Vancouver: A Life* (New York: D. Appleton and Co., 1931), pp. 288-90. The incident is also described more briefly in Cook and King, *Voyage to the Pacific*, III, 39-40.

11. Vancouver, *Voyage of Discovery*, II, 368.

12. Cook and King, *Voyage to the Pacific*, III, 437.

Chapter 2

1. George Vancouver, HMS *Martin*, 9 Dec 1781-16 May 1782, Lieutenant's Logs (Greenwich, Eng.: National Maritime Museum), April 19, 1782.

2. Admiral Hugh Pigot, In Letters, 1780-87 (London: Public Record Office), September 19, 1782.

3. Rear Admiral Alan Gardner, Admiral's Journal, 1786-96 (London: Public Record Office), May 5, 1787.

4. *Regulations and Instructions Relating to His Majesty's Service at Sea* (13th ed.; London: the Admiralty, 1790), pp. 96-97.

5. Belisarius was a Byzantine general under the sixth-century emperor Justinian. After conquering Carthage, Sicily, and Italy he fell from grace, and Justinian seized his fortune. There is a fictional story that near the end of his life he wandered through the streets of Constantinople as a blind beggar.

6. British Museum, *Catalog of Personal and Political Satires* (London, 1949), IX, 801-2.

Chapter 3

1. For detailed accounts of the rise and growth of the fur trade see Hubert H. Bancroft, *History of Alaska, 1730-1885* (San Francisco: A. L. Bancroft and Co., 1886), chapter xi; and *History of the Northwest Coast* (San Francisco: A. L. Bancroft and Co., 1884), Vol. I, chapters vi-xvii.

2. Frederick W. Howay (ed.), *The Dixon Meares Controversy* (Montreal: Ryerson Press, 1929), pp. 16-17. An outline of the East India Company's license to the *Ruby*, 1794, is given.

3. *Ibid.*, p. 11.

4. Since the dates in the English and Spanish accounts of events at Nootka vary by one day, exact dates are avoided here. The difference is due to reckoning longitude and dates east (English) or west (Spanish) of Europe.

5. See Frederick W. Howay (ed.), *The Journal of Captain James Colnett aboard the Argonaut from April 26, 1789, to Nov. 3, 1791* (Toronto: Champlain Press, 1940). This work contains a translation of Martinez' journal from July 2 to July 14, 1789, covering the period from the arrival of the *Argonaut* at Nootka until she was seized and sent to San Blas as a prize.

6. *Ibid.*, pp. 58-60. After returning from his own voyage in 1795 Vancouver talked to Colnett, who then gave him a highly colored version of the affair which differed materially from his own journal; see Vancouver, *Voyage of Discovery*, III, 491-98.

7. Howay, *Colnett Journal*, pp. 310-12.

8. *Ibid.*, p. 207. Vancouver, in *Voyage of Discovery*, II, 497, quotes the viceroy's passport: "I grant a free and safe passport to [the] captains James Colnett and Thomas Hudson, that they may proceed to Macao, or sail to any other place they may choose, with the express prohibition that they shall not put in to any port or bay of our coasts without some very pressing necessity, or establish themselves there, or trade in them with the Indians, because they may do this in other places or islands not the dominions of His Catholic Majesty."

9. Frederick W. Howay (ed.), "Four Letters from Richard Cadman Etches to Sir Joseph Banks," *British Columbia Historical Quarterly*, VI (April, 1942), 133.

10. *Historical Records of Australia* (Sydney: Library Committee of the Commonwealth Parliament), I, 162.

11. Her exact dimensions were as follows: length on the gun deck, 96 feet; length on the keel, 79 feet; breadth, 27 feet, 3¾ inches; depth of hold, 14 feet; tonnage 337. John Charnock, *A History of Marine Architecture* (London: Bye and Law, 1802), III, 263.

12. Joseph Whidbey, Log of Proceedings of His Majesty's Ship Discovery, 1 Jan 1790-20 May 1790 (MS in the Public Record Office, London), pp. 5-11. The different names for cooperage refer to both use and size. The barrel held 32 to 36 gallons, the hogshead about 52 imperial gallons, and the puncheon from 72 gallons for beer to 120 gallons for whisky or rum.

13. William R. Manning, "The Nootka Sound Controversy," *Annual Report of the American Historical Society, 1904*, p. 376.

14. Whidbey, Log, p. 14.

15. Vancouver, *Voyage of Discovery*, I, x.

16. Manning's study traces details and possible consequences of the controversy, including the concern of the United States that a war in Europe over the incident would involve New Orleans and Florida.

Chapter 4

1. Vancouver, *Voyage of Discovery*, I, 1. "Master and Commander" was the rank given to the commander of a ship smaller than a fifth rate.

2. See Edmond S. Meany, *Vancouver's Discovery of Puget Sound* (New York: Macmillan Co., 1907), Appendix, pp. 335-38. Meany gives the official muster roll of the *Discovery* between April 1 (the date of sailing from England) and May 1, 1791. It lists 132 names, including one "widow's man." The pay of that fictitious crew member was credited to a special fund for the relief of poor widows of officers. Vancouver, in *Voyage of Discovery*, I, xii, indicates that there were 100 on board in December, 1790. Peter Puget, in his Journal, I, 11, has a muster list of the *Discovery* on April 1, 1791, of ninety-eight in the crew and two supernumeraries. Puget's list omits the name of a marine who later died at sea, but otherwise it is considered accurate. The official list does not indicate the discharges that were made for various reasons before sailing.

3. Frederick W. Howay, "Notes on Cook's and Vancouver's Ships," *Washington Historical Quarterly*, XXI (October, 1930), 269. The *Chatham*'s dimensions were as follows: length on the keel, 53 feet, 1¾ inches; breadth, 21 feet, 6¾ inches; depth of hold, 10 feet; tonnage, 131. Charnock, *History of Marine Architecture*, III, 275. Her length on the main deck was not given, but it was 60 feet or slightly more.

4. Edward Bell, Journal, I, 1. Little is known of Broughton before this voyage. As a midshipman he was taken prisoner by the colonists of Boston in 1776.

5. Meany, in *Vancouver's Discovery of Puget Sound*, Appendix, pp. 339-40, gives the official muster roll of the *Chatham* from May 1 to June 30, 1791, with fifty-five names. Bell, in his Journal, I, 9, gives the number as forty-five, as does Vancouver, in *Voyage of Discovery*, I, xiii. Here again, the official list does not indicate the discharges before sailing.

6. C. F. Newcombe (ed.), *Menzies' Journal of Vancouver's Voyage April to October 1792* (Victoria: W. H. Cullin, 1923), pp. ix-x. The text of Menzies' instructions is in Richard H. Dillon, "Archibald Menzies' Trophies," *British Columbia Historical Quarterly*, XV (July-October, 1951), 153-55; a draft, dated February 22, 1791, is in Banks Correspondence 1765-1821 (MSS in the British Museum), Vol. III. In a letter to Banks of February 24, 1791, Evan Nepean, secretary of the Home Office, offered Lord Grenville's suggestion that instructions to learn of the "practice of eating human flesh" be deleted and that Menzies should be given private instructions on that subject.

7. Quoted in Godwin, *Vancouver: A Life*, pp. 201-2. The matter was referred to the Admiralty, for at the end of the month Vancouver reported that he had brought about a thorough reconciliation between Menzies and

his messmates. See Godwin, *Vancouver: A Life,* p. 35. Vancouver's original letter is in Captain's In Letters, 1791-98 (MSS in the Public Record Office, London).

8. Newcombe, *Menzies' Journal,* p. x.

9. The astronomical day was used—from noon to noon and twelve hours later than the civil day.

10. Vancouver, in *Voyage of Discovery,* frequently refers to the bad sailing qualities of the *Chatham,* but it is in the personal journals that the signal is so often recorded. The *Chatham*'s lines were very tubby. Her length-to-breadth ratio was only about 2½ to 1, while the *Discovery*'s was nearly 4 to 1. The larger ship was thus much sleeker in lines, although still boxlike by modern standards.

11. Puget, in his Journal, I, 27; Archibald Menzies, in his Journal, p. 15; and Bell, in his Journal, I, 17, agree on the main details and that the English sailors were drunk and started the brawl. Vancouver did not mention the incident.

12. Bell, Journal, I, 25. Thomas Manby, in his Private Journal, states that the Dutch had great respect for people engaged in exploration; this fact contributed to an orderly and abundant supply for the ships.

13. Vancouver, *Voyage of Discovery,* I, 18; Bell, in his Journal, I, 35, blamed the outbreak on bad liquor ashore.

14. Vancouver, *Voyage of Discovery,* I, 63.

15. Whenever possible the modern accepted spelling of names of native origin has been used. In the journals of the expedition such names are spelled according to the author's own phonetic version of the native pronunciation, resulting in several spellings for the same name. "Otaheiti" is one of the few repeated spellings of Tahiti.

16. Vancouver, *Voyage of Discovery,* I, 69-70. According to Manby, in his Private Journal, the water leaked in through tarpaulins at the hatchways from heavy seas on the main deck.

17. Bell, Journal, I, 68.

18. If Captain William Bligh had given such an order he might have averted the mutiny of the *Bounty* in 1789. His only order at Tahiti at that time was to withhold any news of Cook's death. He remained at Tahiti for about five months, and his officers and men mixed freely with the natives. When Bligh sailed into his mutiny in April, 1789, his officers and men were completely demoralized, surely a contributing factor to the mutiny. When he returned to Tahiti in 1792 he issued orders similar to Vancouver's and had no trouble.

19. Bell, Journal, I, 86.

20. Vancouver, *Voyage of Discovery,* I, 105.

21. *Ibid.,* p. 123. The "correction," according to Puget, in his Journal, I, 129, was twenty-four lashes each, and he added that several chiefs present "admired the justice of the punishment."

22. Vancouver, *Voyage of Discovery,* I, 135.

Chapter 5

1. Vancouver, *Voyage of Discovery*, I, 155. The spelling of the Hawaiian names follows the modern practice used by Kuykendall in *The Hawaiian Kingdom,* and by Herbert H. Gowen in *The Napoleon of the Pacific* (New York: Fleming H. Revell Co., 1919). Vancouver spelled the names of these two chiefs Taiana and Tamaahmaah. Others spelled Kamehameha's name Tamaihamaiha, Tomaiho maiho, and with other phonetic variations. The use of "t" for the Hawaiian "k" is noticeable in the accounts of these early English visitors. There were variations in accent among the islands, and the Hawaiians could not distinguish among the sounds of the English "l," "r," and "d."

2. Vancouver, *Voyage of Discovery*, I, 156.

3. Bell, Journal, I, 138.

4. Vancouver, *Voyage of Discovery*, I, 161. In Charles T. Stuart's Log of the Discovery, 12 July 1791-28 July 1794 (MS in the Public Record Office, London), facing p. 83, is a "Scetch of Wytete Bay." Made from just under Diamond Head, it shows clearly the entrance to Honolulu Harbor.

5. Vancouver, *Voyage of Discovery*, I, 166. With the Englishmen's tendency to render the native "k" sound as a "t," this spelling gives us approximately "*Kow*-ai"; the syllable "Att" was as close as Vancouver could come to the native pronunciation of the name of the island.

6. Kuykendall, *The Hawaiian Kingdom*, pp. 85-86.

7. Vancouver, *Voyage of Discovery*, I, 174.

8. *Ibid.*, p. 175. This mild deception, a safety precaution, is one of the very few instances in which Vancouver was not completely frank and honest with the Hawaiian chiefs.

9. Manby, Personal Journal, March 13, 1792.

10. Bell, Journal, I, 158. Vancouver gave a much more moderate account of the incident.

11. See William Laird Clowes (ed.), *The Royal Navy—A History* (Boston: Little, Brown and Co., 1899-1903), IV, 145.

12. Menzies, Journal, p. 383.

13. The portrait cannot be relied on entirely, for in 1953 the assistant keeper of the National Portrait Gallery in London cast doubt on the identity of the subject of the portrait. He stated that the history of the painting cannot be traced back beyond a sale in 1878, and that, since the subject is not in uniform and there is no other portrait of Vancouver with which to compare it, the identification cannot be absolutely established. Evidence within the picture tends to confirm that the subject was Vancouver. The books on the shelf, *Cook's Voyages* and *Magellan's Voyage,* associate the subject with exploration; the map on the globe is that of Vancouver's master chart for the west coast of North America and cannot be associated with any other

explorer. The fact that he was on half pay (the portrait was probably done toward the end of his life) and the goiterlike appearance of the neck could explain why the subject was not in uniform, although there is no record of a portrait of a naval officer on half pay who was not in uniform. At the time when the portrait was probably painted, Vancouver was living under a cloud, in a state bordering on disgrace, and for this reason he might well have put aside his uniform. Another factor pointing to the validity of the identification is a portrait of Vancouver's brother John, reproduced in George Godwin's *Vancouver: A Life.* Although John was much leaner than George, the portraits show a strong family resemblance.

14. Vancouver, *Voyage of Discovery*, I, 187.

15. Menzies, Journal, pp. 201-2; Bell, Journal, I, 155. George C. Mackenzie, in the Log of the Discovery, March 20, 1792 (MS in the Public Record Office, London), gives the formal charge as "disobedience of orders Insolence & Disrespect to Captain Vancouver on the Quarter Deck."

16. See Cook, *Voyage towards the South Pole,* I, 38.

17. Vancouver, *Voyage of Discovery,* I, xviii. See the Appendix to this work for the full text of his instructions.

18. *Ibid.,* p. xix.

19. Frequent references in the journals and in Vancouver's account to "keeping to the continental shore" and the way in which the survey was conducted show that he was guided by this idea.

20. Each compass bearing had to be corrected for the magnetic variation from true north. This, in turn, varied as the ship's position changed, and it had to be determined regularly by astronomical observation.

21. Latitude 39°27' North, longitude 124°18.5' West. Vancouver, *Voyage of Discovery,* I, 196. Vancouver reckoned his longitudes east of Greenwich, but here, conforming to modern usage, they are transposed to west longitudes. These events occurred before the adoption of standard time and the international date line. There is also a discrepancy of one day in dates, for the same reason.

22. Vancouver, *Voyage of Discovery,* I, 210.

23. Manby, Personal Journal, April 27, 1792.

24. Frederick W. Howay, *Voyages of the Columbia to the Northwest Coast, 1787-1790* (Massachusetts Historical Society Collections, Vol. LXXIX [Boston, 1941]), p. 396. The river mouth was first seen by the Spaniard Heceta in 1775, but he did not explore it. The Spaniards called it *Ensenada de Heceta.*

Chapter 6

1. Vancouver, *Voyage of Discovery,* I, xix.

2. Cook and King, *Voyage to the Pacific,* II, 263.

3. Henry R. Wagner, "Apocryphal Voyages to the Northwest Coast of

America," *Proceedings of the American Antiquarian Society,* XLI (April, 1931), 179-234.

4. Vancouver, *Voyage of Discovery,* I, 214.

5. Puget, Journal, I, 185.

6. Menzies, Journal, p. 223.

7. Manby, Personal Journal, April 29, 1792.

8. Frederick W. Howay, "Early Navigation of the Strait of Juan de Fuca," *Oregon Historical Quarterly,* XII (March, 1911), 8. See also W. Kaye Lamb, "The Mystery of Mrs. Barkley's Diary," *British Columbia Historical Quarterly,* VI (January, 1942), 31-33.

9. For the location of the several anchorages of the *Discovery* in the Puget Sound region, plotted on modern charts, see Robert B. Whitebrook, "Vancouver's Anchorages on Puget Sound," *Pacific Northwest Quarterly,* LXIV (July, 1953), 115-24.

10. Vancouver, *Voyage of Discovery,* I, 224. For Broughton's account of this examination see J. Neilson Barry (ed.), "Broughton's Reconnaissance of the San Juan Islands in 1792," *Washington Historical Quarterly,* XXI (January, 1930), 55-60.

11. Vancouver, *Voyage of Discovery,* I, 275. For Puget's account of the boat expedition see Bern Anderson (ed.), "The Vancouver Expedition. Peter Puget's Journal of the Exploration of Puget Sound, May 7-June 11, 1792," *Pacific Northwest Quarterly,* XXX (April, 1939), 195-205.

12. Manby, in his Personal Journal, May, 1792, reported that he shot a flying crow with his shotgun to impress the Indians. It had some success, but the swivel gun was fired to impress them still further with the white man's power.

13. Vancouver, *Voyage of Discovery,* I, 289. Menzies, in his Journal, p. 272, and Bell, in his Journal, also describe this event, which all seemed to think of great importance. A marker commemorating it is now in the park in the city of Everett. See Whitebrook, "Vancouver's Anchorages on Puget Sound," pp. 125-26.

14. Vancouver, *Voyage of Discovery,* I, 259.

15. Menzies, Journal, pp. 275-76.

16. Hardin Craig, Jr. (ed.), "A Letter from the Vancouver Expedition," *Pacific Northwest Quarterly,* LXI (October, 1953), 354.

17. A possible alternate route, the narrow and dangerous Deception Passage at the northern end of Whidbey Island, was not noticed until a later boat expedition under Whidbey.

18. Sir Gerald Burrard, in "The Naming of Burrard Inlet," *British Columbia Historical Quarterly,* X (April, 1946), 143, presents a family tradition that the Burrard honored was an elderly Sir Harry Burrard, who died shortly after Vancouver sailed from England. W. Kaye Lamb, in the same volume, presents the case for a younger heir who joined the *Expedition* in the Caribbean as second lieutenant in September, 1787. He inherited the

title before Vancouver returned from his voyage and prepared the final draft of his narrative.

19. Manby, Personal Journal, June 23-24, 1792.

20. Henry R. Wagner, in *Spanish Explorations in the Strait of Juan de Fuca* (Santa Ana, Calif.: Fine Arts Press, 1933), pp. 51, 215, quotes Spanish journals to the effect that Vancouver pressed his suggestion to the point where it would have been embarrassing to decline it. But José Espinosa y Tello, in *A Spanish Voyage to Vancouver and the Northwest Coast of America*, trans. Cecil Jane (London: The Argonaut Press, 1930), p. 56, saw in this joining of forces an advantage in that it would speed up the survey and enable the Spaniards to return south sooner.

21. According to Spanish usage he should be called Bodega or Bodega y Quadra. All English records refer to him, however, as Quadra, and since this name is preserved in the region, and there are indications that he himself preferred and used that form, it is used here.

22. Puget, Journal, I, 236-37. Manby noted the flood tide setting in from the north earlier at the ship's anchorage (Personal Journal, June 26, 1792).

Chapter 7

1. Menzies, Journal, p. 354.
2. Wagner, *Spanish Explorations in the Strait of Juan de Fuca*, p. 53.
3. Bell, Journal, I, 205.
4. Menzies, Journal, p. 397.
5. Meany, *Vancouver's Discovery of Puget Sound*, pp. 50-60.
6. Vancouver, *Voyage of Discovery*, I, 385.
7. Howay, *Voyages of the Columbia*, p. 411.
8. Manning, The Nootka Sound Controversy, pp. 454-55.
9. Vancouver, *Voyage of Discovery*, I, xxiii.
10. The words were italicized by Vancouver in *Voyage of Discovery*, I, 388.
11. *Ibid.*, p. 394.
12. *Ibid.*, p. 401. Menzies, in Journal, p. 386, also mentions the agreement, but he was not present at the meeting.
13. See plate depicting Nootka, opposite p. 85. The section of beach in question is marked by the letters ABC on the right-hand side of the plate.
14. Bancroft, *History of the Northwest Coast*, I, 288.
15. Wagner, *Spanish Explorations in the Strait of Juan de Fuca*, p. 66.
16. Letter from Vancouver to Evan Nepean, January 7, 1793; quoted in Godwin, *Vancouver: A Life*, pp. 219-23.
17. Vancouver, *Voyage of Discovery*, I, 407.

Chapter 8

1. Bell, Journal, I, 241.
2. Manby, Personal Journal, September, 1792.
3. Bell, Journal, I, 207; Puget, in his Journal, I, 285, briefly mentions the incident.
4. Puget, Journal of the Proceedings of the Chatham, January 15, 1794-September, 1795 (MS in the British Museum, Add MSS 17548). This is a greatly edited rough journal containing a fragment of a rough journal for September, 1792, on page 51. Vancouver did not mention this incident.
5. Frederick W. Howay, in "Voyage of the Hope," *Washington Historical Quarterly*, XI (January, 1920), 25-56, gives Captain Ingraham's charges that Captain Butterworth was robbing the Indians and having fights with them, and that Magee came to his rescue and drove off the Indians. The reader of such partisan accounts of the early fur trade can only conclude that no hands were spotless in that trade.
6. Menzies, Journal, p. 383.
7. Vancouver, *Voyage of Discovery*, I, 398. Vancouver was wrong, but see chapter 14 for a discussion of the point.
8. See J. Neilson Barry, "Who Discovered the Columbia River?" *Oregon Historical Quarterly*, XXXIX (June, 1938), 152-61, for a discussion.
9. Vancouver, *Voyage of Discovery*, II, 52 (Broughton's account). The entrance is now improved by dredging, with breakwaters and a complete system of buoys; but it is still a dangerous crossing in sea conditions such as Vancouver described.
10. According to Heddington, Log of the Chatham, I, November 3, 1792, lack of provisions alone kept him from continuing.
11. See J. Neilson Barry, "Broughton up the Columbia River," *Oregon Historical Quarterly*, XXXII (December, 1934), 301-12, for a discussion of the exact location of Point Vancouver.
12. Vancouver, *Voyage of Discovery*, II, 66.
13. Menzies, Journal, p. 413.
14. Hubert H. Bancroft, *History of California* (San Francisco: A. L. Bancroft and Co., 1884), I, 510, note.

Chapter 9

1. Manby, Personal Journal, December, 1792.
2. Vancouver, *Voyage of Discovery*, II, 38.
3. Letter from Vancouver to Governor Phillip, October 15, 1792, in *Historical Records of Australia*, I, 429. He requested the return of the *Daedalus* the following summer. See also his *Voyage of Discovery*, II, 40.

4. David Collins, *An Account of the English Colony in New South Wales* (London: T. Cadell and W. Davies, 1798), p. 292. Lieutenant Hanson also picked up about one hundred hogs at Tahiti. The only survivors were four sheep and about eighty hogs in poor condition. The loss of the cattle was attributed in part to the dry hay and grain diet, to which they were not accustomed, on board ship.

5. Vancouver, *Voyage of Discovery*, II, 47.

6. See chapter 16 for a discussion of Vancouver's discipline.

7. Menzies, Journal, p. 465.

8. Puget, Journal, II, 1. Quadra's generosity in supplying Vancouver's expedition with men was extraordinary.

9. Vancouver, *Voyage of Discovery*, I, xix.

10. *Ibid.*, II, 104.

11. Jean François de Galaup, Comte de la Pérouse, *A Voyage round the World in the Years 1785, 1786, 1787, and 1788* (London: J. Johnson, 1799), II, 31. Nearly all world atlases have a map showing the general current movement in the Pacific Ocean.

12. *Ibid.*, II, 34.

13. E. W. Dahlgren, *Were the Hawaiian Islands Discovered by the Spaniards before Their Discovery by Captain Cook in 1778?* (Stockholm: Almquist and Wiksells, 1916), pp. 212-13.

14. Menzies, Journal, p. 484.

15. *Ibid.*, pp. 486-87.

16. Manby, Personal Journal, March 8, 1793. Manby was strengthened in his opinion by the story of a native historian that it was legendary that a few generations back white men visited the islands, and that the Hawaiian royal family was descended from these men, a tale lacking factual basis.

Chapter 10

1. Manby, in his Personal Journal, February 22, 1793, estimated that there were thirty thousand people around the *Discovery* and the *Chatham* that morning. This was, no doubt, much too high an estimate; nevertheless it must have been an impressive sight.

2. Vancouver, *Voyage of Discovery*, II, 127. Manby noted that Kamehameha called the animals "large hogs."

3. See Kuykendall, *The Hawaiian Kingdom*, pp. 24-25, for a detailed account of the men; also Vancouver, *Voyage of Discovery*, II, 132-45. Puget, in his Journal, II, 19, was skeptical of Young's story of how he happened to be ashore at the time, implying that he might have deserted.

4. Puget, Journal, II, 36.

5. Bell, Journal, II, 75.

6. Puget, Journal, II, 31.

7. Bell, Journal, II, 77.

8. Manby, Personal Journal, March 10, 1793. Menzies, in his Journal, p. 539, also discusses Kamehameha's conditions.

9. Ebenezer Townsend, Jr., "Diary of a Voyage around the World in the Sailing Ship Neptune, 1796-99" (*Papers of the New Haven Colonial Society*, Vol. VI [New Haven, 1888]), p. 74.

10. Menzies, Journal, pp. 547-48. Bell, in his Journal, II, 84-85, also had critical comments on Vancouver's attitude toward the treatment of the man.

11. Menzies, Journal, p. 558. This does not agree with Vancouver, in *Voyage of Discovery*, II, 183-84, in which he indicates that he reviewed the matter at his first meeting with Kahekili. It seems probable, however, that he wanted to avoid friction until his business at Maui was well in hand.

12. Vancouver, *Voyage of Discovery*, II, 180.

13. Manby, Personal Journal, March 8, 1794.

14. Vancouver, *Voyage of Discovery*, II, 199.

15. Menzies, Journal, p. 561.

16. Vancouver, *Voyage of Discovery*, II, 204-5. The most detailed account of the Hergest incident is found in Bell, Journal, I, 209 ff. It differs in some details from Vancouver's version, but not in essentials.

17. Menezies, Journal, pp. 567-68.

18. Bell, Journal, II, 129-30.

19. Kuykendall, in *The Hawaiian Kingdom*, p. 44, states that a ringleader, a minor chief, escaped all punishment.

20. Contrast this with the handling of a comparable case, the "Olowalu Massacre," by the American Captain Metcalfe, of the *Eleanora*, at Maui in 1790. In revenge for the theft of a boat and the killing of a seaman, he enticed many canoes alongside for trade and suddenly discharged a broadside of cannon loaded with musket balls into them, killing more than one hundred natives. See Kuykendall, *The Hawaiian Kingdom*, p. 24.

21. Vancouver, *Voyage of Discovery*, II, 216.

Chapter 11

1. Puget, Journal, II, 76.

2. Copy of an unsigned letter to Meares, dated "Whitehall, June, 1793" (MS in the Public Record Office, London, CO 5/187).

3. Menzies, Journal, p. 607. Vancouver's own account is silent on these measures.

4. Alexander Mackenzie, *Voyages from Montreal, on the River St. Lawrence, through the Continent of North America to the Frozen and Pacific Oceans, in the Years 1789 and 1793* (London: W. Creech, 1802).

5. The *Dictionary of National Biography* states that Charles Vancouver was born in America, although obviously not on Vancouver Island as the editor's source indicated. That he was actually George Vancouver's brother is clearly established in a letter from John Tiotts to the Reverend Thomas

NOTES

Martin written in July, 1793. The letter, found in the Banks Papers (MSS in the Sutro Branch, California State Library, San Francisco), is quoted in full in Richard H. Dillon (ed.), "Charles Vancouver's Plan," *Pacific Northwest Quarterly*, XLI (October, 1950), 356-57.

6. Puget, Journal, II, 126.

7. *Ibid.*, p. 146.

8. Vancouver, *Voyage of Discovery*, II, 364.

9. Puget, Journal, II, 181. The "hour of Departure" was daylight in every case.

10. Bell, Journal, II, 214.

11. Letter from the acting governor to Dundas, April 21, 1793, *Historical Records of Australia*, I, 428.

12. Letter from Vancouver to Stephens, December 6, 1793 (MS in the Public Record Office, London, Adm 1/2629).

13. Letter from Arrillaga to Vancouver, November 3, 1793. The full correspondence relating to this incident is quoted in Godwin, *Vancouver: A Life*, pp. 231-50.

14. Puget, Journal, II, 220.

15. Bancroft, *History of California*, I, 519-21. Bancroft was critical of Vancouver in all of his histories that referred to the captain.

16. Puget, Journal, II, 220.

17. Menzies, Journal, p. 734.

18. Vancouver, *Voyage of Discovery*, II, 459-61. Puget, in his Journal, II, 245, noted that the Indians feared the British and were alarmed when Father Vincente took passage in the *Discovery*. They were overjoyed when he landed safely at his mission. The fear of Englishmen probably stemmed from Anson's buccaneering voyage in the 1740's. Bell, in his Journal, II, 293-94, expressed a similar opinion.

19. At Santa Barbara, Vancouver bought two horses to take to Hawaii, but he returned them on the hint by Goycochea that they were contraband. Bell, Journal, II, 270.

20. Vancouver, *Voyage of Discovery*, II, 485.

Chapter 12

1. Bell, Journal, II, 301-2. Less specific, Vancouver, in his *Voyage of Discovery*, III, 5-6, had no doubt "of soon finding amongst the other islands some chief" who would assist him.

2. Puget, Journal, II, 284.

3. Gowen, *The Napoleon of the Pacific*, p. 222.

4. Menzies, Journal, p. 820.

5. Vancouver, *Voyage of Discovery*, III, 22.

6. *Ibid.*, p. 67. It is probable that they claimed to be Americans in order to evade possible seizure and impressment by Vancouver.

7. *Ibid.,* p. 31.

8. Bell, Journal, II, 346.

9. Bell, in his Journal, II, 350, listed the chief of Hamakua, the remaining district of Hawaii, as also present.

10. Vancouver, *Voyage of Discovery,* III, 56.

11. *Ibid.*

12. *Ibid.,* pp. 56-57. In reply to an inquiry Professor Kuykendall stated that this plate has not been found and that he knows of no record of its having been seen by later visitors (letter to the author, July 6, 1953).

13. Kuykendall, *The Hawaiian Kingdom,* pp. 41-42.

14. *Ibid.,* p. 76.

15. Letter from Croker to Planta, Admiralty Office, July 5, 1824. James A. Williamson, *A Short History of British Expansion* (London: Macmillan and Co., 1927); *Correspondence Relating to the Sandwich Islands, 1823-1843* (London: published privately for use of the Cabinet, [*ca.*] 1843), p. 3.

16. *Ibid.,* p. 13, Byron's report, May 30, 1825. For a detailed discussion of early Hawaiian-British relations see Kuykendall, *The Hawaiian Kingdom,* chapters iii-viii.

17. Vancouver, *Voyage of Discovery,* III, 57.

18. Ebenezer Townsend, Jr., "Diary of a Voyage," p. 74. In May, 1799, Sir Joseph Banks, writing to a "Rev Sir," agreed that the idea of sending missionaries to the Sandwich Islands was a good one. Banks Correspondence 1765-1821 (MSS in the British Museum, Add MSS 33980).

19. William R. Broughton, *A Voyage of Discovery to the North Pacific Ocean* (London: T. Cadell and W. Davies, 1804), p. 34.

20. Gowen, *The Napoleon of the Pacific,* p. 215.

Chapter 13

1. MS in the British Museum, Add MSS 17549, April 20, 1794.

2. Vancouver, *Voyage of Discovery,* III, 334. In November, 1794, at Monterey, he wrote of "the very debilitated state of my health, under which I have severely laboured during the eight preceding months."

3. *Ibid.,* p. 125.

4. *Ibid.,* p. 140.

5. Bancroft, *History of Alaska,* pp. 342-44.

6. Vancouver, *Voyage of Discovery,* III, 204.

7. Floating ice, carried by the tides from live glaciers in Glacier Bay, about fifteen miles inland from Cross Sound, is common in the sound and connecting Icy Strait in the summer months.

8. Vancouver, *Voyage of Discovery,* III, 285.

9. "Post Captain" was the first step in the rank of captain; the appointee

held this rank while he was "posted" to a ship normally commanded by a captain.

10. Vancouver, *Voyage of Discovery*, III, 285.

11. *Ibid.,* p. 295.

12. *Ibid.,* p. 272.

13. "In Need of Financial Help," *Washington Historical Quarterly*, XVII (April, 1926), 56.

14. This letter is in the Collection of Western Americana, Yale University Library, and is quoted with the permission of that library.

15. Puget, Journal, II, 204.

16. MS in the British Museum, Add MSS 17550, p. 23.

17. *Ibid.,* p. 26.

18. Vancouver, *Voyage of Discovery*, III, 395.

Chapter 14

1. W. G. Perrin (ed.), *The Keith Papers* (Publications of the Navy Records Society, Vol. LXII [London, 1927, 1950]), I, 330-32; letter from Vancouver to Elphinstone, July 13, 1795.

2. Vancouver, *Voyage of Discovery*, III, 479-81. The *Macassar* reached England in November.

3. Perrin, *The Keith Papers,* I, 334. Letter from Brooke to Elphinstone, July 12, 1795.

4. Letter from Menzies to Sir Joseph Banks, September 14, 1795, quoted in Godwin, *Vancouver: A Life,* pp. 139-41. Writing after Vancouver left the ship in home waters, Menzies anticipated a court-martial and expected that Sir Joseph would intercede for him. According to Menzies, when he complained of being unfairly treated Vancouver "immediately flew in a rage, and his passionate behaviour and abusive language . . . prevented any further explanation." This may have been another manifestation of Vancouver's hyperthyroid condition, but Menzies was also defending his own conduct.

5. Vancouver, *Voyage of Discovery*, III, 484.

6. *The London Chronicle,* October 17, 1795. Humphreys' journal, the only one that runs to the last day of the voyage, gives the date as October 17. At St. Helena, Vancouver adjusted his dates after having gained a day sailing around the world from west to east. The same adjustment was presumably not made on the *Chatham,* for Vancouver also reported her arrival on October 17. The news item reporting her arrival opens as follows: "Plymouth, Oct. 16. This morning arrived here the tender Chatham. . . ."

7. In May, 1794, Laurie and White of Fleet Street published "A New

Map of the Whole Continent of America," which used the results of Vancouver's 1792 survey.

8. *The Annual Register,* XXXVII (1795), 35.

9. Vancouver, *Voyage of Discovery,* Vol. I, "Advertisement."

10. Letter from Vancouver to Nepean, January 6, 1796 (MS in the Public Record Office, London, Adm 1/2629), quoted in Godwin, *Vancouver: A Life,* pp. 278-80.

11. Meany, *Vancouver's Discovery of Puget Sound,* p. 20.

Chapter 15

1. The *Dictionary of National Biography* credits Sir Joseph Banks with charging that Camelford was flogged three times, put in bilboes, and cast ashore. This source also gives the date of the challenge as early 1797, but the caricature referred to later in this study is dated October 1, 1796; the incident, therefore, must have occurred no later than September.

2. *The Life, Adventures, and Eccentricities of the Late Lord Camelford* (London, 1804), p. 4.

3. *Ibid.,* p. 3.

4. This amazing incident is described in the record of Camelford's court-martial, reproduced in full in *The Navy Chronicle,* XXII (1809), 314.

5. *Life . . . of the Late Lord Camelford,* p. 4.

6. Quoted in Godwin, *Vancouver: A Life,* p. 284.

7. Menzies, Journal, p. 694.

8. Quoted in Godwin, *Vancouver: A Life,* p. 223.

9. Michael Lewis, *England's Sea Officers* (London: G. Allen and Unwin, 1939), p. 197.

10. MS in the British Museum, Add MSS 17551, December 1, 1794. It has already been noted that Vancouver did not feel free to discuss events of the voyage in a letter to his brother.

Chapter 16

1. Letter from Vancouver to Nepean, February 9, 1797 (MS in the Public Record Office, London, Adm 1/2630), quoted in Godwin, *Vancouver: A Life,* pp. 143-45. The orders for seizing Dutch ships were issued in February, 1795, and the *Macassar* was taken in July, so there is no question of the legality of the capture. What Vancouver probably referred to was a provision for restoring neutral property shipped in Dutch ships when Holland was still an ally. See Alfred T. Mahan, *The Influence of Sea Power upon the French Revolution and Empire* (1st ed.; Boston: Little, Brown and Co., 1895), I, 170.

2. Letter from Vancouver to Nepean, September 4, 1797 (MS in the Public Record Office, London, Adm 1/2630).

3. *Ibid.;* the letter is quoted in Godwin, *Vancouver: A Life,* p. 161.

4. The *Dictionary of National Biography* gives the date of his death as May 10. In the Public Record Office Index for 1798 is indexed a letter of May 12 with the notation "dead" under the subject. The original letter was destroyed before 1800. Vancouver's service record also gives the date of his death as May 12, and it is used here since it is probably correct.

5. See Godwin, *Vancouver: A Life,* pp. 166-67.

6. *The Annual Register,* XL (1798), 495-96; *The Navy Chronicle,* I (1799), 221. The entire review extends through twenty-six pages in vols. I, II, and III.

7. For the origins of geographical place names on the northwest coast, and for biographical sketches of the men honored by many of them, see Edmond S. Meany, *Origin of Washington Geographic Names* (Seattle: University of Washington Press, 1923), and John T. Walbran, *British Columbia Coast Names* (Ottawa: Government Printing Bureau, 1906).

8. Godwin, *Vancouver: A Life,* p. 158.

9. This is probably the only complete collection in existence. It is more complete than those in the British Museum or the Library of Congress.

10. *Gentleman's Magazine,* LXVIII, Part I (May, 1798), 447.

11. *The Navy Chronicle,* XII (1805), 277.

12. Unsigned memorandum, probably written by Phillip Stephens, attached to Vancouver's letter of September 20, 1792 (MS in the Public Record Office, London, Adm 1/2628), and quoted in Godwin, *Vancouver: A Life,* pp. 132-33.

13. Robert Greenhow, *The History of Oregon and California and the Other Territories on the Northwest Coast of America* (Boston: C. C. Little and J. Brown, 1844).

14. Travers Twiss, *The Oregon Question Examined* (London: Longman, Brown, Green and Longmans, 1846).

15. *Ibid.,* p. 379.

16. Robert Kerr, *A General History and Collection of Voyages and Travels* (Edinburgh: W. Blackwood, 1811-24).

17. Alexander C. Findlay, *A Directory for the Navigation of the Pacific* (London: R. H. Laurie, 1851), p. xiii.

18. Edward Heawood, *Geographical Discovery in the Seventeenth and Eighteenth Century* (Cambridge, Eng.: Cambridge University Press, 1912), p. 297.

19. J. N. L. Baker, *A History of Geographical Discovery and Exploration* (London: G. G. Harrap and Co., 1931), p. 175.

20. Charles Wilkes, *Narrative of the United States Exploring Expedition during the Years 1838, 1839, 1840, 1841, 1842* (Philadelphia: Lea and Blanchard, 1849), IV, 298.

NOTES

21. Meany, *Vancouver's Discovery of Puget Sound,* p. 21.
22. William H. Dall, *Alaska and Its Resources* (Boston: Lee and Shepard, 1870), p. 316.

Appendix

1. George Vancouver, *Voyage of Discovery,* Introduction, pp. xvii-xviii.

Bibliography

UNPUBLISHED MANUSCRIPT SOURCES

Admiral's In Letters, Public Record Office, London, hereafter abbreviated as PRO.

  Commodore Alan Gardner, 1782-89, Adm 1/243.

  Admiral Hugh Pigot, 1780-87, Adm 1/313.
Admiral's Journals, PRO.

  Rear Admiral Alan Gardner, 1786-96, Adm 50/61.
Captain's Logs and Journals, PRO.

  HMS *Courageux*, 22 July 1790-15 Feb 1791, Adm 51/206.

  HMS *Europa*, 28 Oct 1784-14 Sept 1789, Adm 51/294.

  HMS *Expedition*, 23 Jan 1786-29 Nov 1788, Adm 51/321.

  HMS *Fame*, 1 Dec 1764-2 July 1783, Adm 51/343.

  HMS *Martin*, 11 June 1771-22 Apr 1784, Adm 51/581.
Lieutenant's Logs, George Vancouver, in the National Maritime Museum, Greenwich, England.

  HMS *Europa*, 24 Nov 1787-14 Sept 1789.

  HMS *Fame*, 17 May 1782-3 July 1783.

  HMS *Martin*, 9 Dec 1781-16 May 1782.
Journals and Logs kept in HMS *Chatham*, 1790-95

  Bell, Edward (Clerk). 2 vols., in the Alexander Turnbull Library, Wellington, New Zealand; microfilm copy in possession of the author. Extracts from this journal have been published in a number of journals; see below.

  Heddington, Thomas (Mid). 2 vols., in PRO Adm 55/15 and 16.

  Puget, Peter (Commanding Officer after January, 1793). 2 vols., 4 Jan 1791-14 Jan 1793 in PRO Adm 55/27; vol 2, 15 Jan 1793-5 Feb 1794 in PRO Adm 55/17.

  ———. A collection of Puget's rough journals and notes in the British Museum (hereafter referred to as BM) Add MSS 17542-17552.

Scott, James W. (Mid). 3 Mar 1791-17 Aug 1791, in PRO Adm 51/4534; 10 Aug 1791-29 Mar 1795 in PRO Adm 55/14.

Journals and Logs kept in HMS *Discovery*, 1790-95

Brown, John Aisley (Mid). 1 Jan 1791-26 Mar 1795, in PRO Adm 51/4533.

Baker, Joseph (Third, second, and first lieutenant). 22 Dec 1790-27 Nov 1792 in PRO Adm 55/32; 28 Nov 1792-1 July 1795 in PRO Adm 55/33.

Ballard, Volant V. (Mid). 1 Mar 1791-2 July 1795 in PRO Adm 55/28.

Dobson, Thomas J. (Mid). 15 Mar 1794-2 July 1795 in PRO Adm 51/4534.

Humphreys, Harry (Mid, master's mate, and master of the *Chatham*). 16 Dec 1790-17 Oct 1795 in PRO Adm 55/26.

Manby, Thomas (Master's mate, master of the *Chatham*, and third lieutenant). 16 Dec 1790-26 Sept 1792 and 26 Nov 1794-2 July 1795 in PRO Adm 53/403.

————. A personal journal in the form of letters to a friend in the Collection of Western Americana, Yale University Library.

McKenzie, George C. (Mid). 26 Nov 1791-25 Feb 1794 in PRO Adm 51/4534.

Menzies, Archibald (Botanist and surgeon). A narrative journal in BM Add MSS 32641 Dec 1791-16 Feb 1794.

Mudge, Zachary (First lieutenant). 1 Jan 1791-1 Oct 1792 in PRO Adm 51/4533.

Orchard, Henry M. (Clerk). 1 Dec 1792-30 Nov 1794 in PRO Adm 55/32.

Pigot, Robert (Mid). 7 Jan 1791-7 Jan 1795 in PRO Adm 55/30; 8 Jan 1795-2 July 1795 in PRO Adm 51/4534.

Roberts, Edward (Mid). 19 Feb 1791-12 Apr 1794 in PRO Adm 51/4534.

Stewart, John (Mid and master's mate). 1 Jan 1791-2 July 1795 in PRO Adm 51/4533.

Stuart, Charles (Mid). 12 July 1791-28 July 1794 in PRO Adm 55/28.

Swaine, Spelman (Master's mate, third and second lieutenant). 18 Dec 1790-2 July 1795 in PRO Adm 51/4532.

Sykes, John (Mid). 18 Dec 1790-28 Feb 1795 in PRO Adm 55/25.

Vancouver, George (Captain). In Letters, Captain's U-V 1771-92 in PRO Adm 1/2628; 1793-96 in Adm 1/2629; 1797-98 in Adm 1/2630.

————. Captain Vancouver's Original Despatches 1791-93 in PRO C.O. 5/187.

Whidbey, Joseph (Master). 1 Jan 1790-20 May 1790 in PRO Adm 52/2662.

The Archivo General de la Nacion, Mexico, D.F., *Historia*, Vols. 70-71, has copies of Vancouver's correspondence with Spanish officials at Nootka and in California.

PUBLISHED SOURCES AND REFERENCES

Anderson, Bern (ed.). "The Vancouver Expedition: Peter Puget's Journal of the Exploration of Puget Sound, May 7-June 11, 1792," *Pacific Northwest Quarterly*, XXX (April, 1939), 195-205.

Annual Register, XXXVII (1795), 35; XL (1798), "Chronicle," 10-11; XLI (1799), 21.

Baker, J. N. L. *A History of Geographical Discovery and Exploration*, London: G. G. Harrap and Co., 1931.

Bancroft, Hubert H. *History of Alaska, 1730-1885*. San Francisco: A. L. Bancroft and Co., 1886.

――――. *History of California*. Vol. I. San Francisco: A. L. Bancroft and Co., 1884.

――――. *History of the Northwest Coast*. Vol. I. San Francisco: A. L. Bancroft and Co., 1884.

Barry, J. Neilson. "Broughton up the Columbia River," *Oregon Historical Quarterly*, XXXII (December, 1934), 301-12.

――――. "Who Discovered the Columbia River?" *Oregon Historical Quarterly*, XXXIX (June, 1938), 152-61.

――――. (ed.). "Broughton's Reconnaissance of the San Juan Islands in 1792," *Washington Historical Quarterly*, XXI (January, 1930), 55-60.

Bell, Edward. Extracts from "Journal, 1 Jan. 1791-26 Feb. 1794," *Honolulu Mercury*, I (June, 1929), 11-25, (September, 1929), 7-26, (October, 1929), 55-69, (November, 1929), 76-90; II (December, 1929), 80-91, (January, 1930), 119-29; *Oregon Historical Quarterly*, XXXIII (March, 1932), 31-42, (June, 1932), 43-55; *Washington Historical Quarterly*, V (October, 1914), 300-308; VI (January, 1915), 50-68.

British Museum. *Catalog of Personal and Political Satires*, Vol. IX. London, 1949.

Brosses, Charles de. *Terra Australis Cognita*. Translated by John Collander. 3 vols. Edinburgh: Harris, Clark and Collins, 1766-68.

Broughton, William R. *A Voyage of Discovery to the North Pacific Ocean*. London: T. Cadell and W. Davies, 1804.

Brown, Lloyd A. *The Story of Maps*. Boston: Little, Brown and Co., 1949.

Burney, James. *A Chronological History of the Voyages and Discoveries in the South Sea or Pacific Ocean*. 5 vols. London: L. Hansard, 1802-17.

Burrard, Sir Gerald. "The Naming of Burrard Inlet," *British Columbia Historical Quarterly*, X (April, 1946), 143-49.

Carrington, Hugh. *Life of Captain Cook*. London: Sidgwick and Jackson, 1939.

Cecil, Russell L. (ed.). *Textbook of Medicine*. 3rd ed. Philadelphia: W. B. Saunders, 1934.

Charnock, John. *A History of Marine Architecture*. 3 vols. London: Bye and Law, 1802.

Clowes, William Laird (ed.). *The Royal Navy—A History*. 7 vols. Boston: Little, Brown and Co., 1899-1903.

Collins, David. *An Account of the English Colony in New South Wales*. London: T. Cadell and W. Davies, 1798.

Connelly, Elsey, and E. M. Coulter. Vol. I of *History of Kentucky*, ed. Charles Kerr. 5 vols. New York: American Historical Society, 1922.

Cook, James. *A Voyage towards the South Pole and round the World*. 2 vols. London: W. Strahan, 1777.

———, and James King. *A Voyage to the Pacific Ocean*. 3 vols. London: G. Nicol and T. Cadell, 1784.

Correspondence Relating to the Sandwich Islands, 1823-1843. London: published privately for the use of the cabinet, [ca.] 1843.

Craig, Hardin, Jr. (ed.). "A Letter from the Vancouver Expedition," *Pacific Northwest Quarterly*, LXI (October, 1953), 352-55.

Dahlgren, E. W. *Were the Hawaiian Islands Discovered by the Spaniards before Their Discovery by Captain Cook in 1778?* Stockholm: Almquist and Wiksells, 1916.

Dall, William H. *Alaska and Its Resources*. Boston: Lee and Shepard, 1870.

Dalrymple, Alexander. *An Account of the Discoveries in the South Pacific Ocean Previous to 1764*. London: printed for the author in 1767, 1769.

Dillon, Richard H. "Archibald Menzies' Trophies," *British Columbia Historical Quarterly*, XV (July-October, 1951), 151-59.

———. "Charles Vancouver's Plan," *Pacific Northwest Quarterly*, XLI (October, 1950), 356-57.

Espinosa y Tello, José. *A Spanish Voyage to Vancouver and the Northwest Coast of America*. Translated by Cecil Jane. London: The Argonaut Press, 1930.

Findlay, Alexander G. *A Directory for the Navigation of the Pacific*. London: R. H. Laurie, 1851.

Forster, George. *A Voyage round the World*. 2 vols. London: B. White, 1777.

Gentlemen's Magazine, LXVII, Part I (February, 1797), 135; LXVIII, Part I (May, 1798), 447.

Gill, Conrad. *The Naval Mutinies of 1797*. Manchester, Eng.: The University of Manchester Press, 1913.

Godwin, George. *Vancouver: A Life*. New York: D. Appleton and Co., 1931.

Gould, Rupert T. *The Marine Chronometer*. London: J. D. Potter, 1923.

Gowen, Herbert H. *The Napoleon of the Pacific*. New York: Fleming H. Revell Co., 1919.

Greenhow, Robert. *The History of Oregon and California and the Other Territories on the Northwest Coast of America*. Boston: C. C. Little and J. Brown, 1844.

Guérin, Léon. *Les navigateurs français*. Paris: Belin-Lepreur et Morizot, 1856.

Hawkesworth, John. *An Account of the Voyages Undertaken by the Orders of His Majesty for Making Discoveries in the Southern Hemisphere and Successively Performed by Commodore Byron, Captain Carteret, Captain Wallis and Captain Cook in the Dolphin, the Swallow, and the Endeavour*. 3 vols. London: W. Strahan and T. Cadell, 1774.

Hazard, Samuel (ed.). *Pennsylvania Archives*. Ser. 1, Vol. X. Philadelphia: J. Severns and Co., 1854.

Heawood, Edward. *Geographical Discovery in the Seventeenth and Eighteenth Centuries*. Cambridge, Eng.: Cambridge University Press, 1912.

Historical Records of Australia. Ser. 1, Vol. I. Sydney: Library Committee of the Commonwealth Parliament, 1914.

Hoon, Elizabeth S. *The Organization of the English Customs Systems, 1696-1786*. New York: D. Appleton and Co., 1938.

Howay, Frederick W. (ed.). *The Dixon Meares Controversy*. Montreal: Ryerson Press, 1929.

———. "Early Navigation of the Strait of Juan de Fuca," *Oregon Historical Quarterly*, XII (March, 1911), 1-32.

——— (ed.). "Four Letters from Richard Cadman Etches to Sir Joseph Banks," *British Columbia Historical Quarterly*, VI (April, 1942), 125-39.

——— (ed.). *The Journal of Captain James Colnett aboard the Argonaut from April 26, 1789, to November 3, 1791*. Toronto: Champlain Press, 1940.

———. "Notes on Cook's and Vancouver's Ships," *Washington Historical Quarterly*, XXI (October, 1930), 268-70.

——— (ed.). "Voyage of the Hope," *ibid.*, XI (January, 1920), 3-28.

——— (ed.). *Voyages of the Columbia to the Northwest Coast, 1787-1790*. (Massachusetts Historical Society Collections, Vol. LXXIX.) Boston, 1941.

"In Need of Financial Help," *Washington Historical Quarterly*, XVII (April, 1926), 125-28.

Jane, Fred T. *The Imperial Russian Navy*. London: W. Thacker and Co., 1899.

Kerr, Robert. *A General History and Collection of Voyages and Travels*. 18 vols. Edinburgh: W. Blackwood, 1811-24.

Kippis, Andrew. *The Life of Captain James Cook*. London: G. Nicol and G. G. J. and J. Robinson, 1788.

Kuykendall, Ralph S. *The Hawaiian Kingdom, 1778-1854*. Honolulu: University of Hawaii Press, 1938.

Lamb, W. Kaye. "Burrard of Burrard's Channel," *British Columbia Historical Quarterly*, X (January, 1946), 273-78.

———. "The Mystery of Mrs. Barkley's Diary," *ibid.*, VI (January, 1942), 31-59.

La Pérouse, Jean François de Galaup, Comte de. *A Voyage round the World in the Years 1785, 1786, 1787, and 1788*. 3 vols. London: J. Johnson, 1799.

"A Letter from Antigua," *Annual Register*, XL (1798), 10-11.

Lewis, Michael A. *England's Sea Officers*. London: G. Allen and Unwin, 1939.

———. *The Navy of Britain*. London: G. Allen and Unwin, 1948.

The Life, Adventures, and Eccentricities of the Late Lord Camelford. London, 1804.

The London Chronicle, September 17, 1795; October 5, 15, 16, 23, 1795.

Lorenz, Lincoln. *John Paul Jones, Fighter for Freedom and Glory*. Annapolis, Md.: U.S. Naval Institute, 1943.

Lyons, Sir Henry. *The Royal Society, 1660-1940*. Cambridge, Eng.: Cambridge University Press, 1944.

MacKenzie, Alexander. *Voyages from Montreal, on the River St. Lawrence, through the Continent of North America to the Frozen and Pacific Oceans, in the Years 1789 and 1793*. 2 vols. London: W. Creech, 1802.

Mahan, Alfred T. *The Influence of Sea Power upon the French Revolution and Empire*. 2 vols. 1st ed. Boston: Little, Brown and Co., 1895.

———. *The Life of Nelson, the Embodiment of the Sea Power of Great Britain*. Boston: Little, Brown and Co., 1897.

Makaness, George. *The Life of Vice Admiral William Bligh*. New York and Toronto: Farrar and Rinehart, 1931.

Manby, Thomas. Extract from Personal Journal, *Honolulu Mercury*, I (June, 1929), 11-25; (July, 1929), 33-45.

Manning, William R. "The Nootka Sound Controversy," *Annual Report of the American Historical Society, 1904*, pp. 279-478.

Masefield, John. *Sea Life in Nelson's Time*. 3rd ed. New York: Macmillan Co., 1920.

Meany, Edmond S. *Origin of Washington Geographic Names*. Seattle: University of Washington Press, 1923.

———. *Vancouver's Discovery of Puget Sound*. New York: Macmillan Co., 1907.

Meares, John. *Memorial of John Meares, Lieutenant in His Majesty's Navy, to the House of Commons.* London, 1790.

———. *Voyages Made in the Years 1788 and 1789 from China to the North-west Coast of America.* London: The Logographic Press, 1790.

Menzies, Archibald. *Hawaii Nei 128 Years Ago.* Honolulu: The New Freedom, 1920.

———. Extract from Journal, December, 1791-16 February, 1794, *California Historical Society Quarterly,* II (January, 1924), 265-340.

Milham, Willis I. *Time and Timekeepers.* New York: Macmillan Co., 1941.

Minutes of a Court Martial on Board H.M.S. Dido, Halifax, 21-23 May 1788. London, [ca.] 1790.

Moore, John Hamilton. *The Practical Navigator and Seaman's Daily Assistant.* 8th ed. London: published by the author, 1784.

The Navy Chronicle. Vols. I (1799), II (1799), III (1800), XII (1805), XXII (1809).

Newcombe, C. F. (ed.). *Menzies' Journal of Vancouver's Voyage, April to October, 1792.* Victoria: W. H. Cullin, 1923.

Perrin, W. G. (ed.). *The Keith Papers.* (Publications of the Navy Records Society, Vol. LXII.) 2 vols. London, 1927, 1950.

——— (ed.). *The Naval Miscellany,* Vol. III. (Publications of the Navy Records Society, Vol. LXIII.) London, 1928.

Recollections of James Anthony Gardner, Commander RN (1775-1814). (Publications of the Navy Records Society, Vol. XXXI.) London, 1906.

Regulations and Instructions Relating to His Majesty's Service at Sea. 13th ed. London: The Admiralty, 1790.

Richardson, William. *A Mariner of England,* ed., Spencer Childers. London: John Murray, 1908.

Schomberg, Isaac. *The Navy Chronology or an Historical Summary of Naval and Maritime Events.* London: T. Egerton, 1802; 2nd ed., 1815.

Schurz, William L. *The Manila Galleon.* New York: Dutton and Co., 1939.

Smith, Edward. *The Life of Sir Joseph Banks.* London: John Lane, 1905.

Sparrman, Anders. *Voyage to the Cape of Good Hope.* 2 vols. Perth: R. Morrow and Son, 1789.

Townsend, Ebenezer, Jr. "Diary of a Voyage around the World in the Sailing Ship Neptune, 1796-99." *(Papers of the New Haven Colonial Society,* Vol. VI.) New Haven, 1888.

Twiss, Travers. *The Oregon Question Examined.* London: Longman, Brown, Green and Longmans, 1846.

United States Navy. Hydrographic Office. *Sailing Directions for the Pacific Islands,* Vol. I. Washington, D.C.: Government Printing Office, 1945.

BIBLIOGRAPHY

Vancouver, George. *A Voyage of Discovery to the North Pacific Ocean and round the World.* 3 vols. London: C. J. and J. Robinson; J. Edwards, 1798.

Wagner, Henry R. "Apocryphal Voyages to the Northwest Coast of America," *Proceedings of the American Antiquarian Society,* XLI (April, 1931), 179-234.

———. *Cartography of the Northwest Coast of America to the Year 1800.* 2 vols. Berkeley: University of California Press, 1937.

———. *Spanish Explorations in the Strait of Juan de Fuca.* Santa Ana, Calif.: Fine Arts Press, 1933.

Walbran, John T. *British Columbia Coast Names.* Ottawa: Government Printing Bureau, 1906.

Weaks, Mabel C. (ed.). *Calendar of the Kentucky Papers of the Draper Collection of Manuscripts.* (Publications of the State Historical Society of Wisconsin, Calendar Series, Vol. II.) Madison, Wis., 1925.

Wharton, W. J. L. (ed.). *Captain Cook's Journal during His First Voyage round the World.* London: E. Stock, 1893.

Whitebrook, Robert B. "Vancouver's Anchorages on Puget Sound," *Pacific Northwest Quarterly,* LXIV (July, 1953), 115-24.

Wilkes, Charles. *Narrative of the United States Exploring Expedition during the Years 1838, 1839, 1840, 1841, 1842.* 5 vols. Philadelphia: Lea and Blanchard, 1845.

Williamson, James A. *A Short History of British Expansion.* London: Macmillan and Co., 1927.

Wright, Thomas, and R. H. Evans. *Historical and Descriptive Account of the Caricatures of James Gillray.* London: Bohn, 1851.

Index